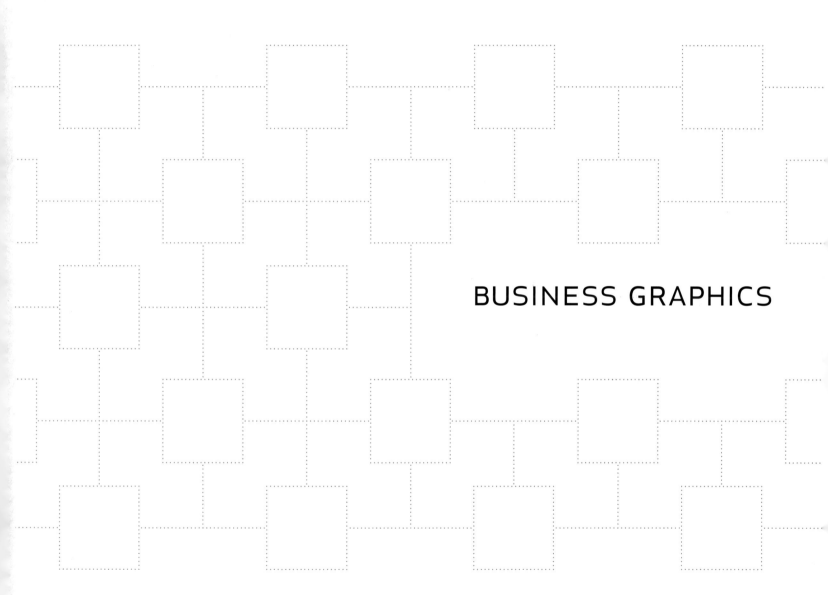

BUSINESS GRAPHICS

ROCKPORT

First published in the United States of America by Rockport Publishers, a member of Quayside Publishing Group
33 Commercial Street
Gloucester, Massachusetts 01930-5089
Telephone: (978) 282-9590
Fax: (978) 283-2742
www.rockpub.com

Library of Congress Cataloging-in-Publication Data
Business graphics : 500 designs that link graphic aesthetics and business savvy / Liska + Associates.
        p.   cm.
    ISBN-13: 978-1-59253-320-6
    ISBN-10: 1-59253-320-5
    1. Commercial art. 2. Graphic arts. 3. Visual communication.
    I. Liska + Associates.
    NC998.B87 2007
    741.—dc22   2006035879
                                                 CIP

Design: Liska + Associates
Cover images (clockwise from top left): mCube, The Valentine Group, Hardy Design, Liska + Associates

Printed in China

BUSINESS
GRAPHICS

500 DESIGNS THAT LINK GRAPHIC AESTHETIC AND BUSINESS SAVVY

STEVEN LISKA, LISKA + ASSOCIATES

GLOUCESTER, MASSACHUSETTS

ROCKPORT PUBLISHERS

CONTENTS

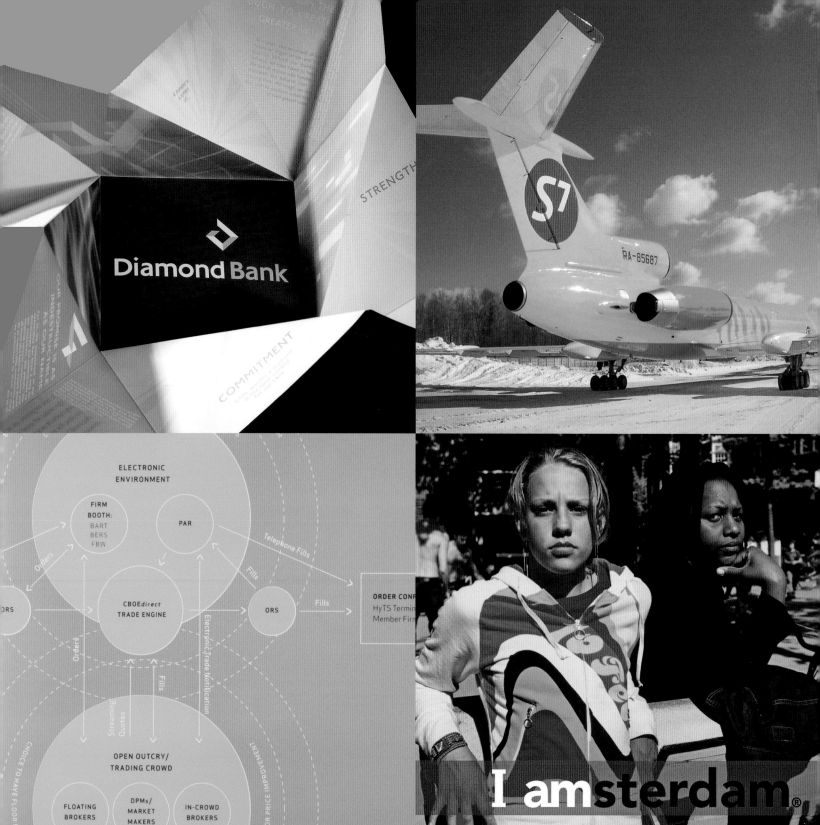

Diamond Bank

STRENGTH

COMMITMENT

S7
RA-85687

ELECTRONIC
ENVIRONMENT

FIRM
BOOTH:
BART
BERS
FBW

PAR

Telephone Fills

Orders

Fills

ORS

CBOEdirect
TRADE ENGINE

ORS

Fills

ORDER CONF
HyTS Termin
Member Firr

Orders

Fills

Streaming
Quotes

Electronic Trade Notification

OPEN OUTCRY/
TRADING CROWD

FLOATING
BROKERS

DPMs/
MARKET
MAKERS

IN-CROWD
BROKERS

I amsterdam.

INTRODUCTION

As professional communicators, designers are critical partners in business development, sustainability, and growth. Designers develop visual and verbal systems that help companies identify, clarify, and communicate who they are, what makes them different, and why customers or clients should choose to buy their product or service. Thoughtful and branded design solutions provide memorable visual representations of a company's core attributes, and serve as the primary voice through which a company communicates.

Providing graphic design for businesses requires strategic thinking and creative discipline. It takes the ability to sift through research, listen well (and often), and thoroughly explore the possibilities and problems a company may face—before any designing takes place. Only after such critical analysis can designers create solutions that communicate the essence of a

company and its differentiating characteristics. Whether creating a comprehensive program or producing a specific project, design teams serve businesses best when the design fits within a unified branding system.

Visual systems and editorial voice must be applied consistently—and incessantly—to be effective. Every customer touch point, from advertising and sales to shipping, offers an opportunity to reinforce the qualities that differentiate one business from another. Designers help companies find these opportunities and maximize their potential through accurate and artful communication programs.

This book features fifteen case studies and hundreds of effective design solutions created for businesses. As we juried the projects and pieces submitted, we needed to determine what

constitutes "business graphics." We concluded
that virtually all graphic design is created for a
business of one type or another. Schools, non-
profits, political parties, cultural institutions,
self-promotional vehicles—at some level, these
are all businesses with similar needs. Each one
has an audience to reach, a story to tell, and a
desire to persuade; most also have products
or services to sell.

We determined that any design project that uses
strategy and aesthetics to solve a client's
communications issue qualifies as an example of
business graphics, which led to an interesting
mix for the contents of this book.

We organized the various projects using the key
ways that business graphics function: *Identify*,
Communicate, *Market*, *Report*, and *Promote*.
A final category, *Other*, shows additional ways
that design supports business communication.

We thank the contributors for inspiring us
with their talent, and Rockport Publishers for
the responsibility of articulating the elements
that comprise effective and compelling
business graphics.

— STEVEN LISKA, LISKA + ASSOCIATES

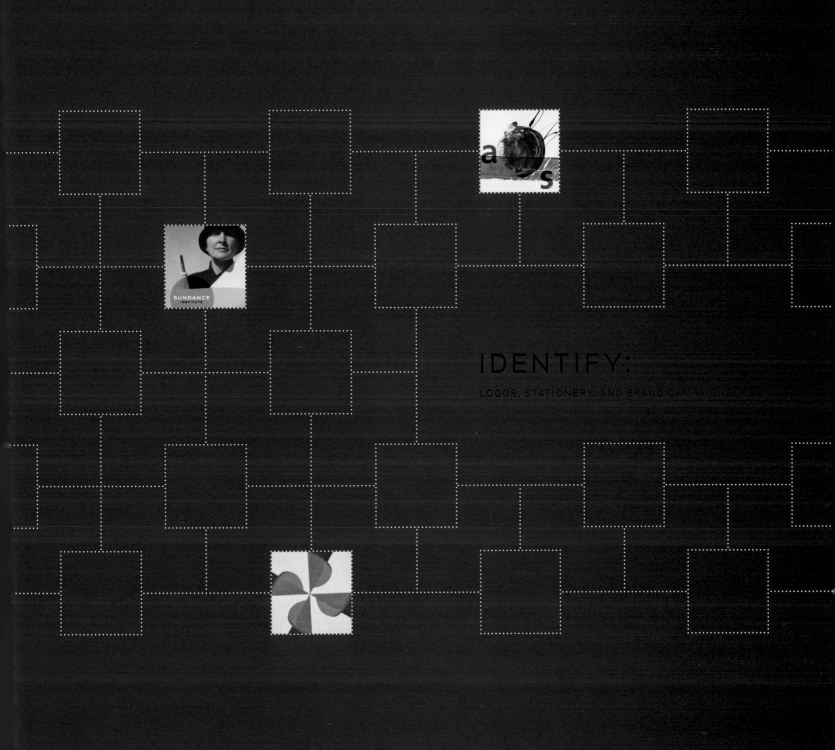

IDENTIFY:

LOGOS, STATIONERY, AND BRAND CAMPAIGNS

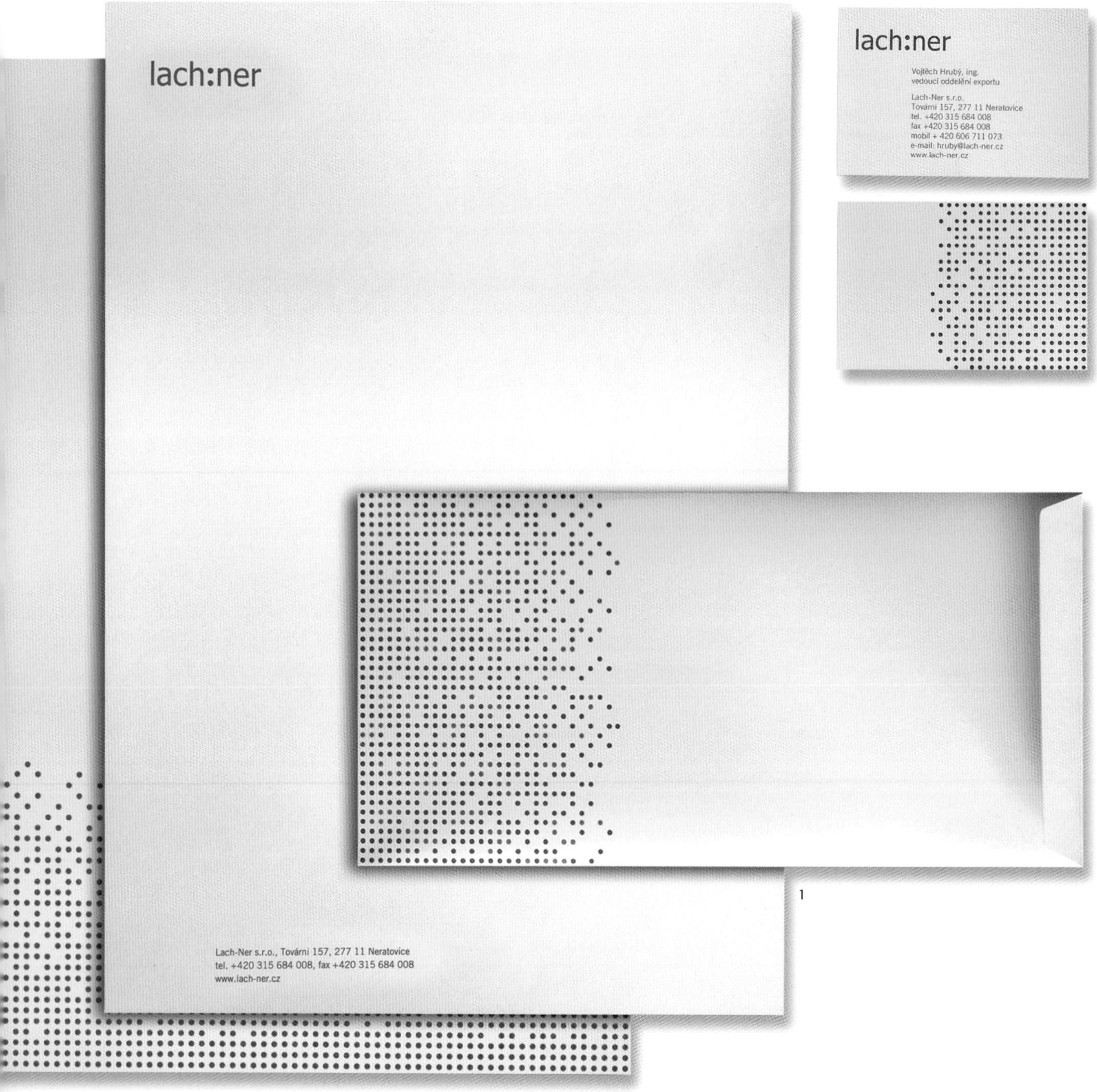

lach:ner

lach:ner

Vojtěch Hrubý, ing.
vedoucí oddělení exportu

Lach-Ner s.r.o.
Tovární 157, 277 11 Neratovice
tel. +420 315 684 008
fax +420 315 684 008
mobil + 420 606 711 073
e-mail: hruby@lach-ner.cz
www.lach-ner.cz

Lach-Ner s.r.o., Tovární 157, 277 11 Neratovice
tel. +420 315 684 008, fax +420 315 684 008
www.lach-ner.cz

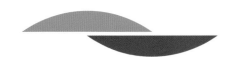

ZEN CONSULTING, LLC

2

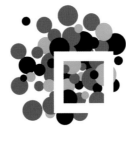

MOMENTUM

3

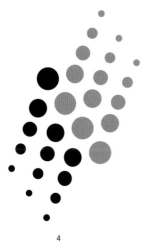

4

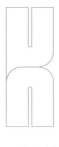

white apron

5

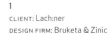

SM

6

n.KATE

7

1
CLIENT: Lach:ner
DESIGN FIRM: Bruketa & Zinic

2
CLIENT: Zen Consulting, LLC
DESIGN FIRM: Valiant Media, Inc.

3
CLIENT: Momentum Builders
DESIGN FIRM: Octavo Design/
Spark Studio

4
CLIENT: Emhz
DESIGN FIRM: Talisman Interactive

5
CLIENT: White Apron
DESIGN FIRM: Hartford Design

6
CLIENT: Keys To...
DESIGN FIRM: Sussner Design Company

7
CLIENT: N. Kate
DESIGN FIRM: Kinetic

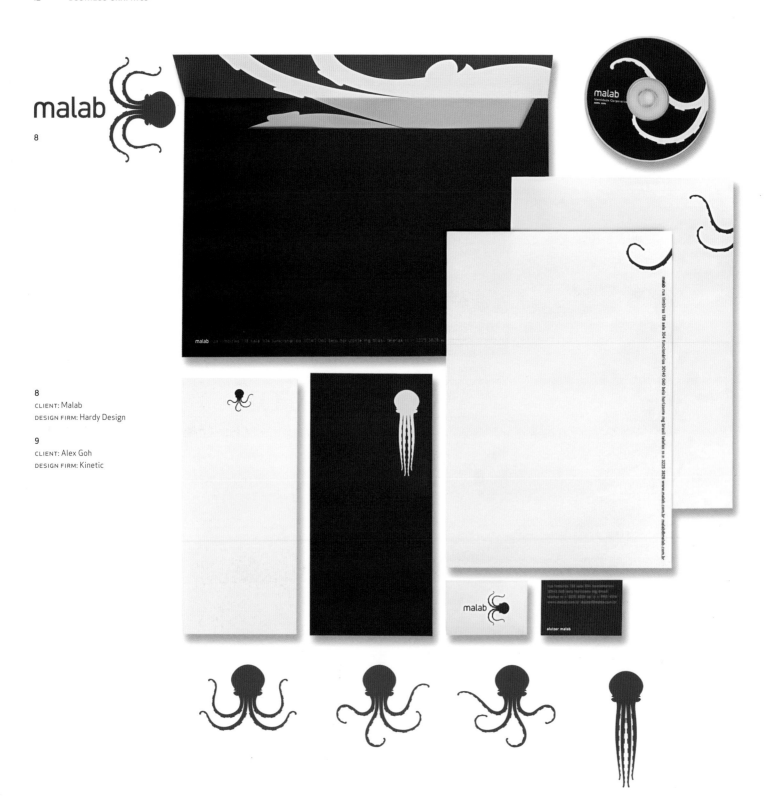

8
CLIENT: Malab
DESIGN FIRM: Hardy Design

9
CLIENT: Alex Goh
DESIGN FIRM: Kinetic

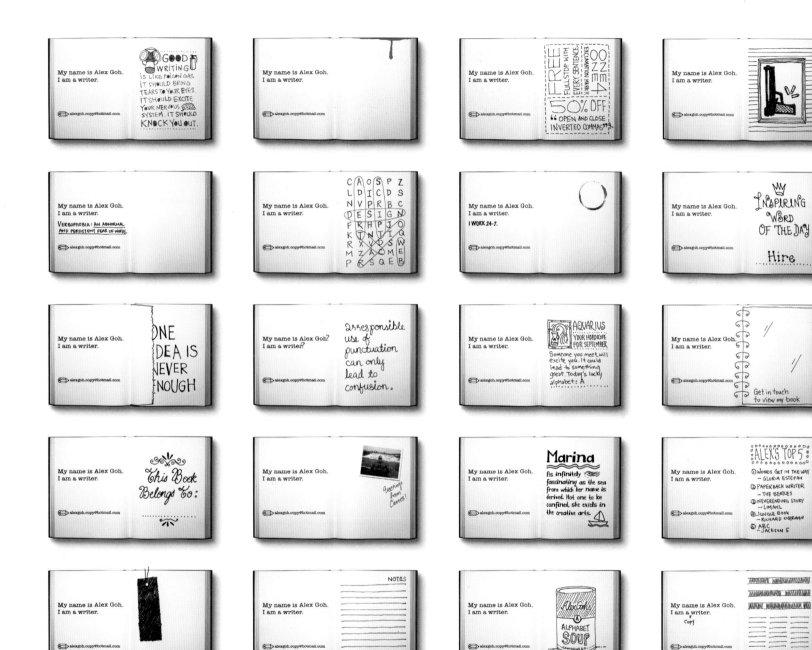

10
CLIENT: Nano-Tex
DESIGN FIRM: Addis Creson

11
CLIENT: BLRB Architects
DESIGN FIRM: Hornall Anderson
Design Works

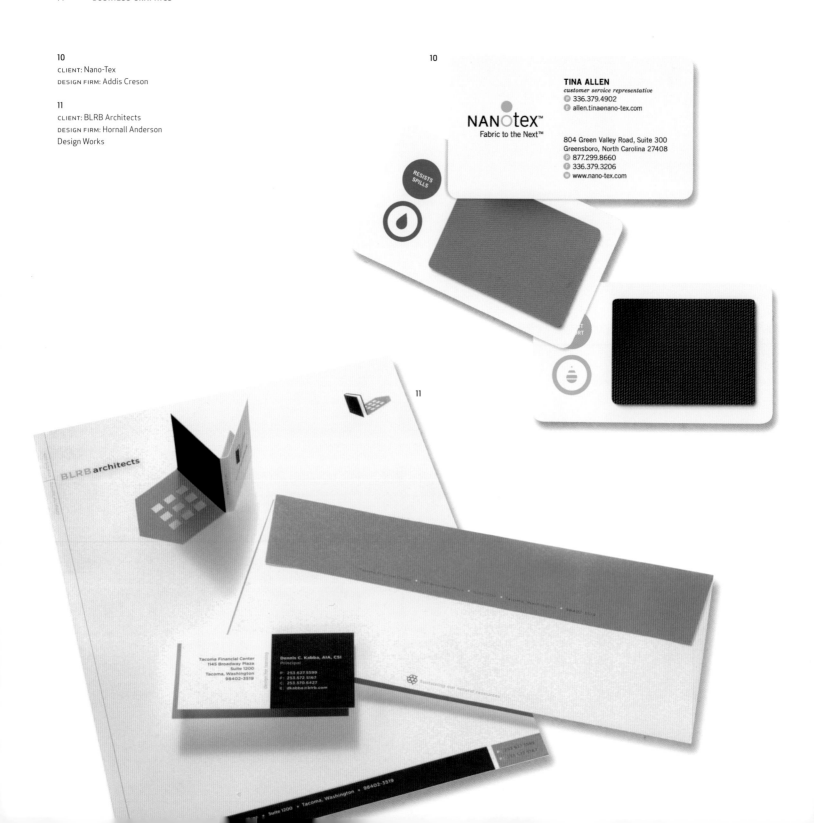

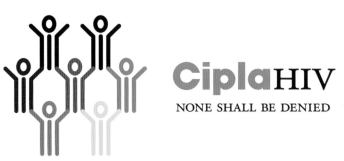

CiplaHIV

NONE SHALL BE DENIED

12

12
CLIENT: Cipla
DESIGN FIRM: mCube

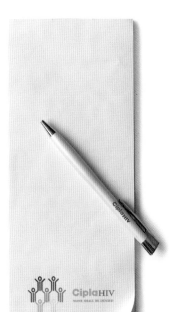

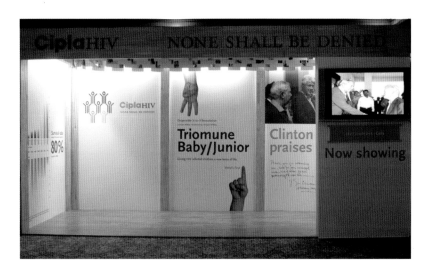

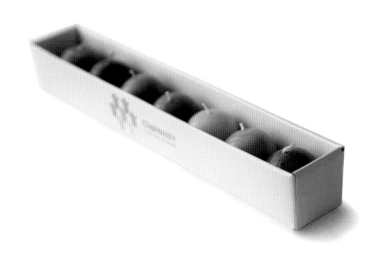

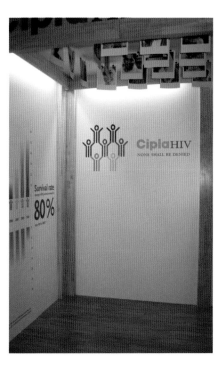

13
CLIENT: 3
DESIGN FIRM: 3

14
CLIENT: Allconnect
DESIGN FIRM: Hornall Anderson
Design Works

15
CLIENT: Nikon
DESIGN FIRM: Mirko Ilić Corp.

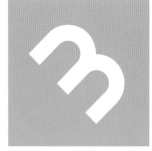

13

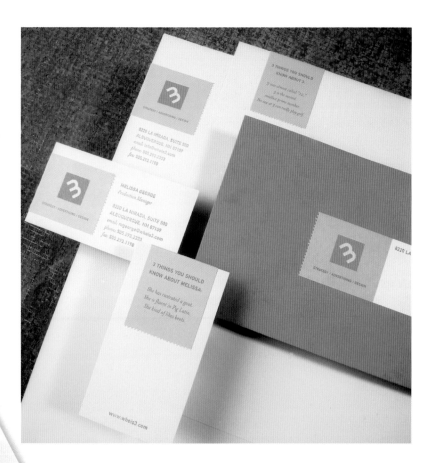

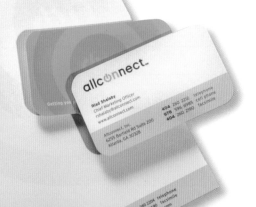

allconnect

14

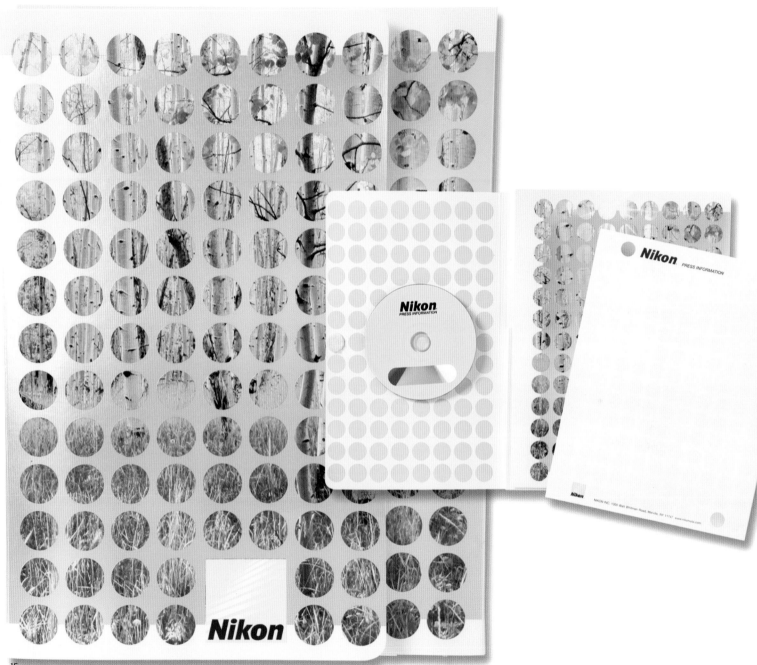

15

16

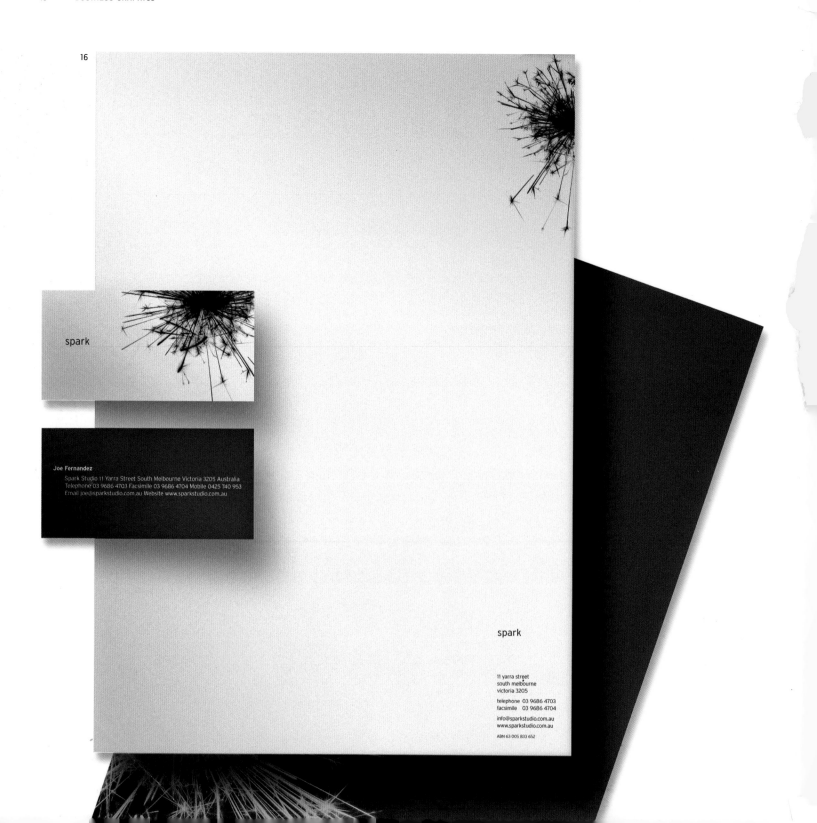

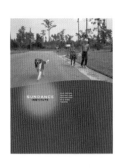
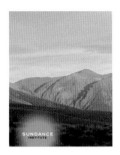
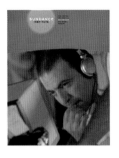
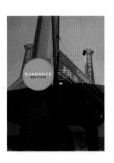

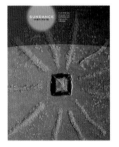
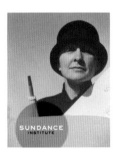
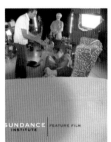
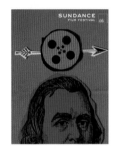

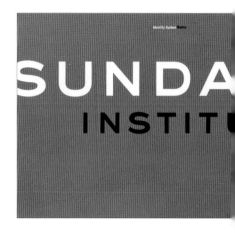

Collateral

Sundance Institute collateral combines multiple elements from
the system to create a diverse but cohesive look. Use of shape
and texture on covers is strongly encouraged.
See Shape and Texture, p. 11

Sundance Institute Identity   21   Usage Examples: Collateral

Sundance Institute promotes
creative diversity, embodying
the ideals of originality and
artistic integrity in support
of independent spirit in the
art of film and theatre.

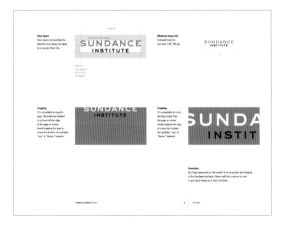
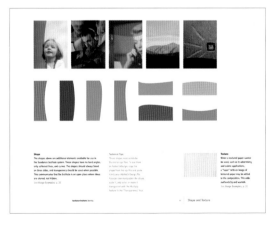
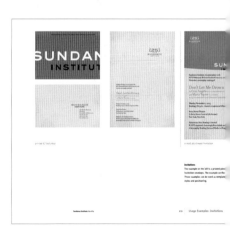

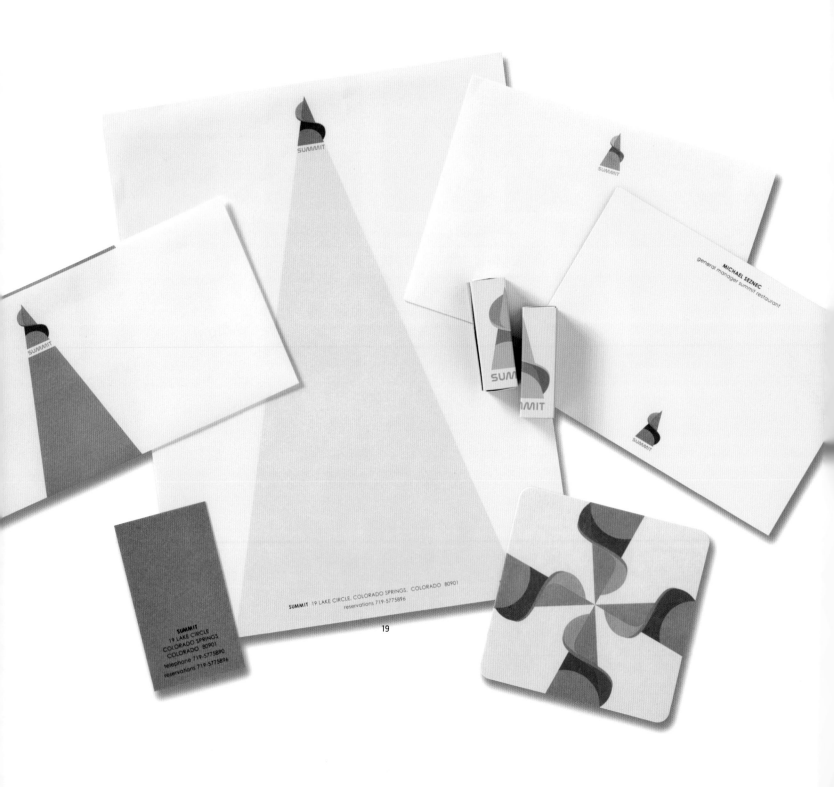

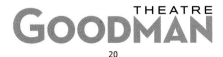

20

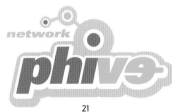

21

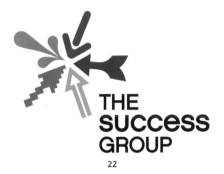

22

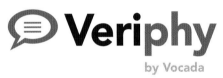

23

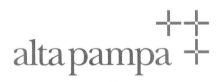

24

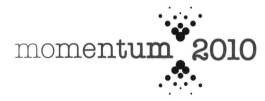

25

19
CLIENT: Summit
DESIGN FIRM: Mirko Ilić Corp.

20
CLIENT: Goodman Theatre
DESIGN FIRM: Liska + Associates

21
CLIENT: ignition, Inc.
DESIGN FIRM: Timber Design Company

22
CLIENT: The Success Group
DESIGN FIRM: Sussner Design Company

23
CLIENT: Vocada, Inc.
DESIGN FIRM: Valiant Media, Inc.

24
CLIENT: Alta Pampa
DESIGN FIRM: Emmi Salonen

25
CLIENT: Rancho Cordova Economic
Development Corp.
DESIGN FIRM: Taber Creative Group

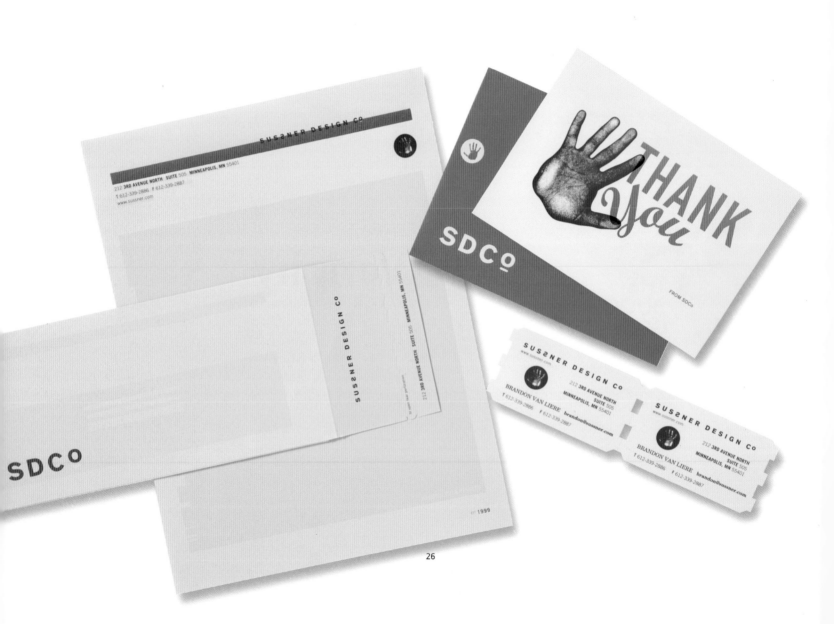

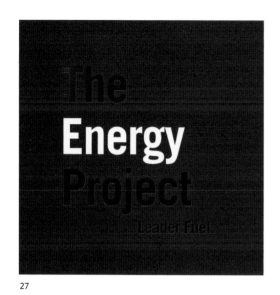

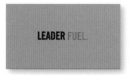
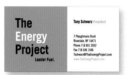
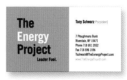

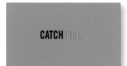
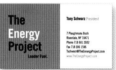

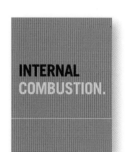

27

26
CLIENT: Sussner Design Company
DESIGN FIRM: Sussner Design Company

27
CLIENT: The Energy Project
DESIGN FIRM: 98pt6

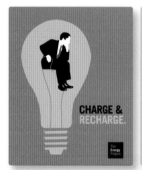
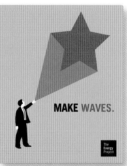

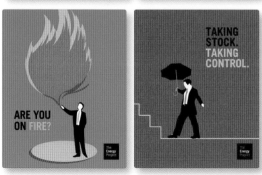

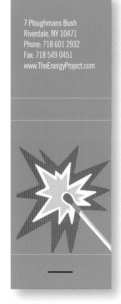
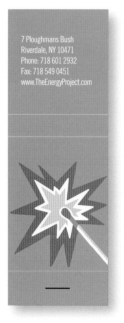
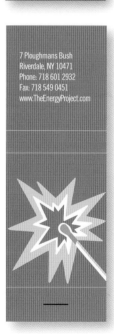

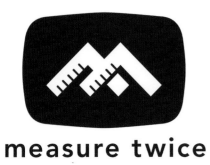

measure twice
YOU ONLY BUILD ONCE.

28

28
CLIENT: Measure Twice
DESIGN FIRM: 3

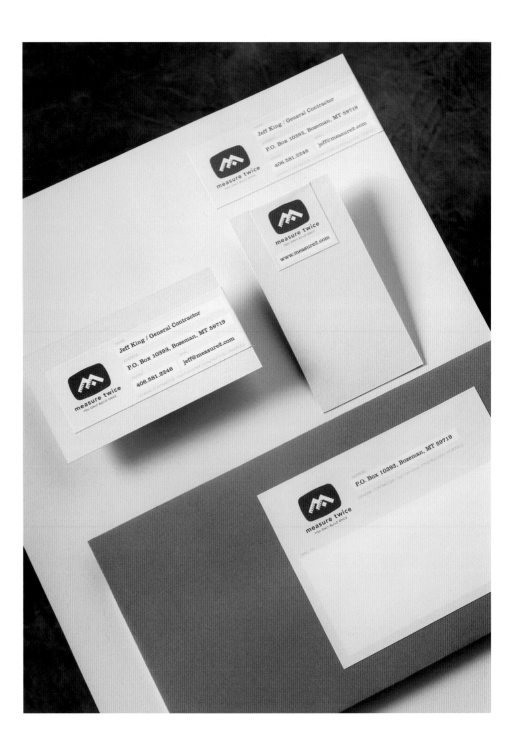

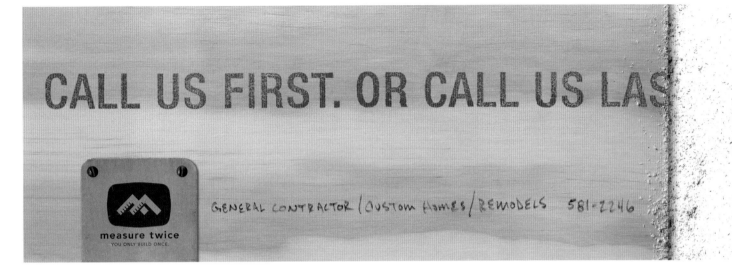

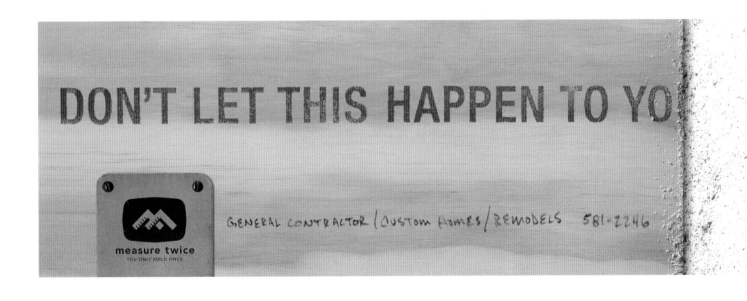

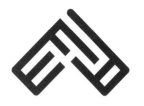

FINNEGAN ERICKSON ASSOCIATES
CONSULTING ENGINEERS

29

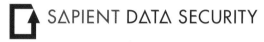

30

THE GROVE HOTEL
DOWNTOWN BOISE

31

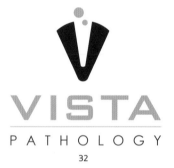

32

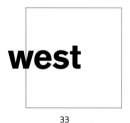

33

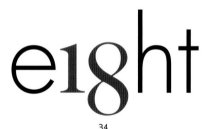

34

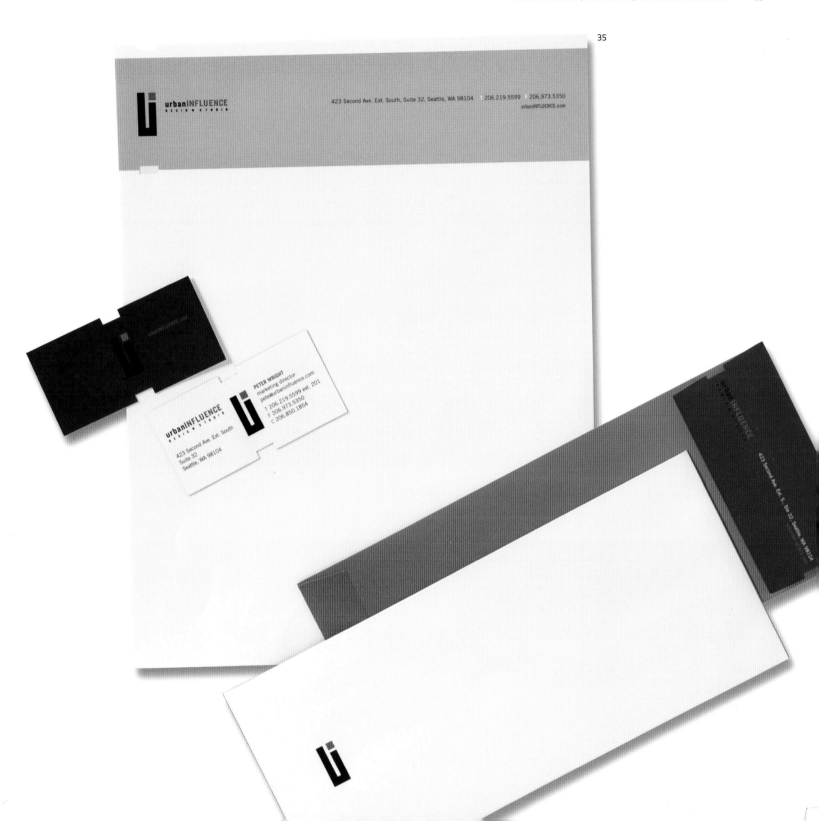

36
CLIENT: Bycor Limited
DESIGN FIRM: p11 Creative

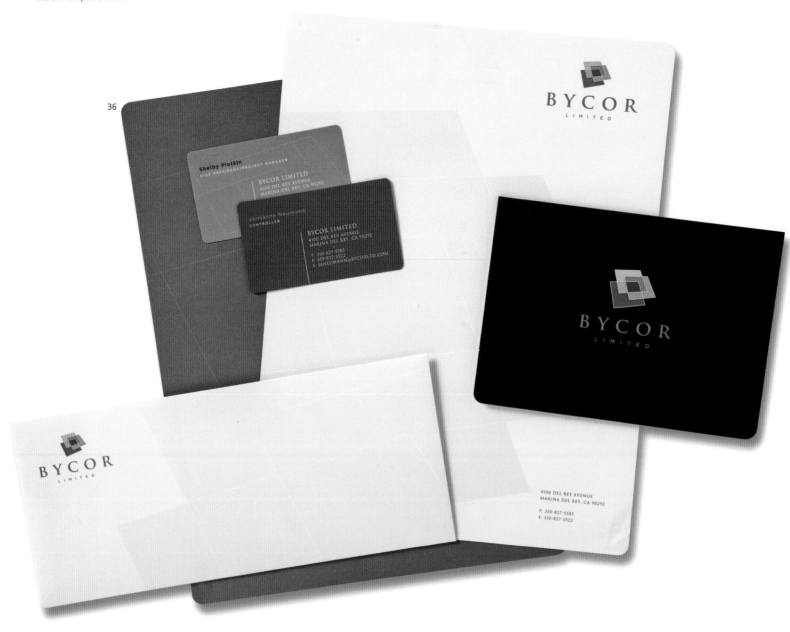

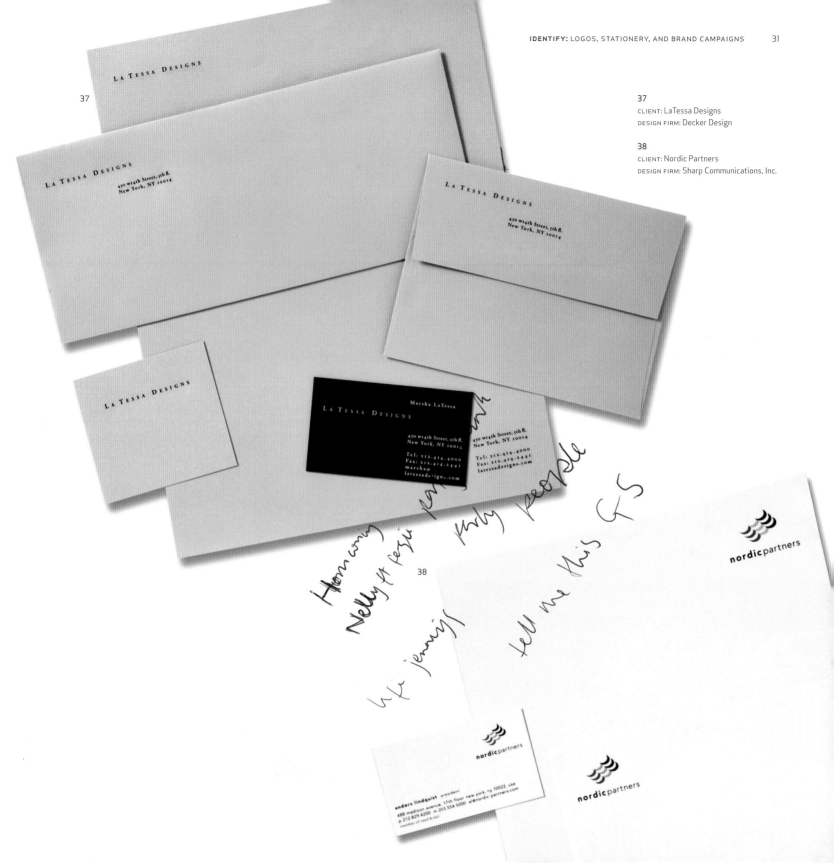

37
CLIENT: LaTessa Designs
DESIGN FIRM: Decker Design

38
CLIENT: Nordic Partners
DESIGN FIRM: Sharp Communications, Inc.

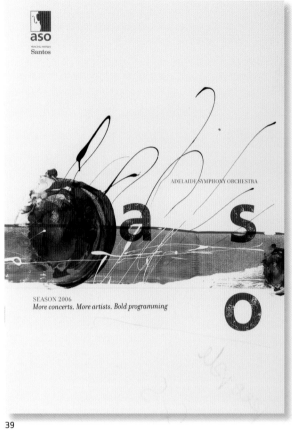

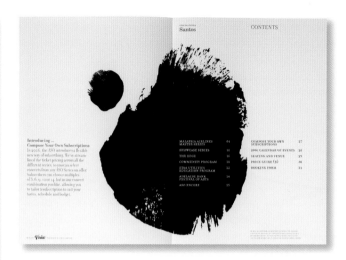

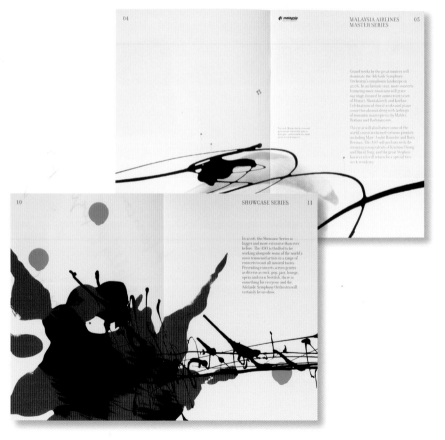

39

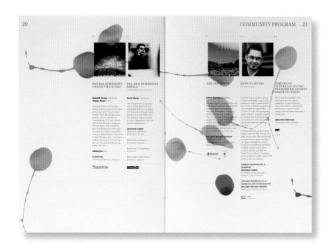

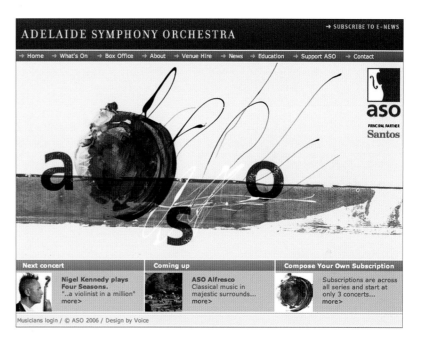

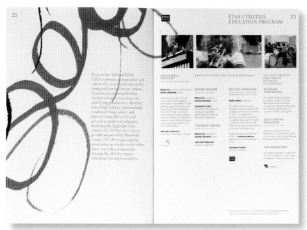

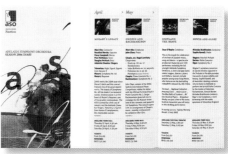

39

CLIENT: Adelaide Symphony Orchestra
DESIGN FIRM: Voice

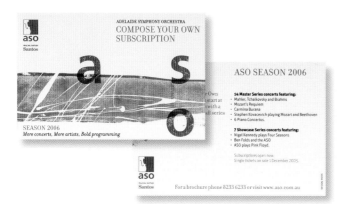

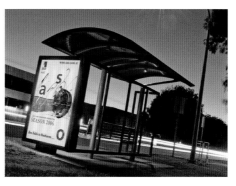

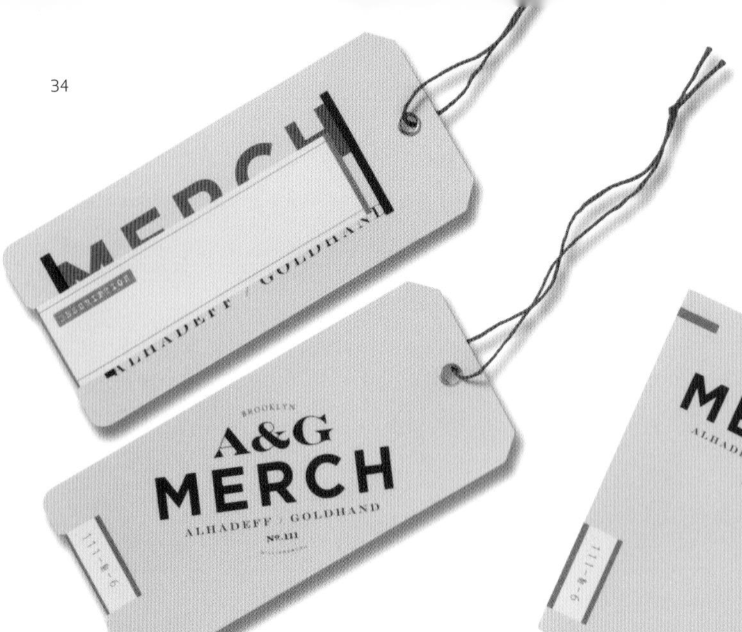

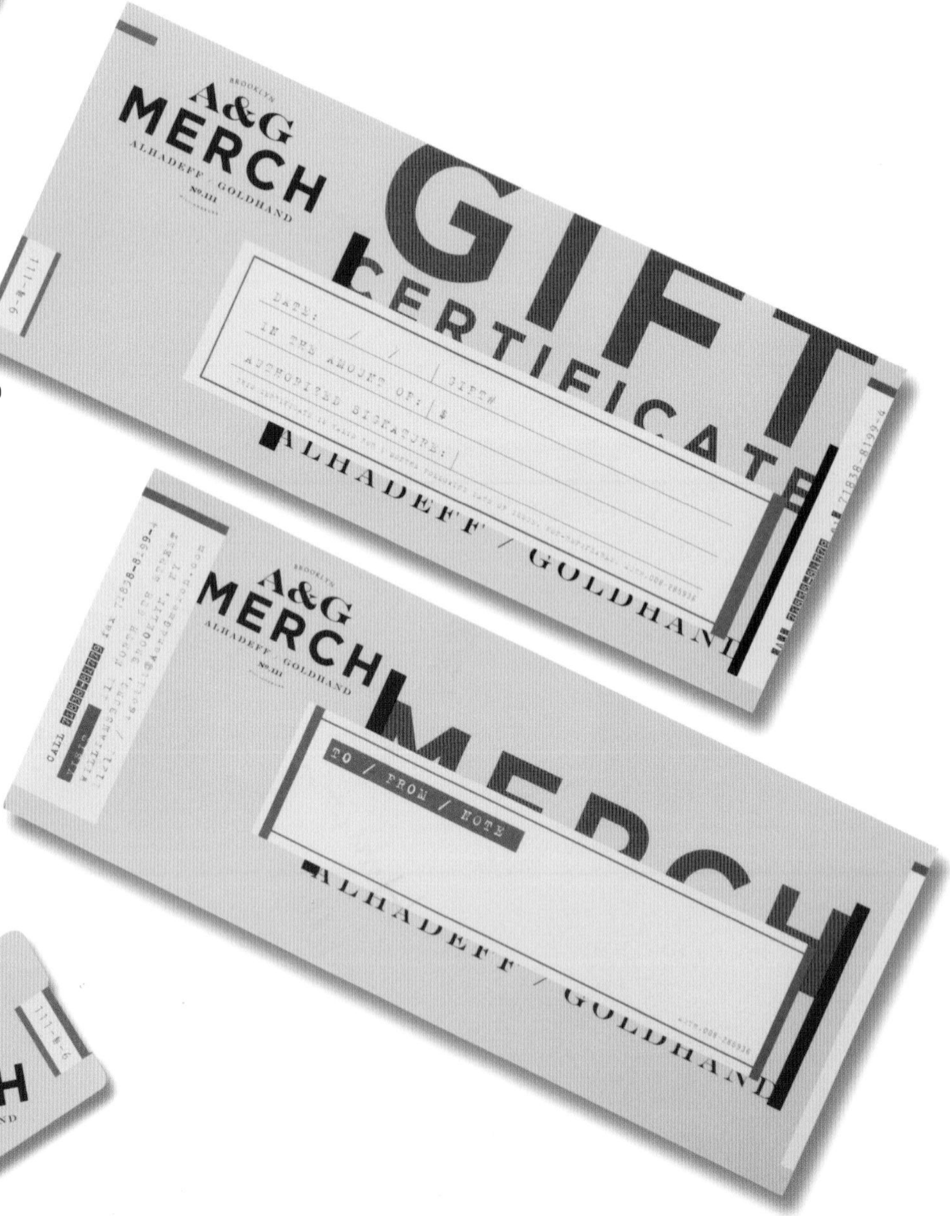

40
CLIENT: A + G Merch
DESIGN FIRM: Nothing: Something: NY

41
CLIENT: Bernardi
DESIGN FIRM: Hardy Design

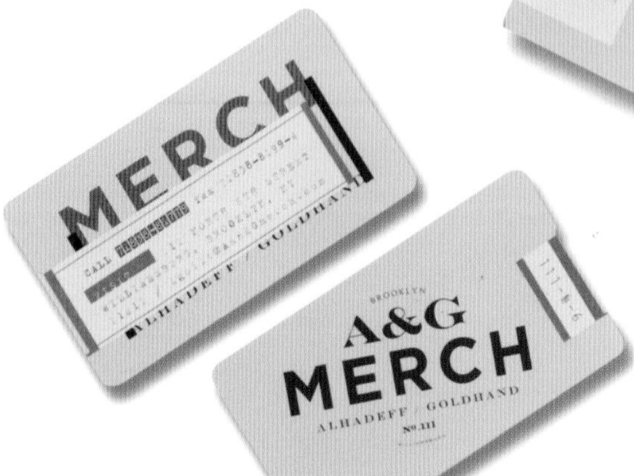

40

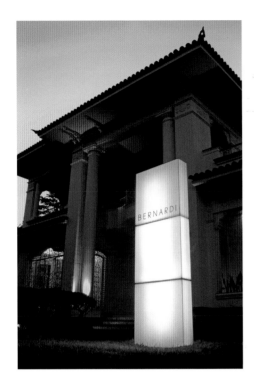

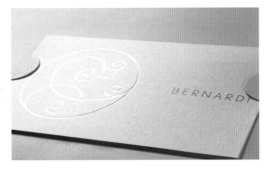

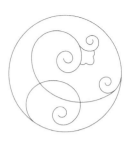

BERNARDI

41

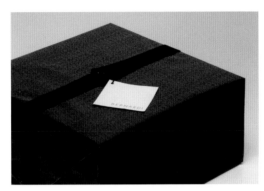

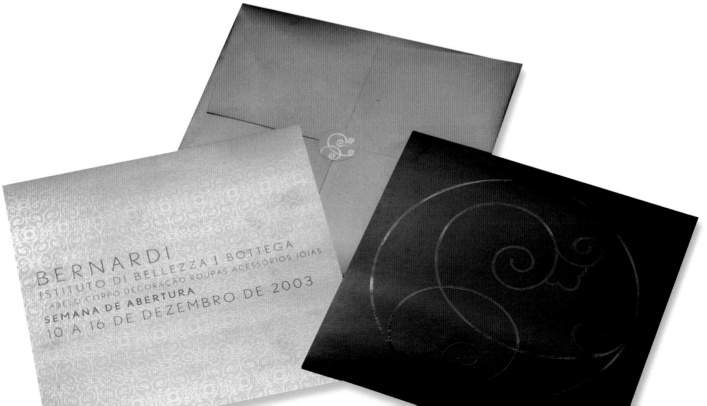

42
CLIENT: Widmer Brothers Brewery
DESIGN FIRM: Hornall Anderson
Design Works

43
CLIENT: 5 Gimnazija
DESIGN FIRM: Bruketa & Zinic

44
CLIENT: Quadragen
DESIGN FIRM: Talisman Interactive

45
CLIENT: Tim Bieber: Director
DESIGN FIRM: Liska + Associates

46
CLIENT: Three Below
DESIGN FIRM: Spark Studio

47
CLIENT: Wet Paint
DESIGN FIRM: Hornall Anderson
Design Works

48
CLIENT: Incognito Sum
DESIGN FIRM: Octavo Design/
Spark Studio

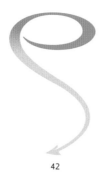

42

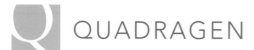

44

gimnazija

43

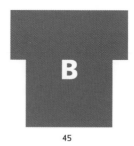

45

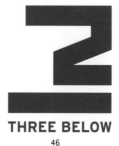

THREE BELOW

46

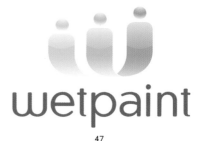

wetpaint

47

48

Incognito Sum
3/50 Tanner Street
Richmond 3121
Victoria Australia

Telephone 03 9421 2025
Facsimile 03 9421 2026
info@incognitosum.com
www.incognitosum.com

incognito sum

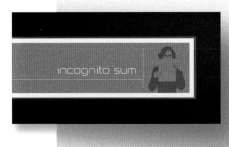

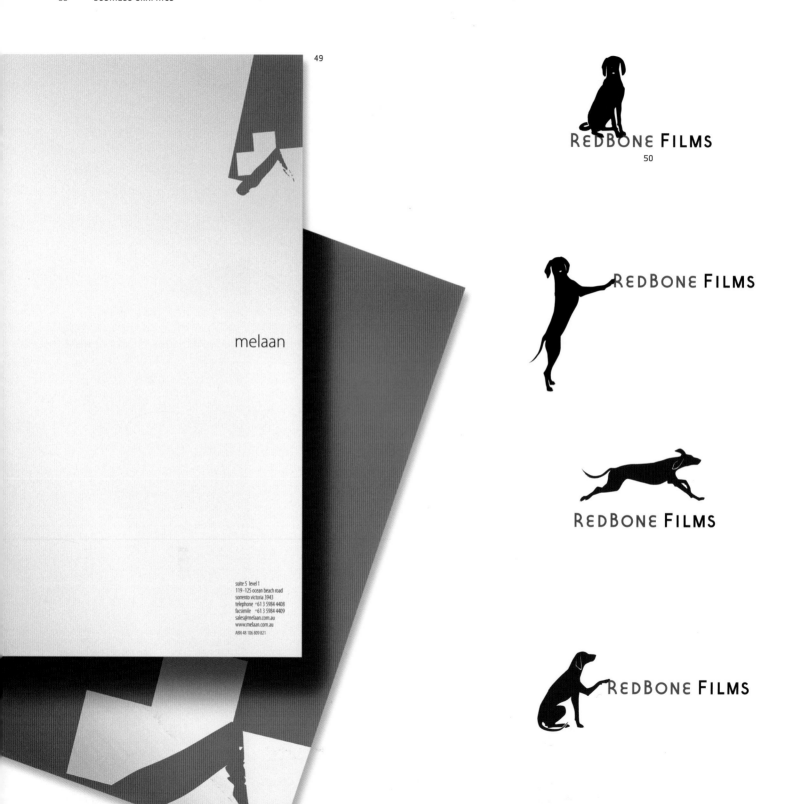

99

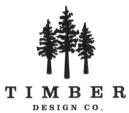

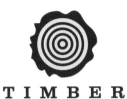

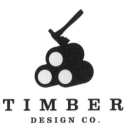

TIMBER
DESIGN CO.

54

TIMBER
DESIGN CO.

TIMBER
DESIGN CO.

53
CLIENT: Sullivan Shuman Freedberg
DESIGN FIRM: Seltzer Design

54
CLIENT: Timber Design Company
DESIGN FIRM: Timber Design Company

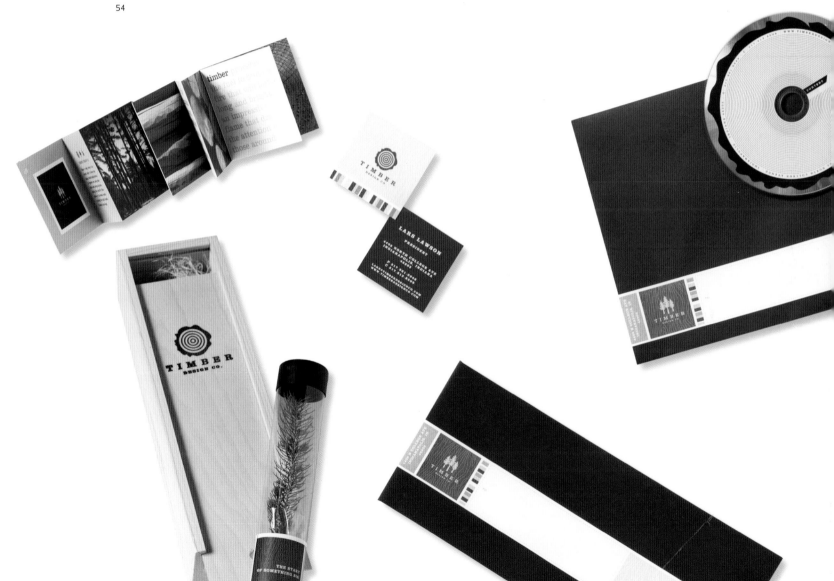

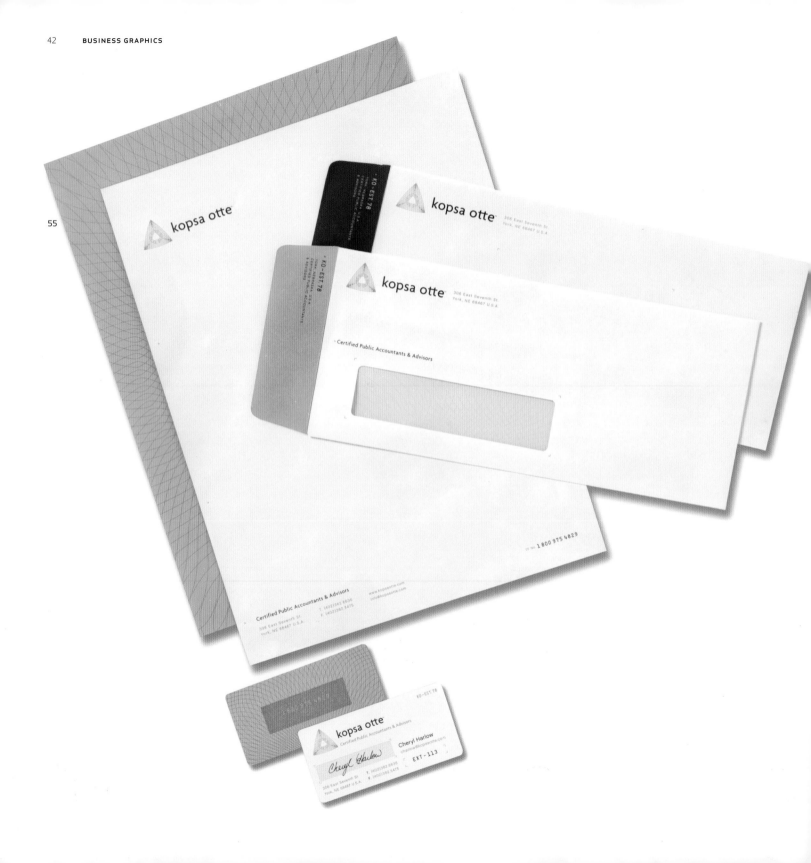

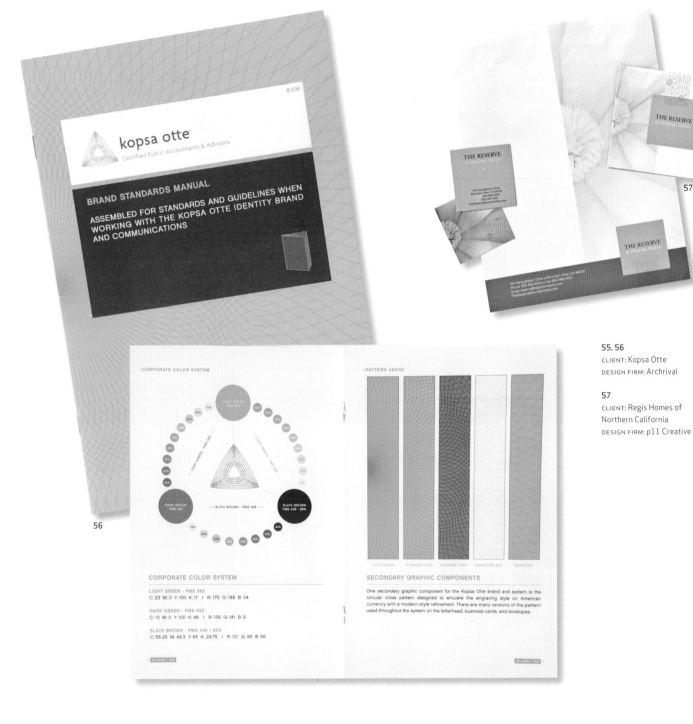

55, 56
CLIENT: Kopsa Otte
DESIGN FIRM: Archrival

57
CLIENT: Regis Homes of
Northern California
DESIGN FIRM: p11 Creative

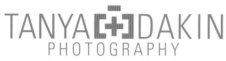

58

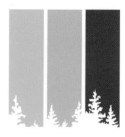

INDIANA URBAN FOREST COUNCIL

59

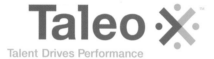

60

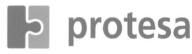

61

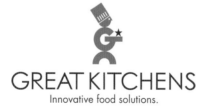

62

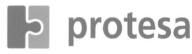

protesa

63

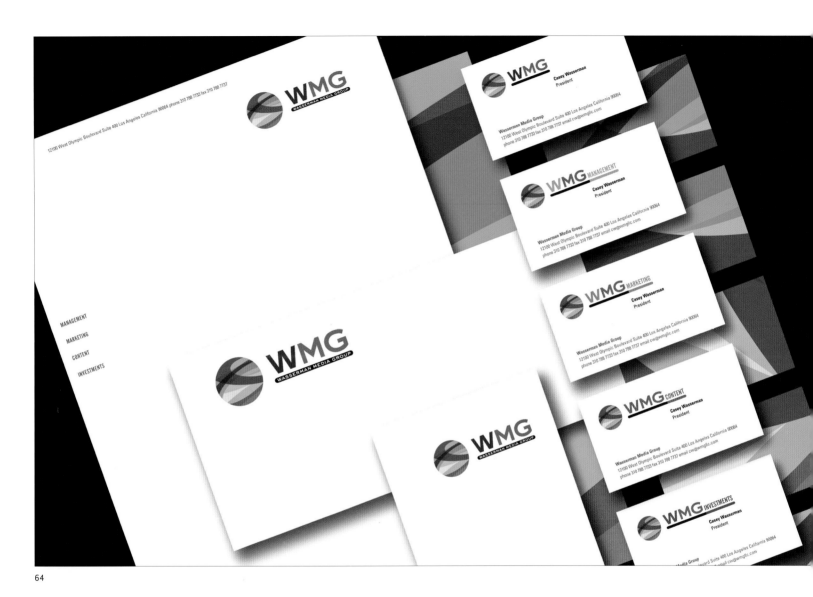

64

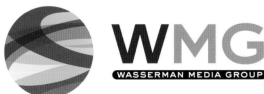

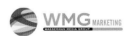

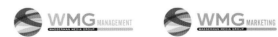

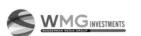

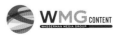

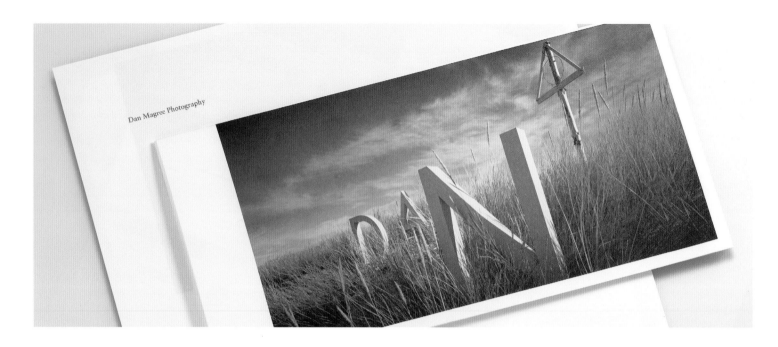

The Bakehouse Studio
2/133-135 Johnston Street
Collingwood 3066
Victoria Australia

Mobile 0416 046 556
Telephone +61 3 9417 6448
Facsimile +61 3 9417 6442
dan@danmagree.com
www.danmagree.com

Dan Magree Photography

65

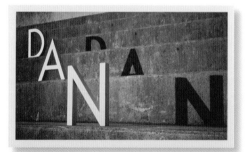

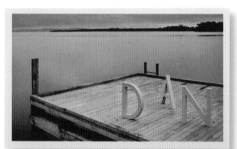

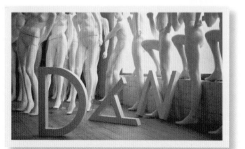

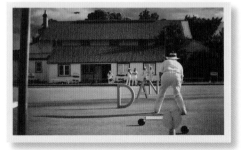

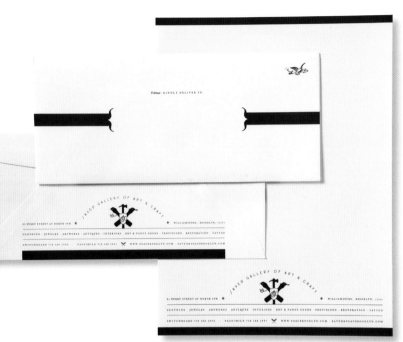

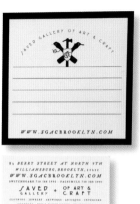

65
CLIENT: Dan Magree Photography
DESIGN FIRM: Davidson Design

66
CLIENT: Saved Gallery of Art + Craft
DESIGN FIRM: Nothing: Something: NY

66

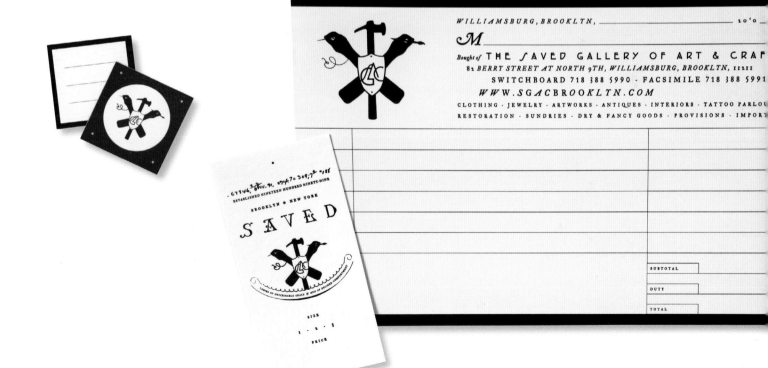

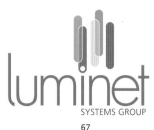

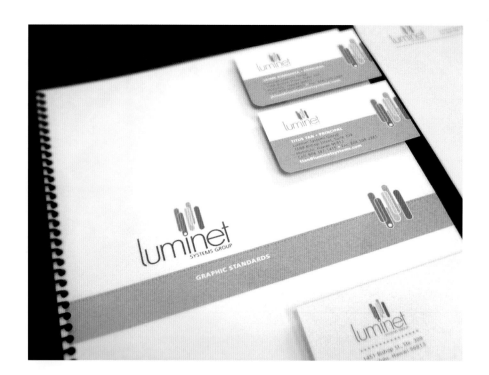

luminet
SYSTEMS GROUP

67

68

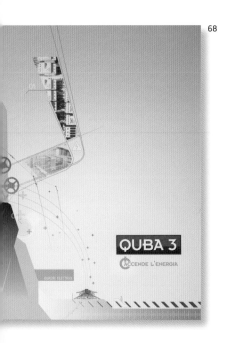

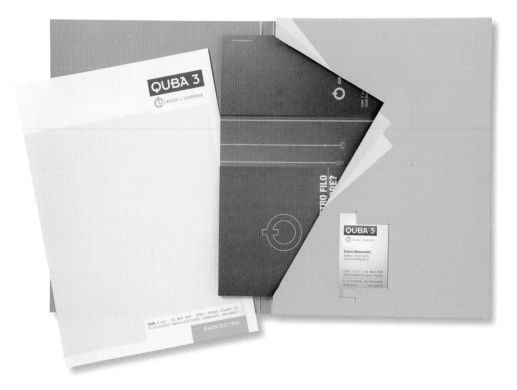

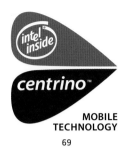

MOBILE
TECHNOLOGY
69

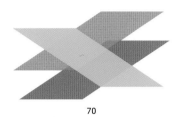

70

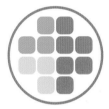

Nokia Global Games Summit
71

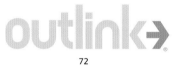

72

67
CLIENT: Luminet
DESIGN FIRM: John Wingard Design

68
CLIENT: Quba 3
DESIGN FIRM: Fluid Design Lab

69
CLIENT: Intel-Centrino
DESIGN FIRM: Addis Creson

70
CLIENT: Xhilarate
DESIGN FIRM: Talisman Interactive

71
CLIENT: Nokia
DESIGN FIRM: Valiant Media, Inc.

72
CLIENT: Outlink
DESIGN FIRM: Hartford Design

73
CLIENT: Tangerine Concepts
DESIGN FIRM: OneMethod Inc.

74
CLIENT: Agency Access
DESIGN FIRM: Matthew Schwartz
Design Studio

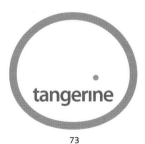

73

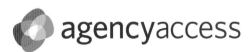

74

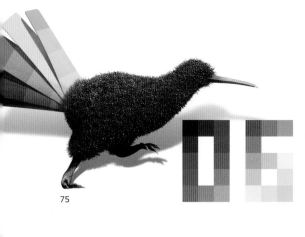

06 New Zealand
International
Arts Festival
24 February – 19 March

75

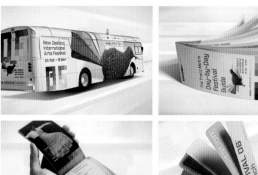

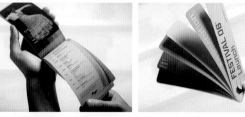

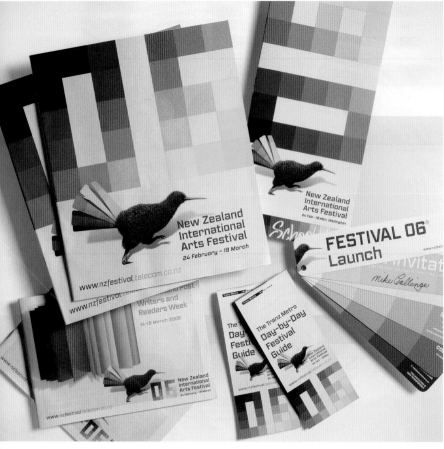

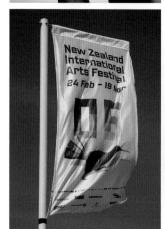

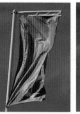

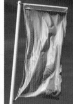

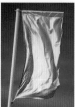

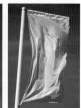

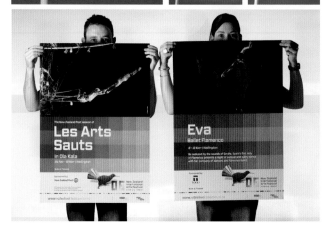

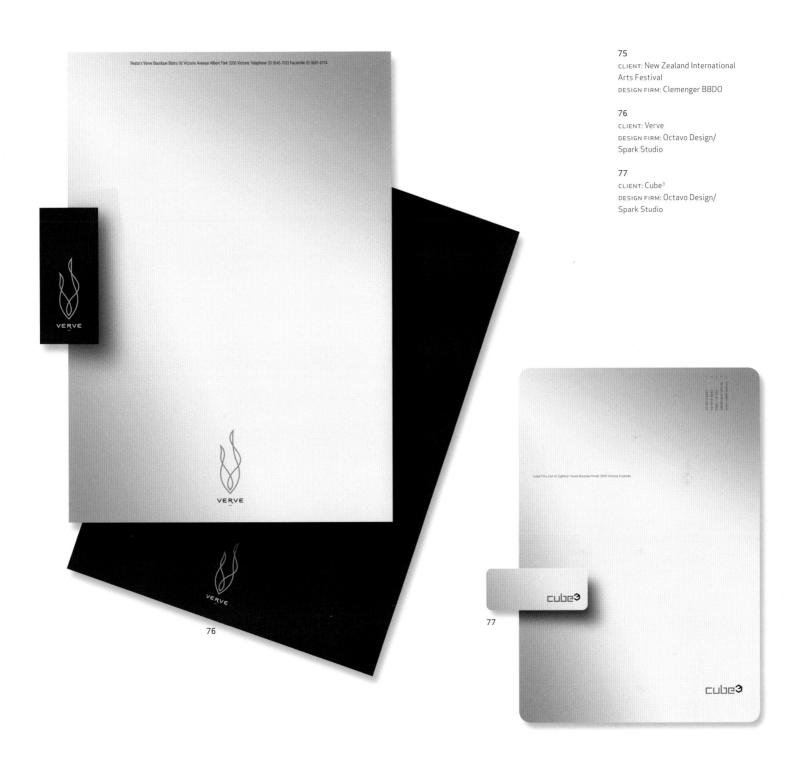

75
CLIENT: New Zealand International
Arts Festival
DESIGN FIRM: Clemenger BBDO

76
CLIENT: Verve
DESIGN FIRM: Octavo Design/
Spark Studio

77
CLIENT: Cube³
DESIGN FIRM: Octavo Design/
Spark Studio

78
CLIENT: America Abroad Media
DESIGN FIRM: Matthew Schwartz
Design Studio

79
CLIENT: Regis Homes of
Northern California
DESIGN FIRM: p11 Creative

80
CLIENT: Food Bank of Alaska
DESIGN FIRM: Mad Dog Graphx

81
CLIENT: Root Idea
DESIGN FIRM: Root Idea

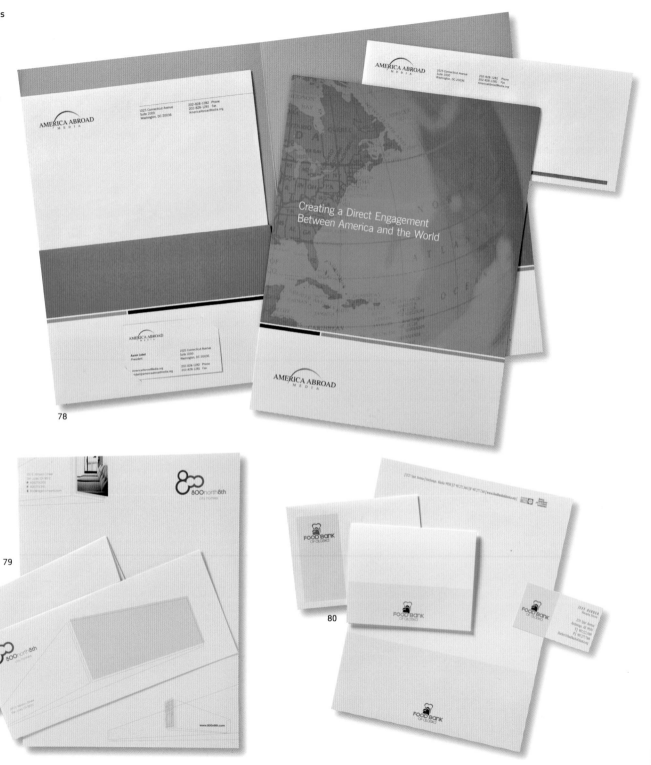

ROOT IDEA

ROOT IDEA

FLAT 2304, PROGRESS COMMERCIAL BLDG
9 IRVING STREET, CAUSEWAY BAY, HK
WWW.ROOTIDEA.COM • WELCOME@ROOTIDEA.COM

KEN LEE
CREATIVE VEGETARIAN

FLAT 2304, PROGRESS COMMERCIAL BLDG
9 IRVING STREET, CAUSEWAY BAY, HK
T 29730056 • M 97070066
WWW.ROOTIDEA.COM • KENLEE@ROOTIDEA.COM

FLAT 2304, PROGRESS COMMERCIAL BLDG, 9 IRVING ST, CAUSEWAY BAY, HK • T 29730056 • F 29730035 • WWW.ROOTIDEA.COM • WELCOME@ROOTIDEA.COM

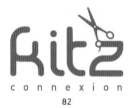

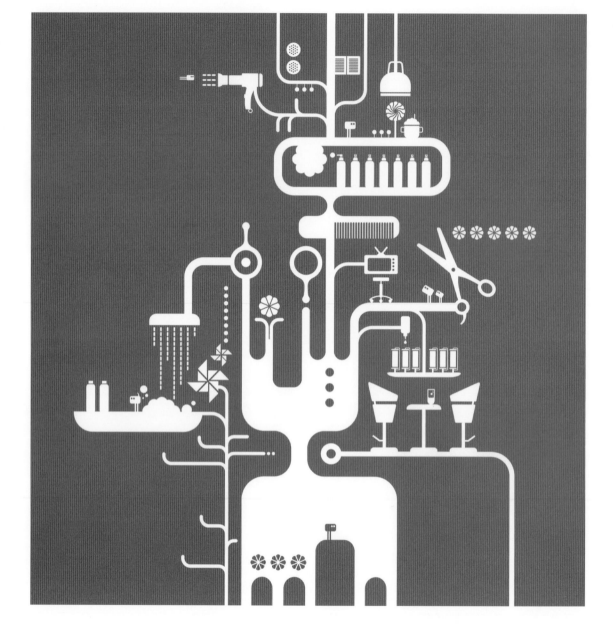

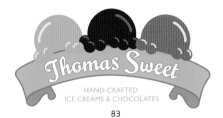

83

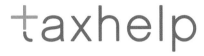

84

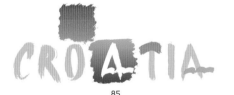

85

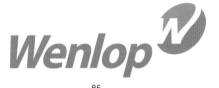

86

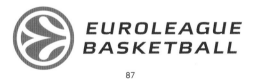

87

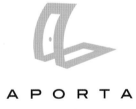

88

82
CLIENT: Kitz
DESIGN FIRM: Kinetic

83
CLIENT: Thomas Sweet
DESIGN FIRM: 98pt6

84
CLIENT: Tax Help
DESIGN FIRM: urbanINFLUENCE
Design Studio

85
CLIENT: Croatian National Tourist Board
DESIGN FIRM: Studio International

86
CLIENT: Wenlop
DESIGN FIRM: Diseño Dos Asociados

87
CLIENT: Euroleague Basketball
DESIGN FIRM: Sockeye Creative

88
CLIENT: Laporta
DESIGN FIRM: Diseño Dos Asociados

89
CLIENT: Goodness
DESIGN FIRM: Clemenger BBDO

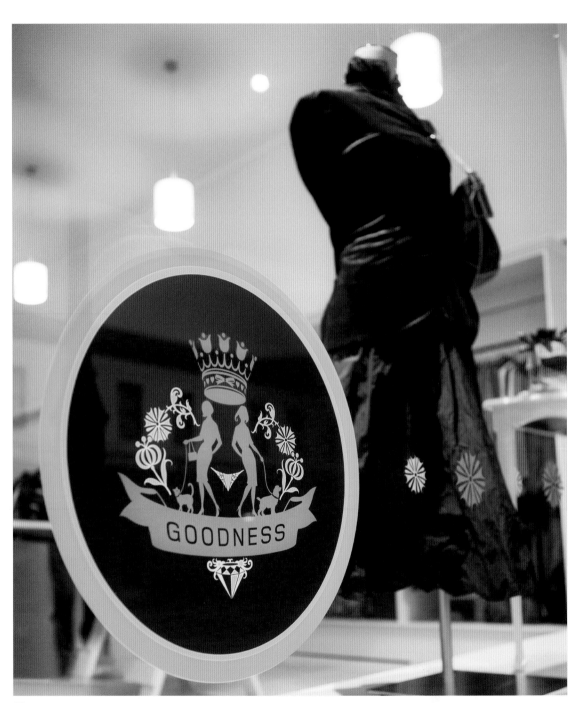

89

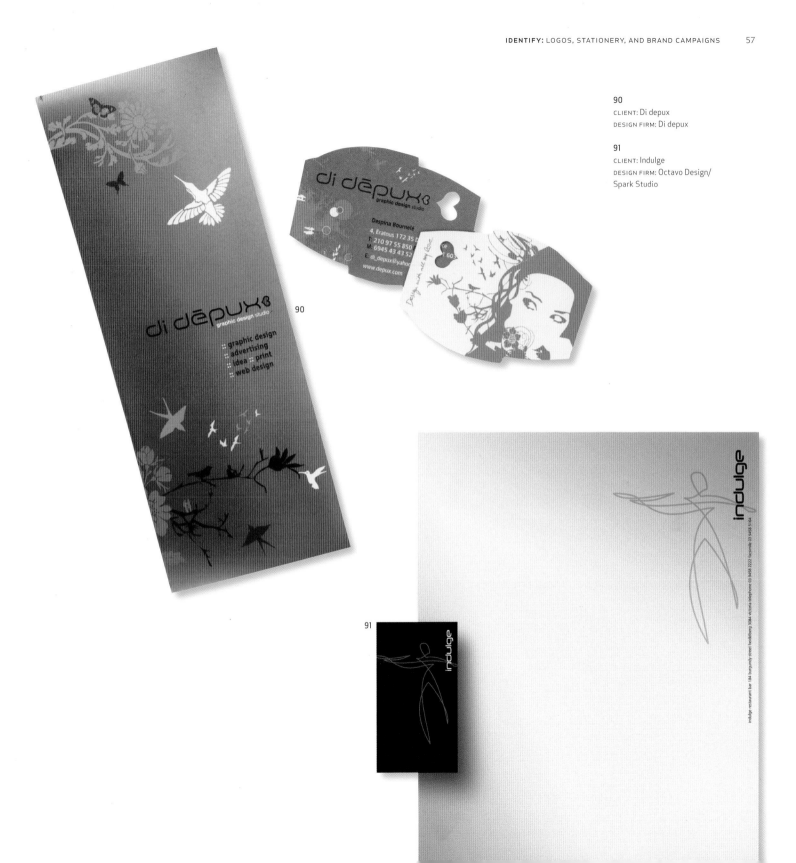

90
CLIENT: Di depux
DESIGN FIRM: Di depux

91
CLIENT: Indulge
DESIGN FIRM: Octavo Design/
Spark Studio

90

91

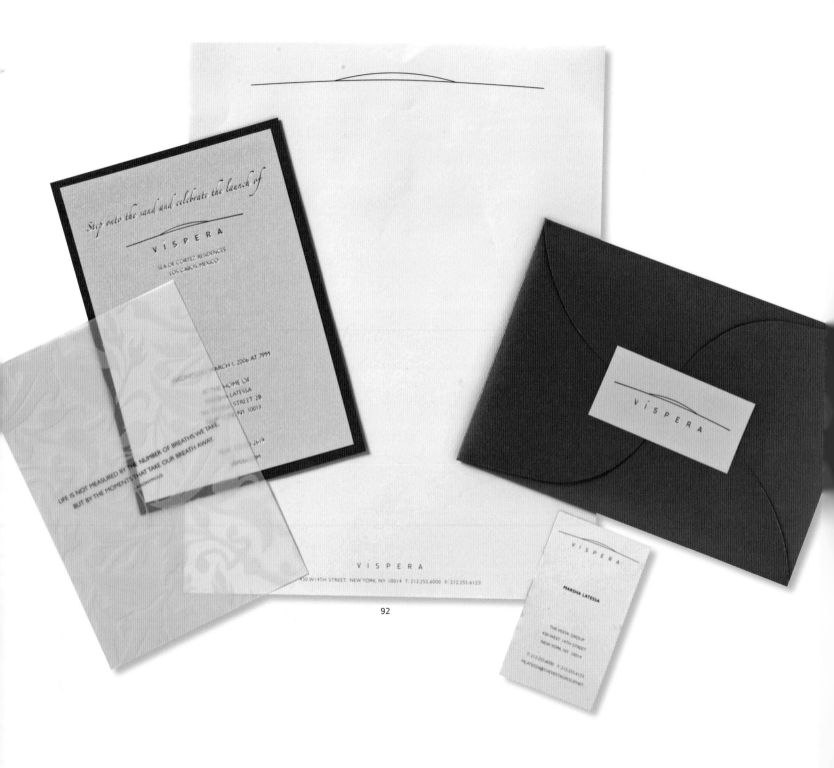

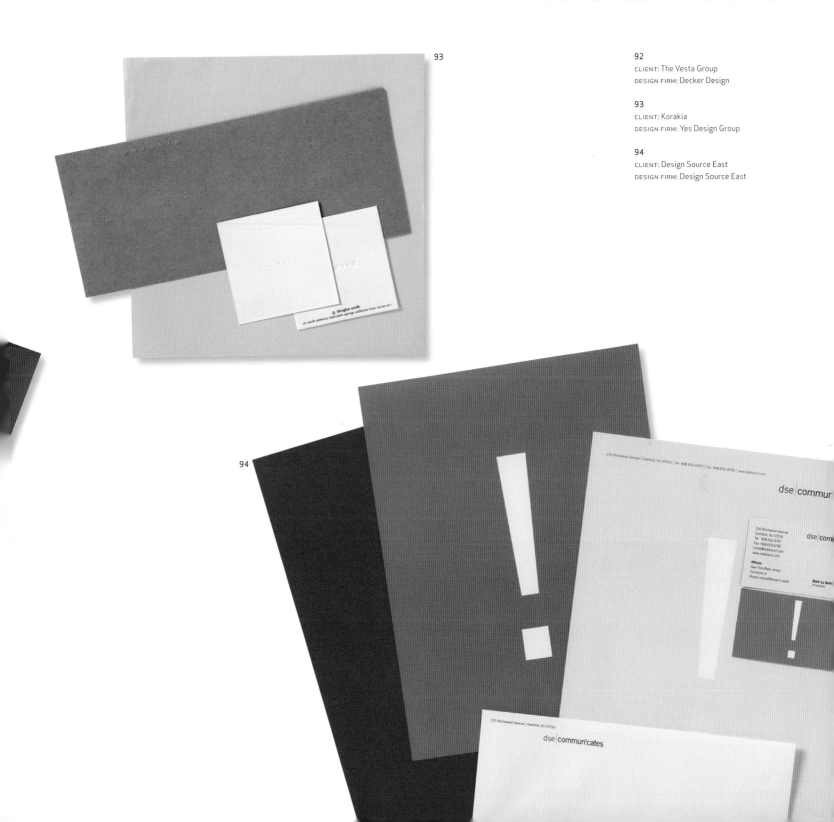

93

92
CLIENT: The Vesta Group
DESIGN FIRM: Decker Design

93
CLIENT: Korakia
DESIGN FIRM: Yes Design Group

94
CLIENT: Design Source East
DESIGN FIRM: Design Source East

94

95
CLIENT: Bergen Street Studio
DESIGN FIRM: Poulin & Morris Inc.

96
CLIENT: Routledge Modise Moss Morris
DESIGN FIRM: Enterprise IG

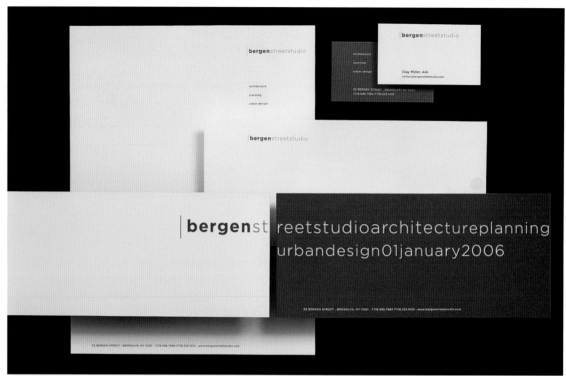

95

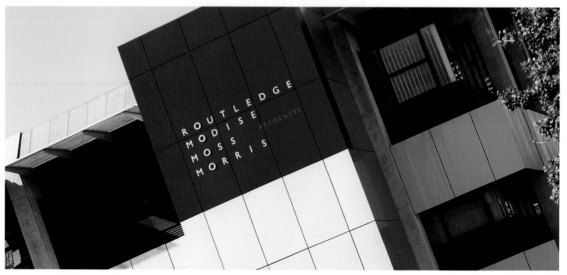

96

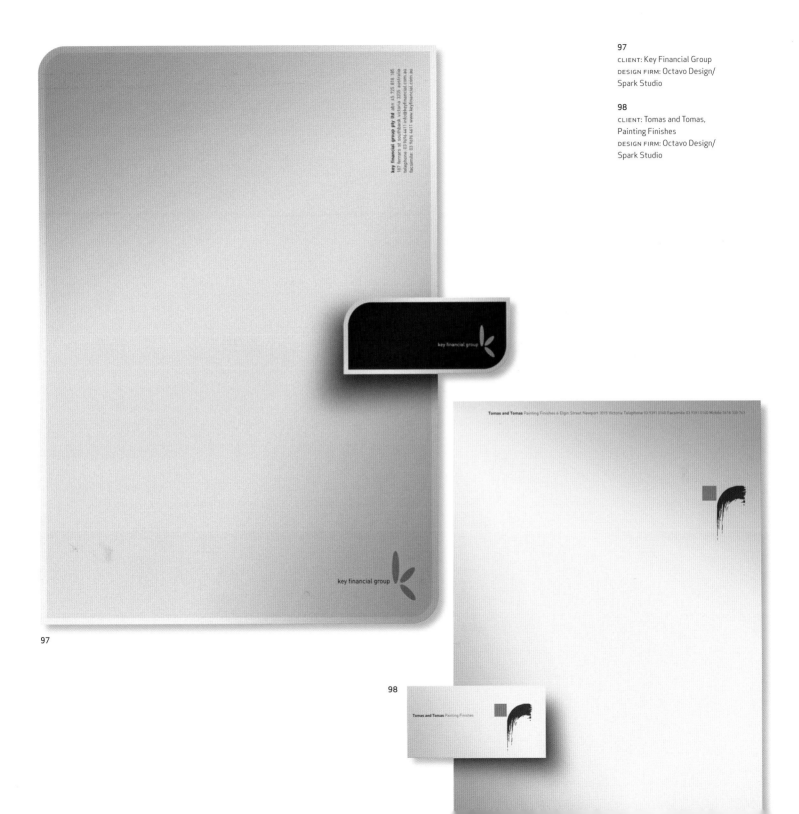

97
CLIENT: Key Financial Group
DESIGN FIRM: Octavo Design/
Spark Studio

98
CLIENT: Tomas and Tomas,
Painting Finishes
DESIGN FIRM: Octavo Design/
Spark Studio

97

98

99
CLIENT: The Giles Agency
DESIGN FIRM: Timber Design Company

100
CLIENT: DIM
DESIGN FIRM: Manasteriotti
Design Studio

101
CLIENT: 16 Candles Bakery
DESIGN FIRM: Talisman Interactive

102
CLIENT: Riat Telecom
DESIGN FIRM: urbanINFLUENCE
Design Studio

103
CLIENT: Alaska State Chamber
of Commerce
DESIGN FIRM: Mad Dog Graphx

104
CLIENT: The Handel Group
DESIGN FIRM: AS|D Labs, Inc.

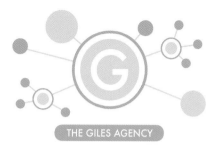

THE GILES AGENCY

99

100

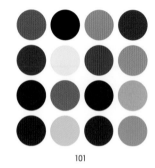

101

RIAT TELEC M

102

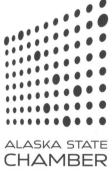

ALASKA STATE
CHAMBER
OF COMMERCE

103

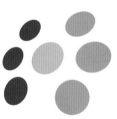

THE HANDEL GROUP

104

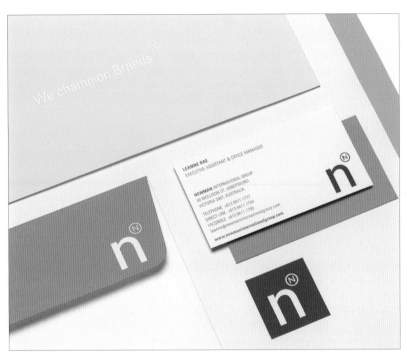

105

105
CLIENT: Newman International
DESIGN FIRM: Davidson Design

106
CLIENT: Holmes Private Investigators
DESIGN FIRM: Kinetic

107
CLIENT: Becky Lucas
DESIGN FIRM: Emmi Salonen

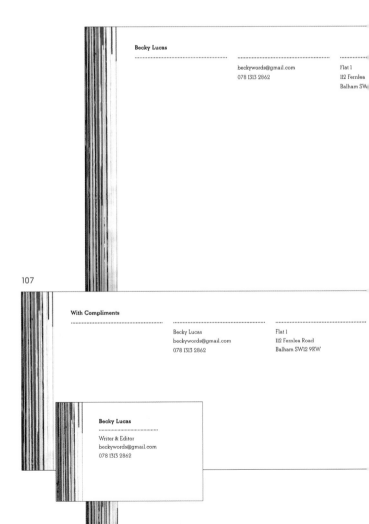

107

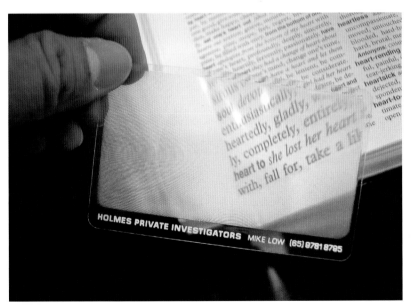

106

108

CLIENT: Truefitt & Hill
DESIGN FIRM: 98pt6

TRUEFITT&HILL

EST. 1805 · ST. JAMES'S · LONDON

◆ ◆ ◆ ◆ ◆

Grooming men for greatness.

108

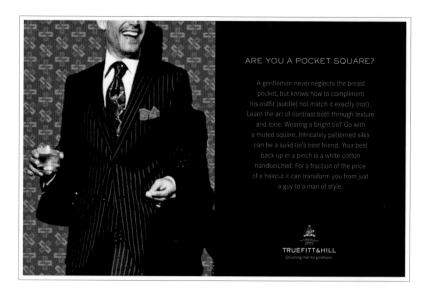

ARE YOU A POCKET SQUARE?

A gentleman never neglects the breast pocket, but knows how to compliment his outfit (subtle) not match it exactly (not). Learn the art of contrast both through texture and tone. Wearing a bright tie? Go with a muted square. Intricately patterned silks can be a solid tie's best friend. Your best back up in a pinch is a white cotton handkerchief. For a fraction of the price of a haircut it can transform you from just a guy to a man of style.

TRUEFITT&HILL
Grooming men for greatness.

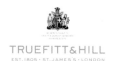

TRUEFITT&HILL
EST. 1805 · ST. JAMES'S · LONDON

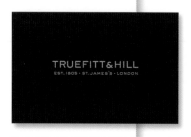

TRUEFITT&HILL
EST. 1805 · ST. JAMES'S · LONDON

TRUEFITT&HILL
EST. 1805 · ST. JAMES'S · LONDON

◆ ◆ ◆ ◆ ◆   **Brian Jacobson**
Chief Fiancial Officer

216 W. Jackson Blvd.   Tel: 312 714 1011
Suite 1040   Cell: 312 597 5138
Chicago IL 60606   Fax: 312 714 1059
www.truefittandhill.com   brian.j@truefittandhill.com

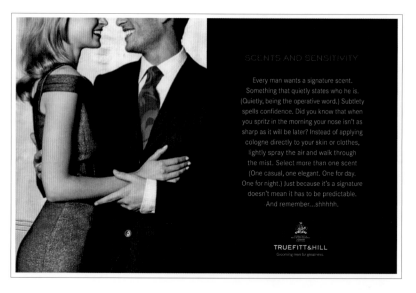

SCENTS AND SENSITIVITY

Every man wants a signature scent. Something that quietly states who he is. (Quietly, being the operative word.) Subtlety spells confidence. Did you know that when you spritz in the morning your nose isn't as sharp as it will be later? Instead of applying cologne directly to your skin or clothes, lightly spray the air and walk through the mist. Select more than one scent (One casual, one elegant. One for day. One for night.) Just because it's a signature doesn't mean it has to be predictable. And remember...shhhhh.

TRUEFITT&HILL
Grooming men for greatness.

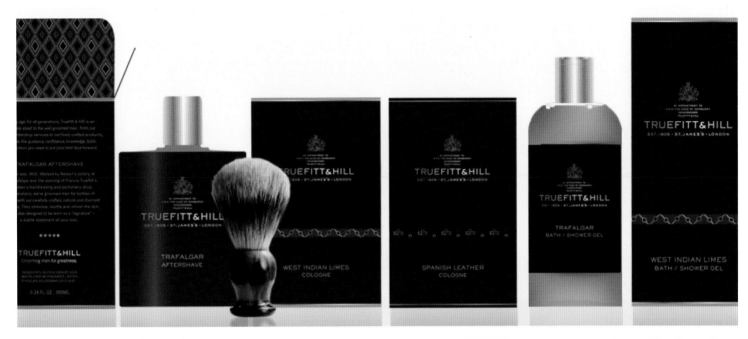

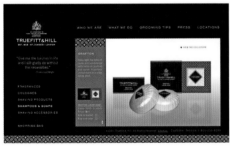

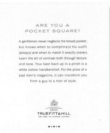

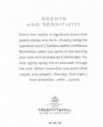

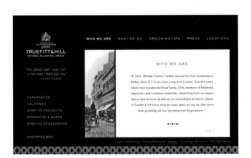

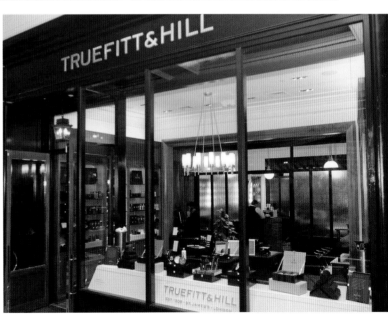

109
CLIENT: FNM Group
DESIGN FIRM: Carré Noir Roma

110
CLIENT: Interior Resource
DESIGN FIRM: Hollis Brand
Communications

111
CLIENT: Thuma Works
DESIGN FIRM: urbanINFLUENCE
Design Studio

112
CLIENT: The Jim Henson Company
DESIGN FIRM: Michele Moore Design

113
CLIENT: Mohomine
DESIGN FIRM: Hollis Brand
Communications

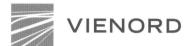 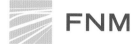 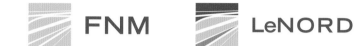

109

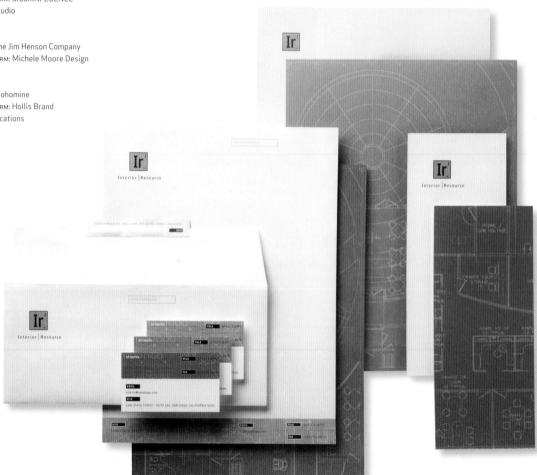

110

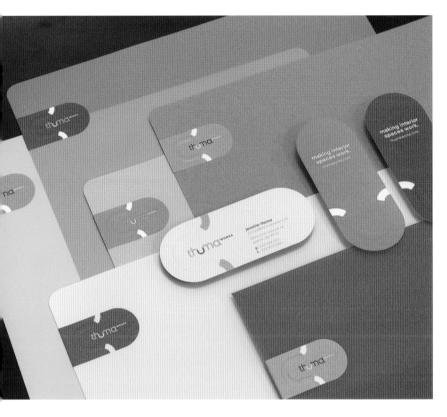

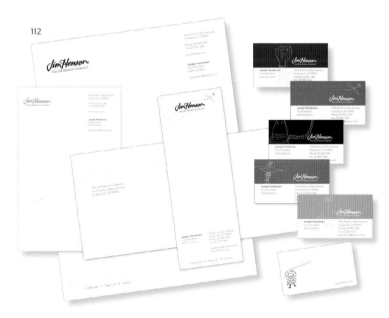

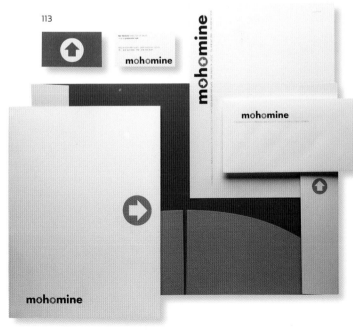

111

112

113

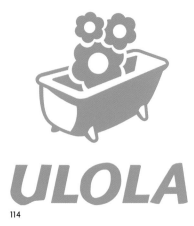

ULOLA

114

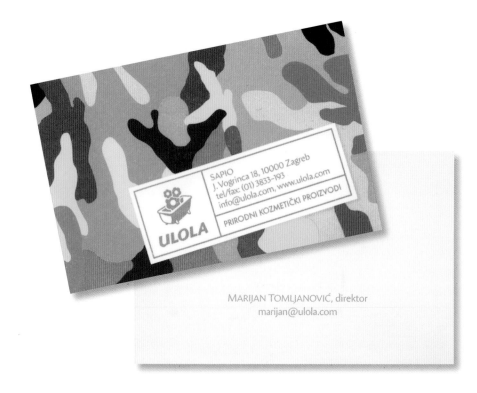

SAPIO
J. Vogrinca 18, 10000 Zagreb
tel/fax: (01) 3833-193
info@ulola.com, www.ulola.com

ULOLA   PRIRODNI KOZMETIČKI PROIZVODI

MARIJAN TOMLJANOVIĆ, direktor
marijan@ulola.com

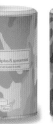
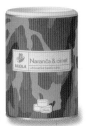
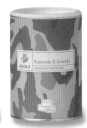

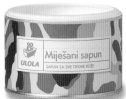
ULOLA   Miješani sapun

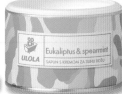
ULOLA   Eukaliptus & spearmint

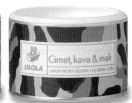
ULOLA   Cimet, kava & mak

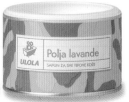
ULOLA   Polja lavande

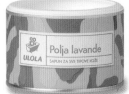
ULOLA   Polja lavande

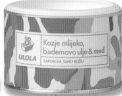
ULOLA   Kozje mlijeko,
bademovo ulje & med

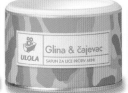
ULOLA   Glina & čajevac

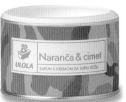
ULOLA   Naranča & cimet

REFLECTIONS

115

114
CLIENT: Ulola
DESIGN FIRM: Elevator

115
CLIENT: Reflections Printing
DESIGN FIRM: Sussner Design Company

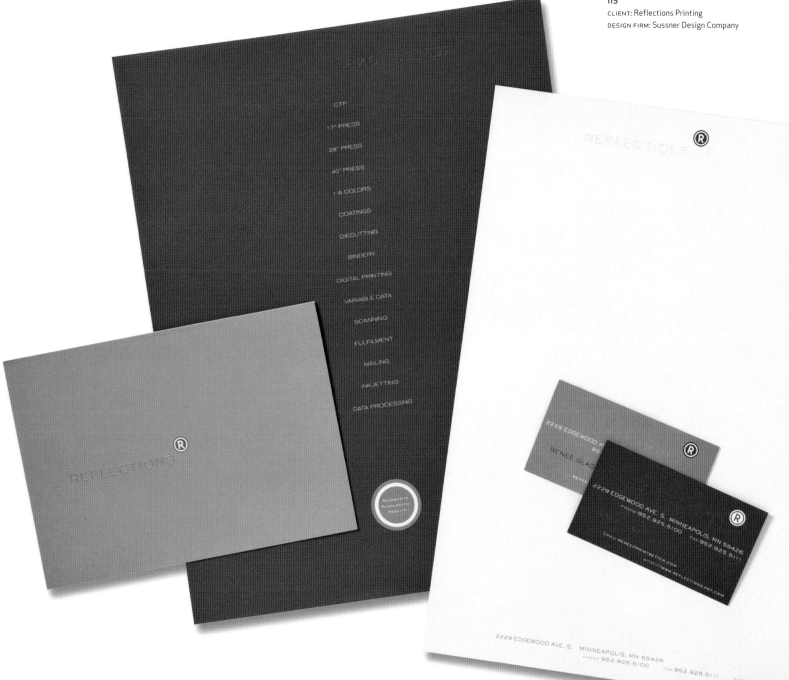

116
CLIENT: Lorenzo's Salon,
Reflections Printing
DESIGN FIRM: Sussner Design Company

117
CLIENT: Otsu
DESIGN FIRM: JDAnthony

118
CLIENT: Kaleidoscope Information
Services, Inc.
DESIGN FIRM: Valiant Media, Inc.

119
CLIENT: Fantela Apartments
DESIGN FIRM: p11 Creative

120
CLIENT: Marinanet
DESIGN FIRM: Manasteriotti Design

121
CLIENT: Arlig Teckna
DESIGN FIRM: Sussner Design Company

122
CLIENT: Axcelerator Home Loans
DESIGN FIRM: Octavo Design/
Spark Studio

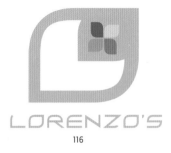

116

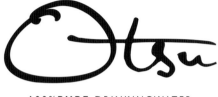

100%PURE DRINKINGWATER

117

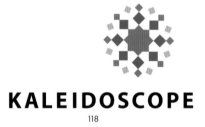

KALEIDOSCOPE

118

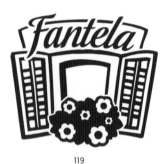

119

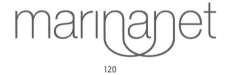

120

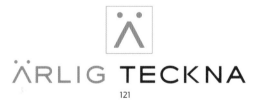

121

122

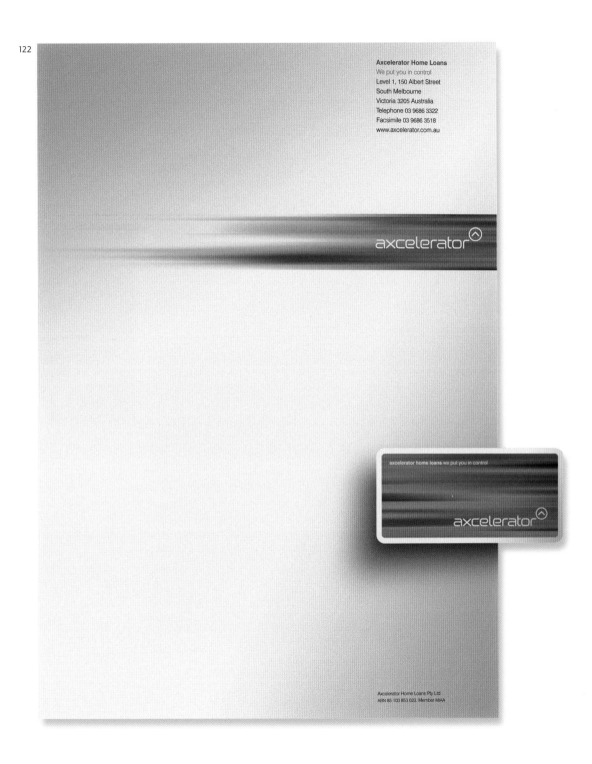

Axcelerator Home Loans
We put you in control
Level 1, 150 Albert Street
South Melbourne
Victoria 3205 Australia
Telephone 03 9686 3322
Facsimile 03 9686 3518
www.axcelerator.com.au

axcelerator

axcelerator home loans we put you in control

axcelerator

Axcelerator Home Loans Pty Ltd
ABN 85 103 853 023. Member MIAA

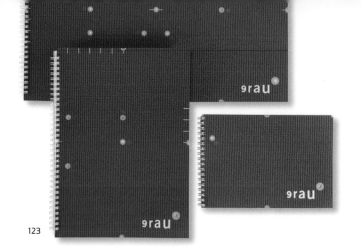

123

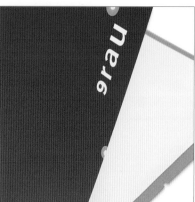

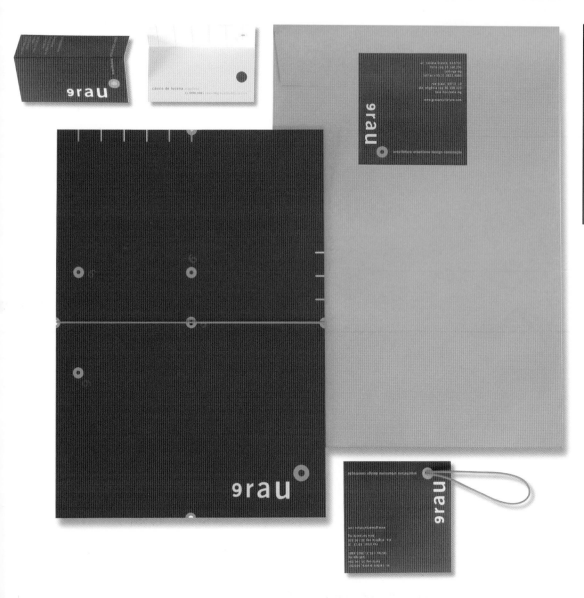

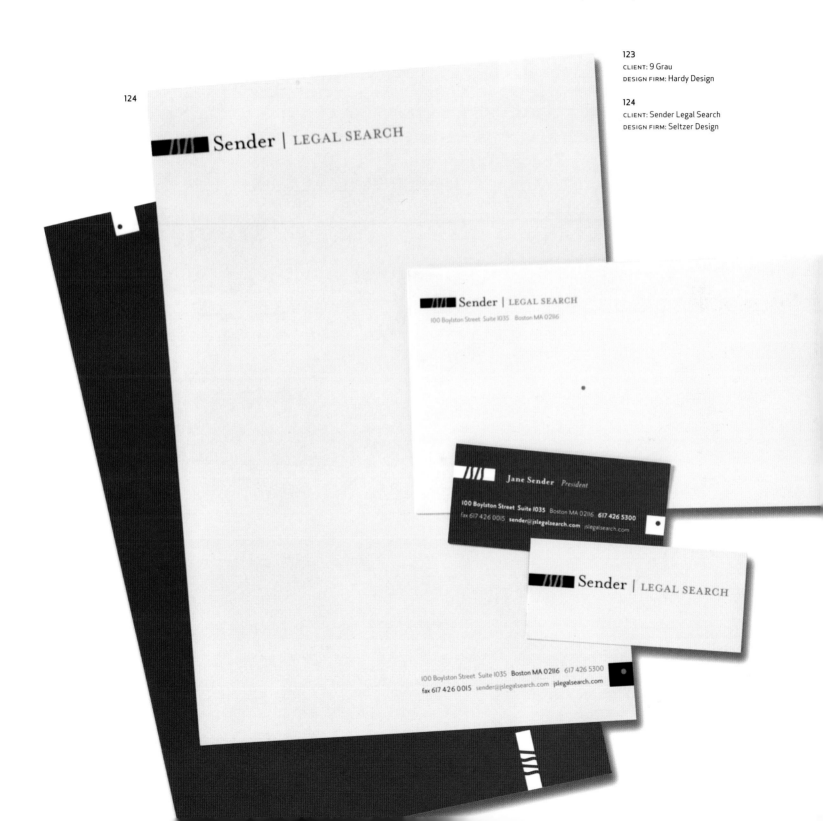

123
CLIENT: 9 Grau
DESIGN FIRM: Hardy Design

124
CLIENT: Sender Legal Search
DESIGN FIRM: Seltzer Design

125
CLIENT: The Moinian Group
DESIGN FIRM: The Valentine Group

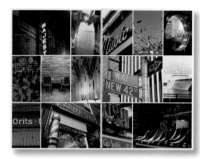

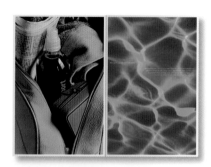

ATELIER

635 WEST 42ND STREET *new york, new york* 10036

125

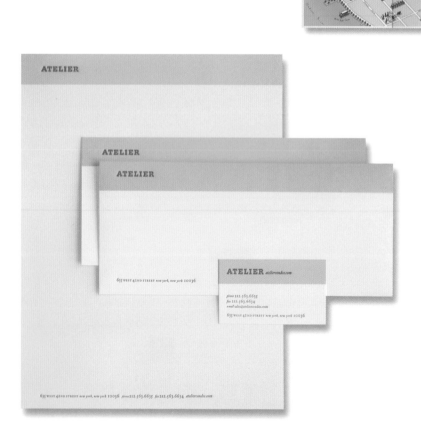

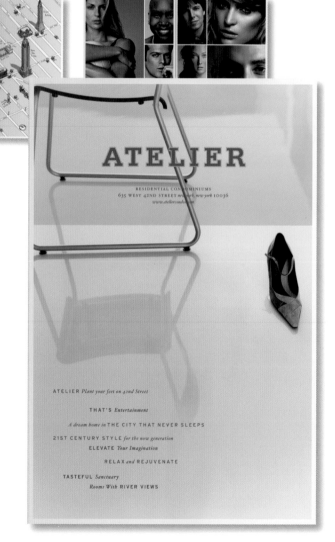

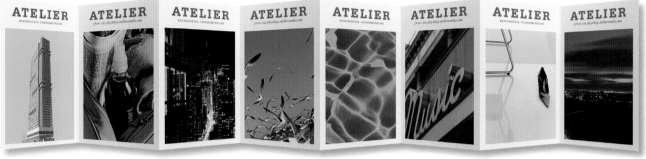

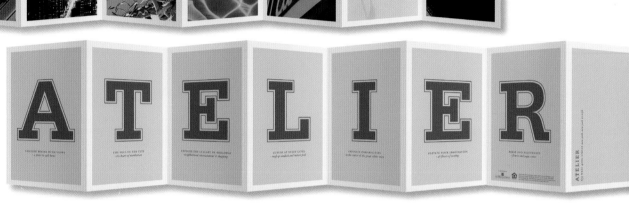

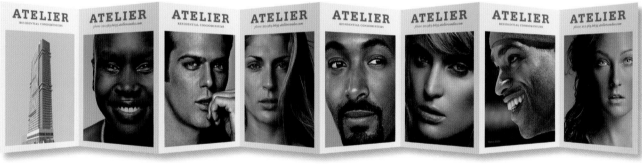

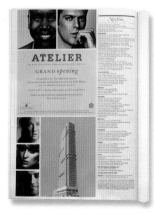

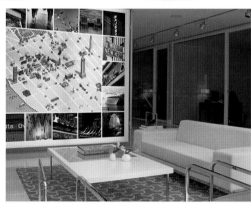

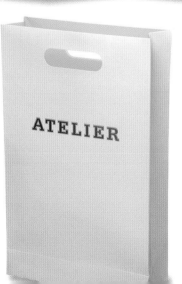

126

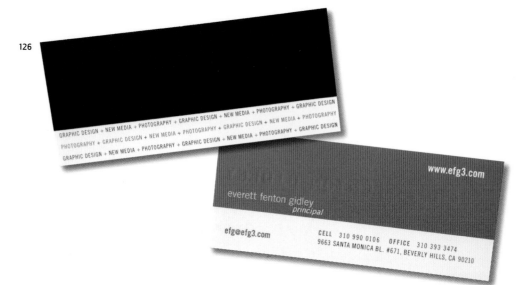

GRAPHIC DESIGN + NEW MEDIA + PHOTOGRAPHY + GRAPHIC DESIGN + NEW MEDIA + PHOTOGRAPHY + GRAPHIC DESIGN
PHOTOGRAPHY + GRAPHIC DESIGN + NEW MEDIA + PHOTOGRAPHY + GRAPHIC DESIGN + NEW MEDIA + PHOTOGRAPHY
GRAPHIC DESIGN + NEW MEDIA + PHOTOGRAPHY + GRAPHIC DESIGN + NEW MEDIA + PHOTOGRAPHY + GRAPHIC DESIGN

www.efg3.com

everett fenton gidley
principal

efg@efg3.com   CELL   310 990 0106   OFFICE   310 393 3474
9663 SANTA MONICA BL. #671, BEVERLY HILLS, CA 90210

127

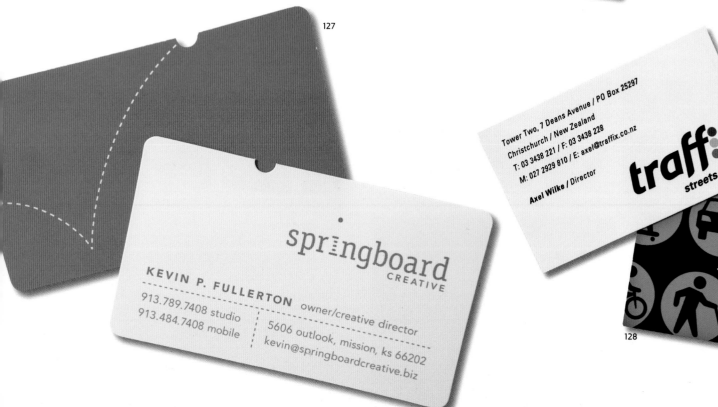

springboard
CREATIVE

KEVIN P. FULLERTON   owner/creative director

913.789.7408 studio
913.484.7408 mobile   5606 outlook, mission, ks 66202

                          kevin@springboardcreative.biz

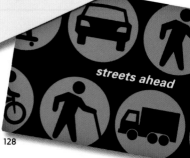

Tower Two, 7 Deans Avenue / PO Box 25297
Christchurch / New Zealand
T: 03 3438 221 / F: 03 3438 228
M: 027 2929 810 / E: axel@traffix.co.nz

Axel Wilke / Director

traff:x
streets ahead

streets ahead

128

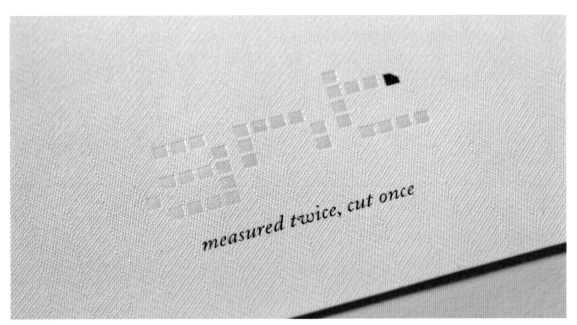

129

126
CLIENT: Everett Fenton Gidley
DESIGN FIRM: Nazy Alvarez

127
CLIENT: Springboard Creative
DESIGN FIRM: Springboard Creative

128
CLIENT: Traffix
DESIGN FIRM: Lloyd's Graphic Design Ltd.

129
CLIENT: Ant Industrial Design Pte Ltd
DESIGN FIRM: Ant Industrial Design Pte Ltd

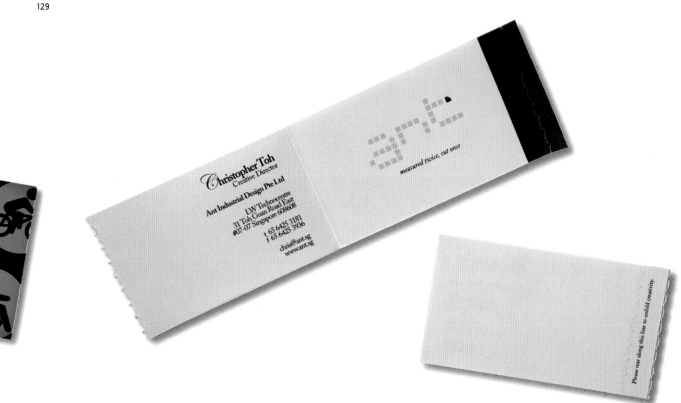

130
CLIENT: Fundação Biominas
DESIGN FIRM: Hardy Design

131
CLIENT: ClariPath
DESIGN FIRM: JDAnthony

132
CLIENT: Galenski
DESIGN FIRM: Elevator

133
CLIENT: Ljekarna Splitsko-dalmatinske
županije
DESIGN FIRM: Elevator

134
CLIENT: Dentos
DESIGN FIRM: Diseño Dos Asociados

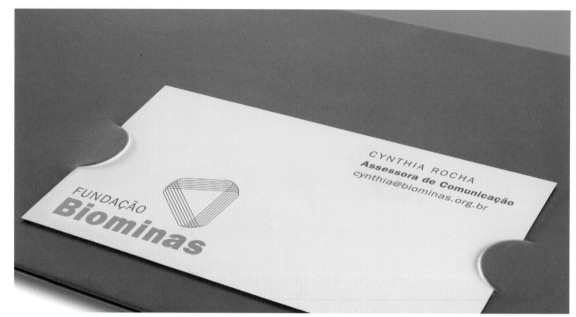

130

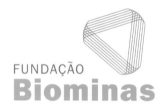

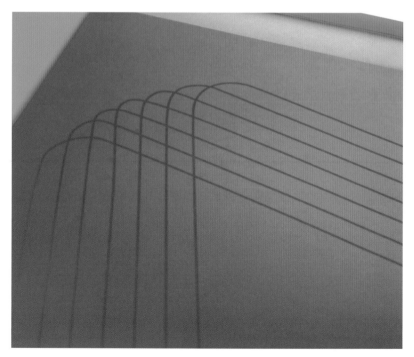

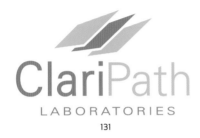

131

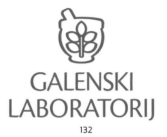

132

Ljekarna Splitsko-dalmatinske županije

133

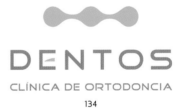

134

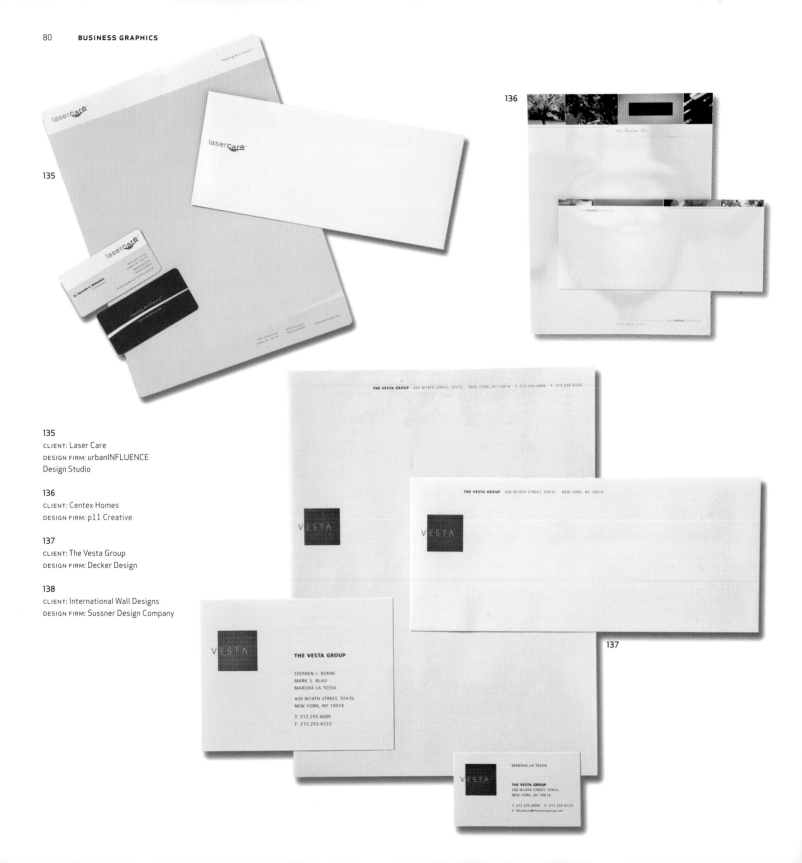

135
CLIENT: Laser Care
DESIGN FIRM: urbanINFLUENCE
Design Studio

136
CLIENT: Centex Homes
DESIGN FIRM: p11 Creative

137
CLIENT: The Vesta Group
DESIGN FIRM: Decker Design

138
CLIENT: International Wall Designs
DESIGN FIRM: Sussner Design Company

138

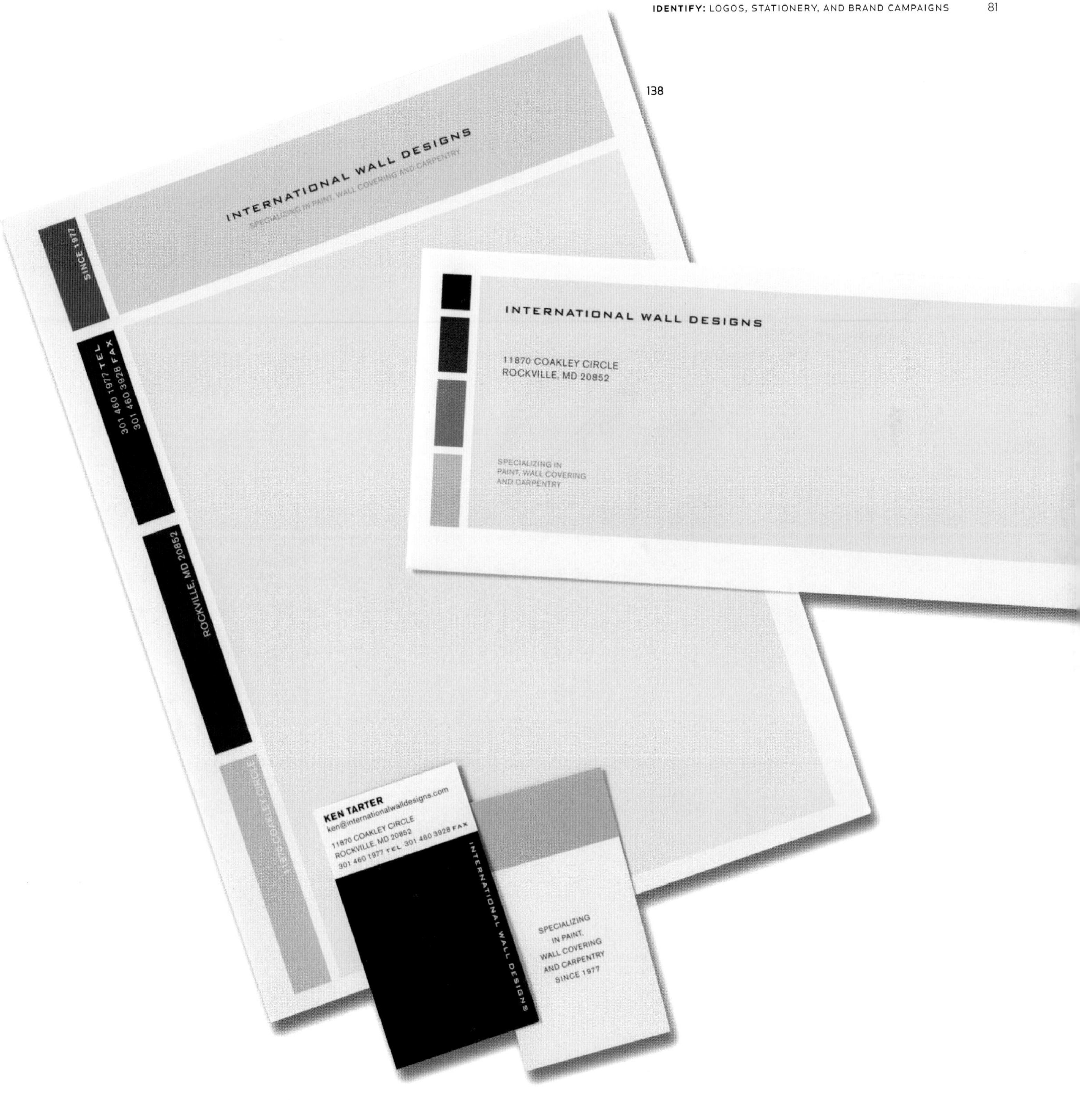

INTERNATIONAL WALL DESIGNS
SPECIALIZING IN PAINT, WALL COVERING AND CARPENTRY

SINCE 1977

301 460 1977 TEL
301 460 3928 FAX

ROCKVILLE, MD 20852

11870 COAKLEY CIRCLE

INTERNATIONAL WALL DESIGNS

11870 COAKLEY CIRCLE
ROCKVILLE, MD 20852

SPECIALIZING IN
PAINT, WALL COVERING
AND CARPENTRY

KEN TARTER
ken@internationalwalldesigns.com
11870 COAKLEY CIRCLE
ROCKVILLE, MD 20852
301 460 1977 TEL 301 460 3928 FAX

INTERNATIONAL WALL DESIGNS

SPECIALIZING
IN PAINT,
WALL COVERING
AND CARPENTRY
SINCE 1977

139
CLIENT: Brigite
DESIGN FIRM: Hardy Design

140
CLIENT: Consolidated Shoe Company
DESIGN FIRM: The Republik

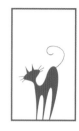

BRIGITE

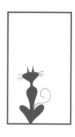

BRIGITE

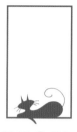

BRIGITE

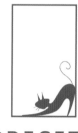

BRIGITE

139

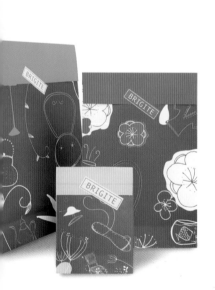

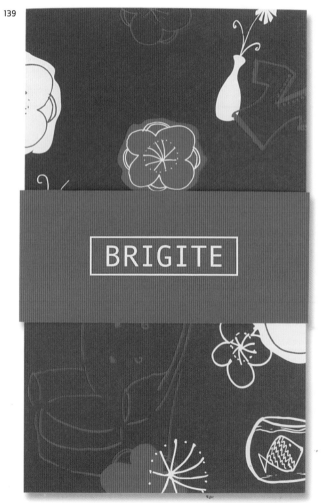

BRIGITE

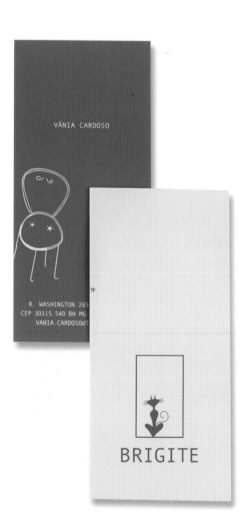

VÂNIA CARDOSO

R. WASHINGTON 265
CEP 30315.540 BH MG
VANIA.CARDOSO@T

BRIGITE

140

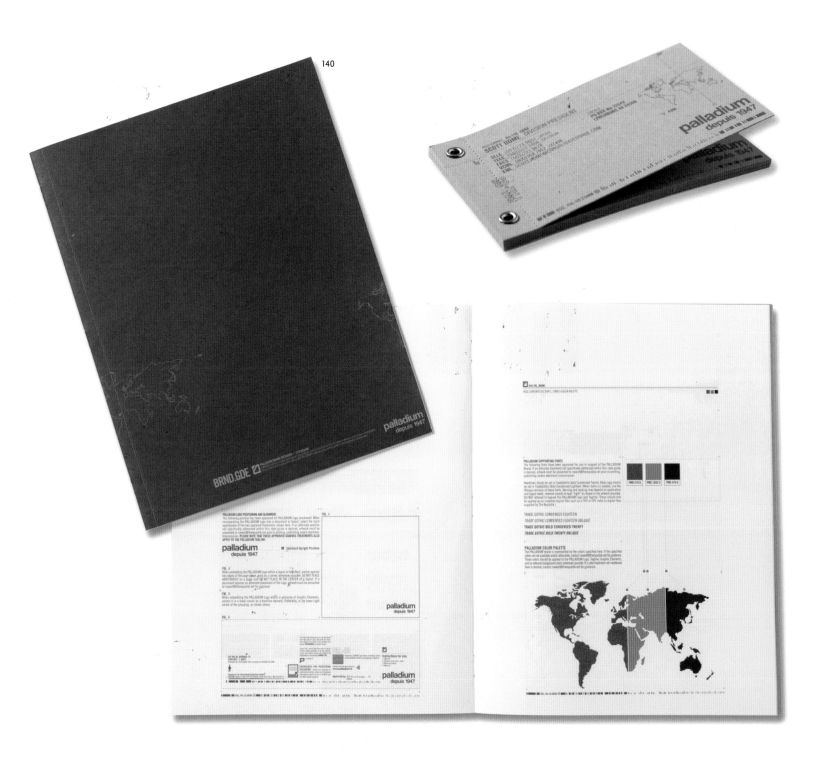

141
CLIENT: Pete's Mountain
DESIGN FIRM: Sockeye Creative

142
CLIENT: JDAnthony
DESIGN FIRM: JDAnthony

143
CLIENT: Mika Ohtsuki, Piano Technician
DESIGN FIRM: Emmi Salonen

144
CLIENT: Cold Standard
DESIGN FIRM: Hornall Anderson
Design Works

145
CLIENT: Diamlink
DESIGN FIRM: Mindseye Creative

146
CLIENT: Černelić-Business Interior
Solutions
DESIGN FIRM: Brandoctor

147
CLIENT: Mineral Image
DESIGN FIRM: Hardy Design

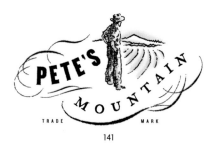

141

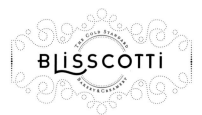

142

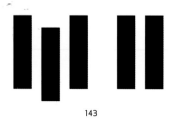

143

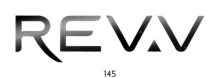

144

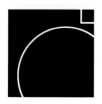

145

146

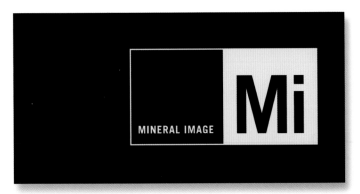

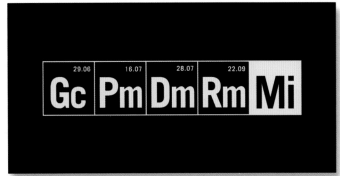

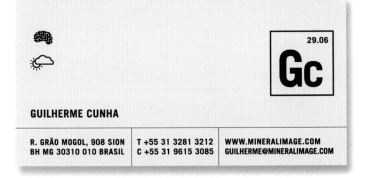

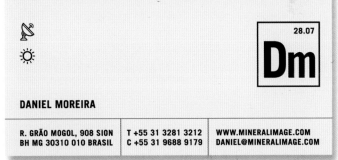

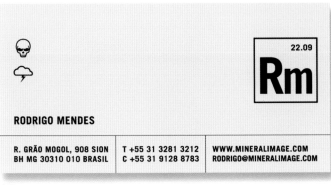

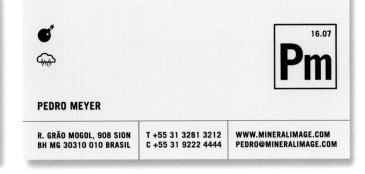

148

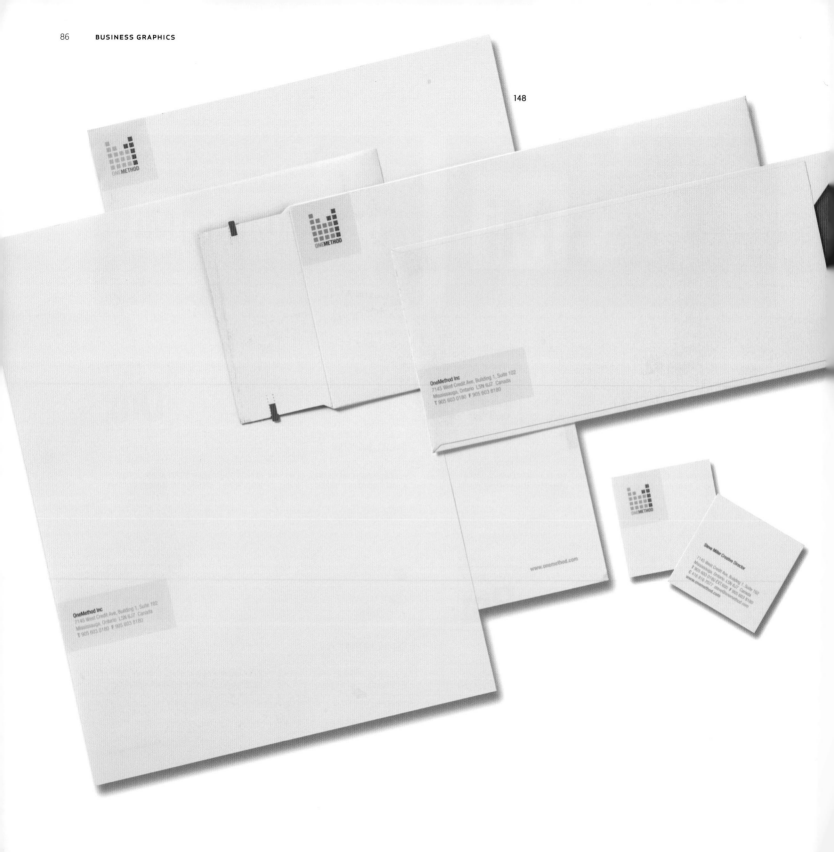

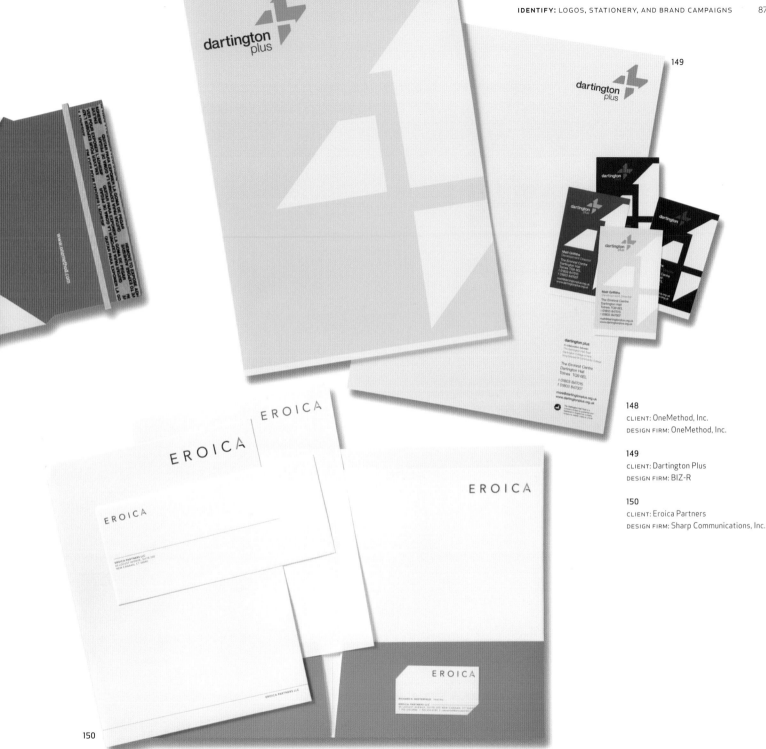

148
CLIENT: OneMethod, Inc.
DESIGN FIRM: OneMethod, Inc.

149
CLIENT: Dartington Plus
DESIGN FIRM: BIZ-R

150
CLIENT: Eroica Partners
DESIGN FIRM: Sharp Communications, Inc.

151

LANG NATURALS, INC. 20 Silva Lane Newport, RI 02842
T 401 848 7700 F 401 848 7701 www.langnaturals.com

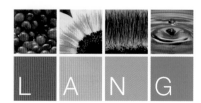

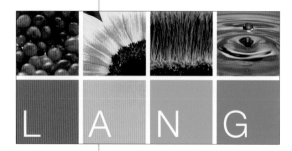

DAVID LANG
dave.lang@naturals.com

LANG NATURALS, INC. 20 Silva Lane Newport, RI 02842
T 401 848 7700 F 401 848 7701 www.langnaturals.com

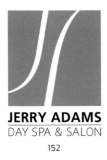

JERRY ADAMS
DAY SPA & SALON
152

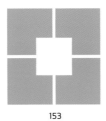

153

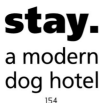

stay.
a modern
dog hotel
154

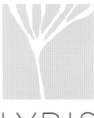

LYRIS
155

156

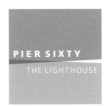

PIER SIXTY
THE LIGHTHOUSE
157

151
CLIENT: Lang Naturals
DESIGN FIRM: Lowercase, Inc.

152
CLIENT: Jerry Adams Day Spa & Salon
DESIGN FIRM: Liska + Associates

153
CLIENT: Vastu Commons
DESIGN FIRM: Lienhart Design

154
CLIENT: Stay. A Modern Dog Hotel
DESIGN FIRM: Liska + Associates

155
CLIENT: Lyris
DESIGN FIRM: Hardy Design

156
CLIENT: Subject Wills & Company
DESIGN FIRM: Talisman Interactive

157
CLIENT: Pier Sixty & The Lighthouse
DESIGN FIRM: Sharp Communications, Inc.

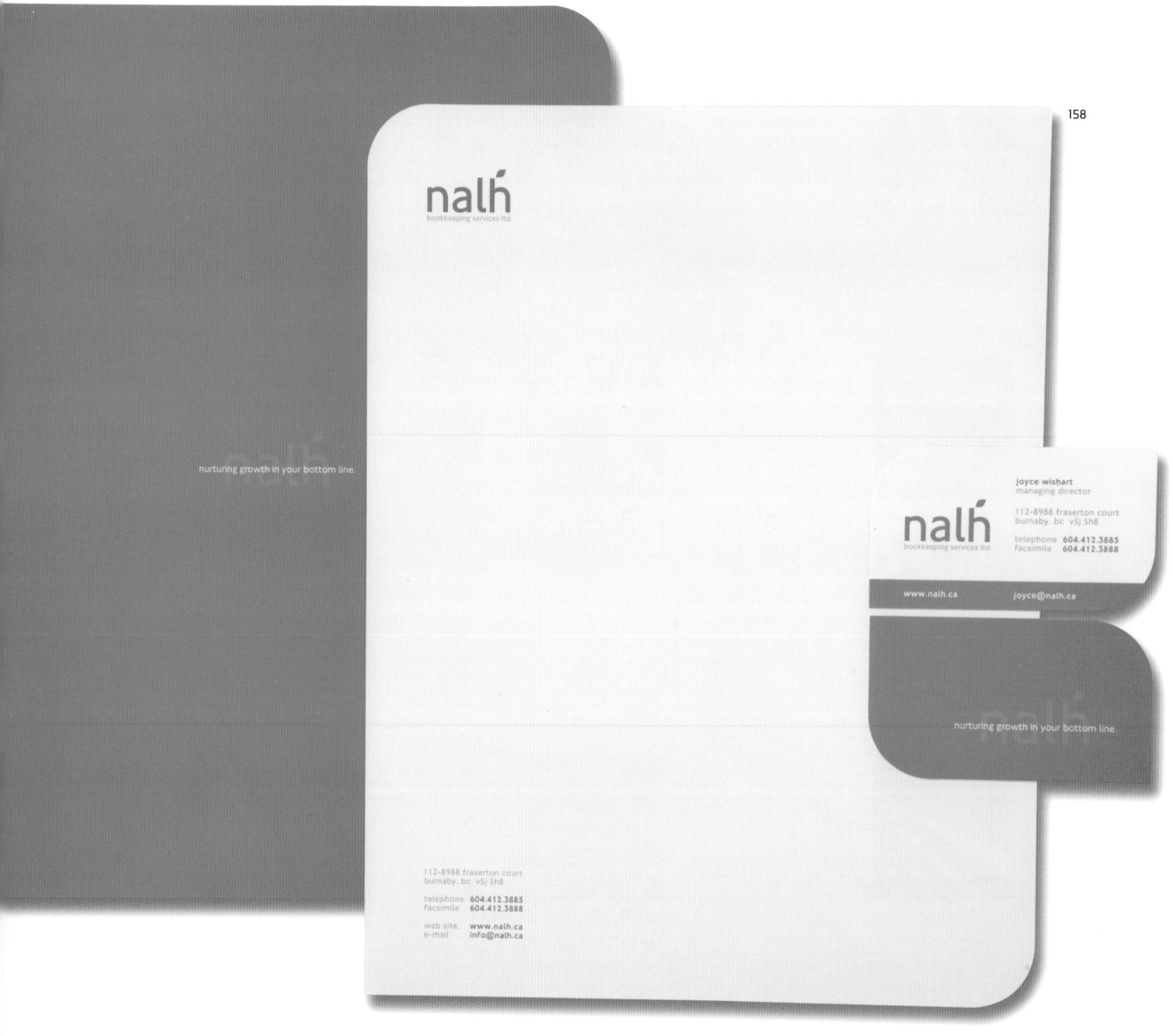

158

nalh
bookkeeping services ltd.

nurturing growth in your bottom line.

joyce wishart
managing director

nalh
bookkeeping services ltd.

112-8988 fraserton court
burnaby. bc v5j 5h8

telephone 604.412.3885
facsimile 604.412.3888

www.nalh.ca   joyce@nalh.ca

nurturing growth in your bottom line.

112-8988 fraserton court
burnaby. bc v5j 5h8

telephone 604.412.3885
facsimile 604.412.3888

web site   www.nalh.ca
e-mail   info@nalh.ca

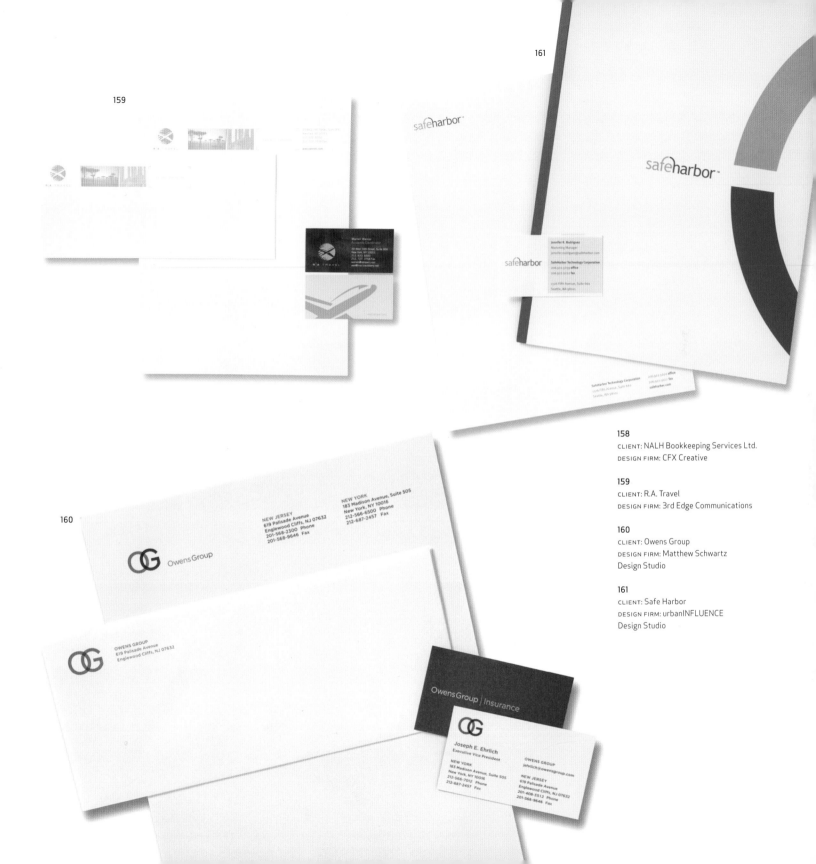

158
CLIENT: NALH Bookkeeping Services Ltd.
DESIGN FIRM: CFX Creative

159
CLIENT: R.A. Travel
DESIGN FIRM: 3rd Edge Communications

160
CLIENT: Owens Group
DESIGN FIRM: Matthew Schwartz
Design Studio

161
CLIENT: Safe Harbor
DESIGN FIRM: urbanINFLUENCE
Design Studio

CO WORKER

that we were independently owned and operated. In a sense, we embraced what has been described as "devolution," a concept that allowed us to operate independently, become even more responsive to our clients needs and create challenging opportunities for young talented architects, while participating in a larger network known as Anshen+Allen.

Was the decision unanimous among the principals in Los Angeles? Absolutely.

When was Anshen+Allen in San Francisco notified? April 18, 2005

What was the reaction? The principals in the San Francisco office were very understanding of the need for our firm to embrace a unique identity. They have been proactive in working with us to assure customers that this is a change in name only, and that the professional standards of both firms remain exceptionally high.

Did the termination of the license agreement involve any financial exchange? No.

How will the firms manage business they now work on jointly? We will work as partners toward a single, unified goal: to exceed our clients' expectations for the projects.

Our clients are paramount and we will do everything in our power to meet this goal.

Will the firms compete? As two completely independent firms working in the same fields it is only natural that we will be submitting for the same projects from time to time.

Will you continue to focus on the academic, science and technology, healthcare, and civic practice areas? Yes. While these markets represent the majority of the projects the firm is awarded, the knowledge and skills amassed as a collaborative team is also fully transferable to any number of other markets.

Will you continue to maintain and expand your expertise in lab design and healthcare planning? Absolutely.

Who will serve as the managing principals of the firm? Will this change? No, our principals will remain the same and will serve in the same roles they did as Anshen+Allen Los Angeles.

How will this change deliver better results for the firm overall? From a pragmatic standpoint, we will broaden our marketing base and submit proposals to clients that we have had an interest in working with. In addition, working under our own name will lessen confusion among the public and our

profession al[...]
Anshen+Allen[...]
change in ide[...]
nurture our v[...]
progressive, [...]
is continually[...]
understandin[...]
ahead of us. [...]
that reflects [...]
and what we [...]
It truly gives[...]
the firm we e[...]

FAQs

Why did we change our name?

We started in 1986 as a regional office of the San Francisco based Anshen+Allen. Ten years later we became a separate firm, autonomous and locally owned. While expressing our own identity in the name Anshen+Allen Los Angeles, we continued to be linked to our origins by remaining in a working alliance with the Anshen+Allen organization.

Will the firm maintain its present location? Yes, not only does Los Angeles provide a relatively central location for our clients, but it also gives our team access to complementary resources that we can leverage on behalf of our clients.

Are there plans to expand into new geographies with new offices? Not at this time.

Will there be any changes in personnel across the board? No.

Will you be hiring? If so, what positions? We are in a constant state of gradual and considered growth, and presently are expanding our team with the best talent available. Our office has grown steadily since it opened in 1986.

How will this arrangement deliver better results for the employees? Our new name, CO Architects, for the first time creates a tangible sense of identity for the office and our team. This name will reinforce our values, fortify our culture and strengthen our vision. Creating our own name that reflects who we are and what we are allows each member of our team to work toward a common set of ideals and gives us the freedom to become the firm we want to be.

How will this change impact proposals that are in review? The basic substance of the proposal does not change, only the name of the firm which submitted the work. We believe it is important that people recognize the broad scope of our work in academics as well as in the science and research, healthcare and civic fields.

Who will "own" projects that have been completed by the Los Angeles office in terms of a portfolio of work? CO Architects will own these projects. They represent the body of expertise and success that our firm has built over the years; the passion and style of our team and our approach to creating lasting projects in a collaborative environment.

Will the current Los Angeles clients be retained by CO Architects? Yes, absolutely.

Will this change cause any delays or extensions in current projects? No, w[...] are conducting business as usual and are committed to consistently deliveri[...] projects that exceed our clients' expe[...] tions in creativity, innovation, purpose[...] and functionality. Our clients will con[...] tinue to see the same discipline in ter[...] of timelines and integrity of process.

When did you notify your clients? C[...] clients were notified of our new name [...] beginning June 6, 2005.

CLIENT:

CO ARCHITECTS

DESIGN FIRM:

ADAMSMORIOKA

An **inquisitive, skillful practice** engaged in a collaborative process of discovery and immersed in the craft and technology of building.

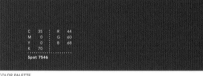

C	35	R	44
M	0	G	60
Y	0	B	68
K	70		

Spot 7546

C	0	R	102
M	50	G	163
Y	50	B	84
K	20		

Spot 617

COLOR PALETTE

A ABCDEFGHJKLMNOPQRSTUVWXYZabcdefghijklmnopqrstuvwxyz
ABCDEFGHJKLMNOPQRSTUVWXYZabcdefghijklmnopqrstuvwxyz

PRIMARY TYPEFACE: AVENIR (TOP) OR ARIAL (BOTTOM)

16 TOOLBOX

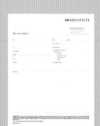

18 TOOLBOX

FAX COVER SHEET (SINGLE)   FAX COVER SHEET (MULTIPLE)   LETTER OF TRANSMITTAL

You can find
K(drive): Of[...]

Approach

We strive to design buildings that enrich the lives of the people who use them; buildings that gracefully fulfill functional and technical expectations, yet appeal as fully to the senses as to the intellect.

We pursue ideas that embody the timeless values of the institutions we serve. We believe good buildings reinforce the coherence of their surroundings and maintain their physical and cultural significance over time.

Clients and consultants are collaborative partners in our persistent search for the solution that best fits the needs of the program and site. Design emerges through a creative, iterative process of discovery.

Our senior staff share a common store of knowledge and experience, developed over nearly two decades, that informs every project. Principals actively lead project teams in a practice founded on a structure of participation.

We couple our depth of experience with a genuine delight in the craft and technology of building. We seek to rise above the exigencies of the program and budget to make memorable places that build community and celebrate the experience of being in a particular place at a particular time.

www.coarchitects.com

COMPANIES GROW AND CHANGE. WHEN A NAME CHANGES, A COMPANY NEEDS A VISUAL SYSTEM TO INTRODUCE, CLARIFY, AND ESTABLISH THE CHANGE. DESIGN FIRMS OFTEN FACE THE CHALLENGE OF DEVELOPING AN IDENTITY SYSTEM AND REBRANDING PROGRAM THAT PROVIDES A CONNECTION TO THE BEST ATTRIBUTES OF THE OLD COMPANY, WHILE INFUSING THE IMAGE WITH FRESHNESS AND VITALITY. THIS CASE STUDY PRESENTS AN INNOVATIVE AND ENERGETIC DESIGN SOLUTION THAT POSITIONS **CO ARCHITECTS** AS BOTH NEW AND ESTABLISHED.

CO ARCHITECTS

1

1
The logo communicates a brand anchored in strength and infused with energy.

CLIENT After several years in business, Anshen+Allen renamed itself CO Architects. CO Architects specializes in large architectural projects in the academic, healthcare, and science/technology fields. Its roster includes some of the most well-known and experienced architects in the United States.

With the name change, CO Architects needed to reintroduce itself to current and future clients and its approximately 110 employees. Company officials have long understood that graphic design is a complex and specialized profession, and looked to AdamsMorioka, the company that created the original identity system for Anshen+Allen in 1999, to rebrand the firm.

PROJECT AdamsMorioka chose a bold and simple visual system for CO Architects. They celebrated and emphasized the unique name wherever

possible and focused on communicating the client's attributes of energy and strength. Designers developed a new logotype, a color palette, a custom font, stationery, project sheet templates, proposal covers, announcement cards, a book cover, merchandise giveaways, and even company wrapping paper.

Feedback from employees and existing clients was overwhelmingly positive, and the rebranding program generated significant interest from potential clients. Recruitment efforts also improved; CO Architects saw a thirty percent jump in new applicants in the year following the rebranding effort.

INTERNAL AUDIENCE Current employees are a critical target audience for any corporate identity and rebranding program. If engaged, informed, and proud of their company's brand,

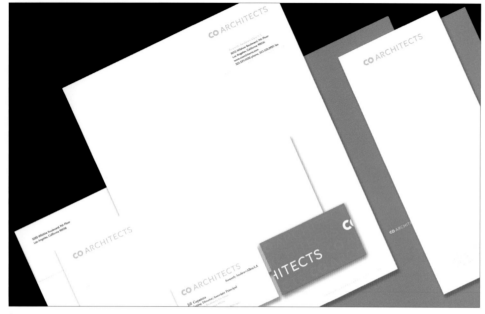

2

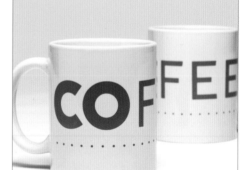

3

employees function as brand ambassadors. AdamsMorioka made sure that the rebranding program included creative and thoughtful ways to introduce the system to employees. They paid careful attention to the design of the employee handbook, internal style guidelines, and the "packaging" of the rebranding program.

At the launch of the rebrand, each employee received a unique bamboo desktop organizer that included business cards, employee handbook, notecards, merchandise, and a coffee mug. This attention to detail and understanding of the important internal audience further established the brand among the firm's most important brand ambassadors—the employees.

STRONG ATTRIBUTES The most valuable visual systems accurately reflect the client's attributes. CO Architects had long been known for being consistent, stable, collaborative, and dedicated to excellence. AdamsMorioka emphasized these elements and designed a new corporate identity and rebranding program that communicates a brand anchored in strength and infused with energy. ■

4

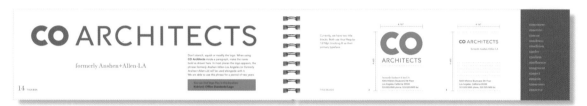

CO ARCHITECTS

formerly Anshen+Allen-LA

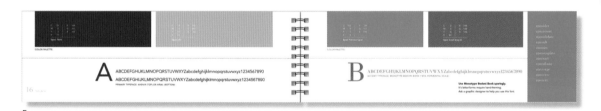

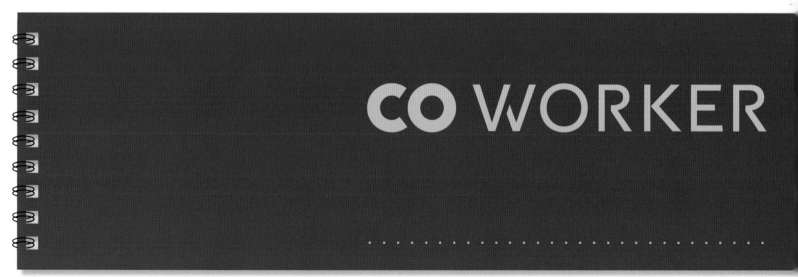

5

6

2

AdamsMorioka used color and style to convey both vitality and stability.

3

AdamsMorioka designed templates that the client could easily adapt to show a variety of projects.

4

Functional office items reinforce the brand.

5

AdamsMorioka extended the rebranding program to the design of the style guidelines.

6

The unusual name lends itself well to a variety of communication pieces.

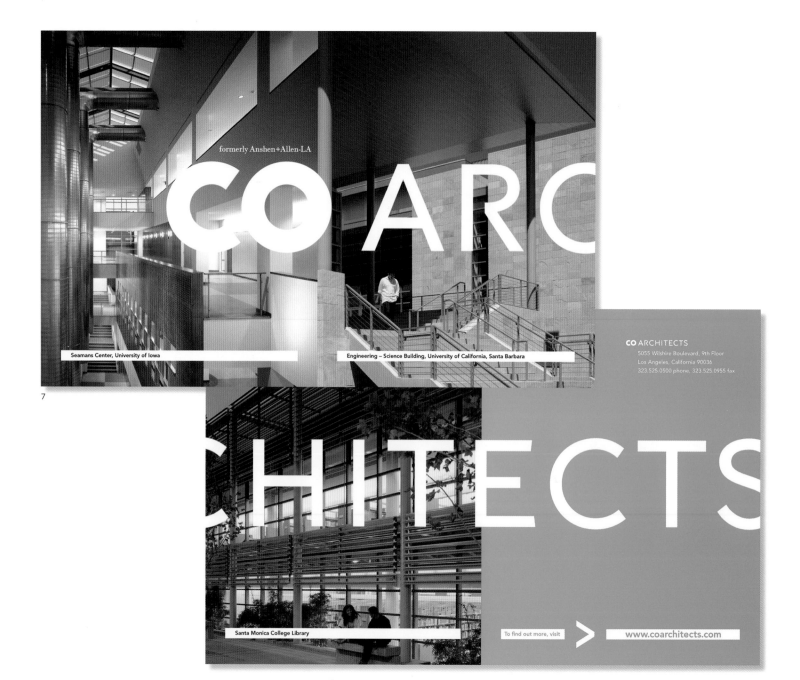

formerly Anshen+Allen-LA

CO ARC

Seamans Center, University of Iowa

Engineering – Science Building, University of California, Santa Barbara

CO ARCHITECTS
5055 Wilshire Boulevard, 9th Floor
Los Angeles, California 90036
323.525.0500 phone, 323.525.0955 fax

CHITECTS

Santa Monica College Library

To find out more, visit > www.coarchitects.com

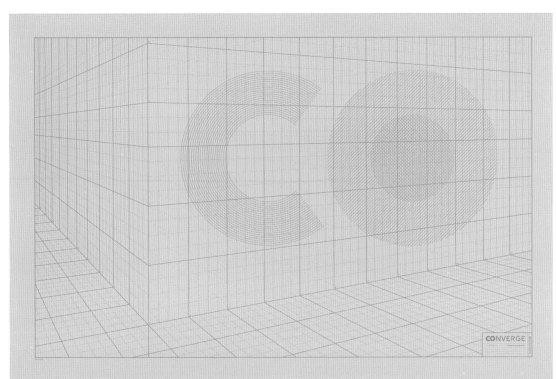

7
Postcards are printed in a way that allows for customized imprinting for featured projects.

8
The design team created wrapping paper to communicate the brand in an unexpected and intriguing way.

9
The interior, in this case, is the brand. AdamsMorioka designed the entrance to the client's office to provide immediate introduction to the new visual language.

10
To introduce and generate excitement about the rebranding program, each employee received a bamboo desk tray filled with branded materials.

CLIENT: CO Architects
DESIGN FIRM: AdamsMorioka
ART DIRECTORS: Sean Adams, Volker Dürre
DESIGNER: Volker Dürre

8

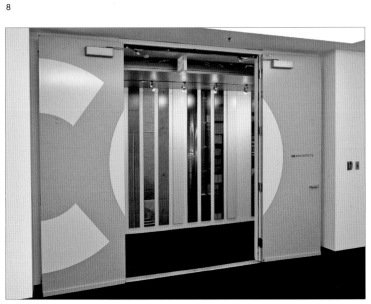

9

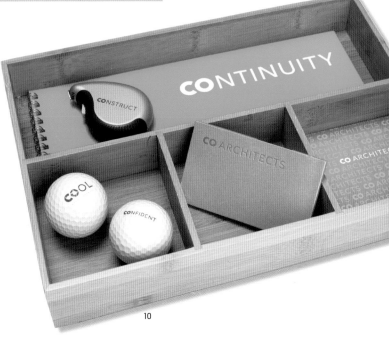

10

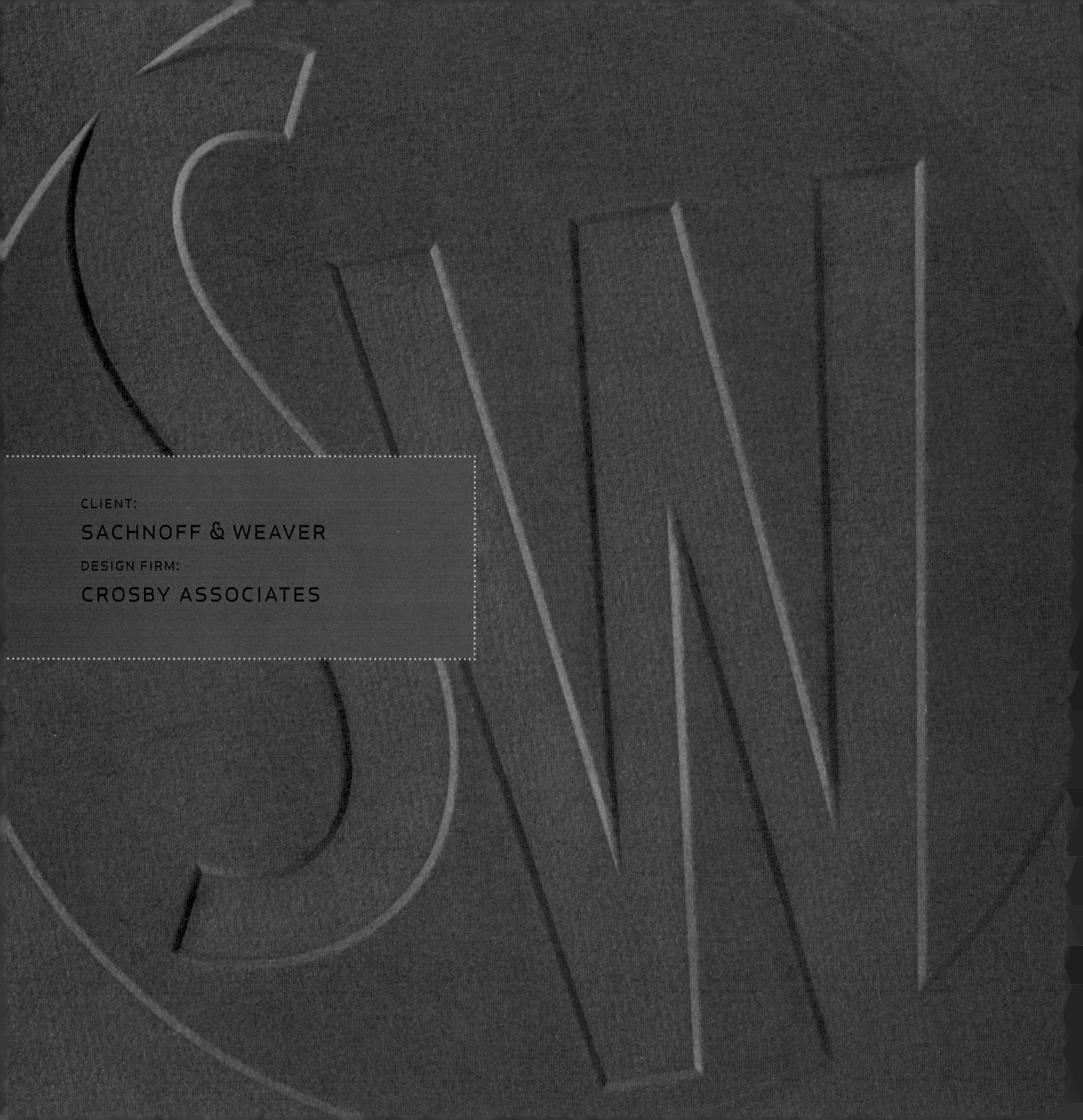

CLIENT:
SACHNOFF & WEAVER
DESIGN FIRM:
CROSBY ASSOCIATES

THOUGHTFUL AND HOLISTIC BRANDING INCREASES AWARENESS AND BUILDS RECOGNITION AMONG A COMPANY'S INTERNAL AND EXTERNAL AUDIENCES. BRANDING DIFFERENTIATES ONE COMPANY FROM ANOTHER AND UNIFIES AND FOCUSES CORPORATE VALUES. THIS THOROUGH, SYSTEMATIC, AND WELL-ARTICULATED IDENTIFICATION AND BRANDING PROGRAM CREATED FOR INTERNATIONAL LAW FIRM **SACHNOFF & WEAVER** ACHIEVES THE PERFECT BALANCE OF CONSISTENCY AND FLEXIBILITY.

Sachnoff&Weaver

CLIENT Sachnoff & Weaver employs more than 140 lawyers and offers a remarkably large array of legal services. The legal industry has undergone corporate consolidation and commoditization of services over the past fifteen years. Business once based on long-term relationships has become more consumer-driven and product-oriented. These changes caused Sachnoff & Weaver to grow in size and scope and face stiffer competition. It needed visual language to support its efforts toward client retention, attorney recruitment, and marketplace differentiation. The company approached Crosby Associates with a request for a consistent corporate identity and a system of communicating its brand across a variety of communication pieces.

PROJECT Crosby Associates developed a strong visual language that emphasizes consistent messaging and flexibility of use. The expansive

program includes the logo design, a typeface, a color palette, stationery, a website, annual reviews, environmental graphics, report covers, notecards, and more. Even with the size of the program, the visual style is brilliantly simple and distinctive. The designers wisely chose a variety of photography, typography, and well-established editorial illustrators to communicate a personality that reflects the law firm's progressive, yet business-oriented style.

VISUAL VARIETY The best branding programs allow for visual variety rooted in consistent messaging—no small task for a design firm. Colors may change, techniques may be combined, and written language may differ in an effort to keep the audience engaged. The corporate website does not have to look exactly like the advertising, and the annual report need not look like the employee holiday party invite. What

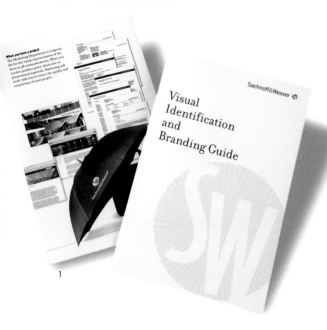

1

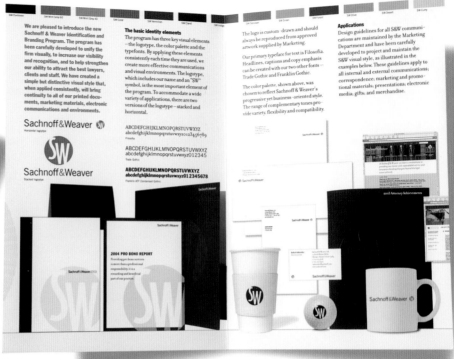

does need to be consistent throughout all the communication media is the core message of the company.

Crosby designed a varied visual language for Sachnoff & Weaver that enhances the depth of the core values of the company. The website looks hip and urban, while the notecards look elegant and refined. However, both indicate that the company is smart, accomplished, significant, and contemporary.

CONSISTENT FLEXIBILITY One of the greatest challenges for any midsize to large company is to develop an identification and branding program that will be implemented by any number of departments, in multiple locations, and by

several vendors. Regardless of what an approved set of style guidelines may require, people will customize presentations, report covers, and corporate coffee cups.

Crosby's designers understood this penchant for customization and designed with it in mind. They developed a program that offers consistency and flexibility through the use of extremely detailed templates with built-in ways of customizing color and adapting the design to various print techniques. Accounting for the way people *really* use program components ensures that the company's core values are always communicated, even when an employee prefers SW Curry over SW Indigo. ∎

2

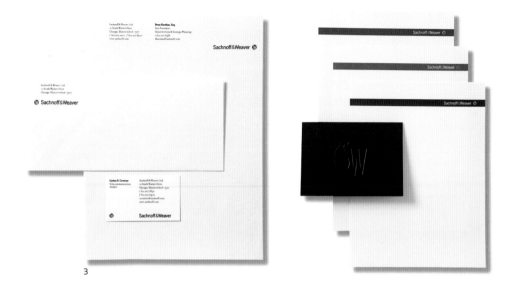

3

1

To introduce the branding initiative to employees, Crosby created a quick reference guide that details the flexibility and breadth of the program.

2

Crosby explored several logo options. The process helped refine ideas and focus concepts.

3

Crosby created a comprehensive stationery system including an embossed notecard and printed or engraved sheets for imprinting.

4

Highly detailed templates provide consistency across all corporate communications.

All measurements are in points

48   24
9   31
26   4
138

Corporate Governance Team
September 12, 2003
www.sachnoff.com

Height of the "W" = 12.453
Symbol Height = 15.568

30

Sachnoff&Weaver

15.5

Client Advisory

39

Are You Compensating Your Directors Appropriately?

36

Overview

18

Following the enactment of the Sarbanes-Oxley Act of 2002, compensation paid to outside directors, and their corresponding duties, has received more attention than in the past. Previously, outside directors generally received cash stipends, some form of equity or equity-based compensation and, occasionally, were eligible to participate in a non-qualified deferred compensation or retirement program. Because of the increase in expected time commitment, the greater risk, visibility and focus on corporate governance issues, and the supply and demand of qualified "financial experts," the role of outside directors, as well as their compensation, is now coming under increased scrutiny.

27.5

Increased Expectations

It is clear that the expected role and the corresponding time commitment for outside directors of public companies has increased. Indeed, recent studies suggest that the average outside director's workload has increased annually from 175 hours to about 300 hours. because of this increased workload, and attendant risk, the question of how to compensate outside directors (and the amount) is gaining greater prominence.

Adjusting Components of Director's Compensation

More and more companies are reviewing and adjusting the compensation packages of their directors. The types of adjustments that companies are considering include the following:

17.5

- Adjusting the board retainer fees, both with respect to the amount of the fee and the manner in which it is paid (i.e., cash versus equity)

5

Editorial illustrations added a level of creative sophistication and personality to the Annual Review.

6

The photography and color palette support the brand, while giving the website an intuitive and progressive feel.

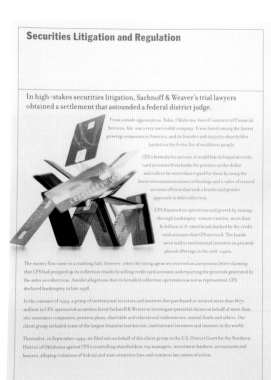

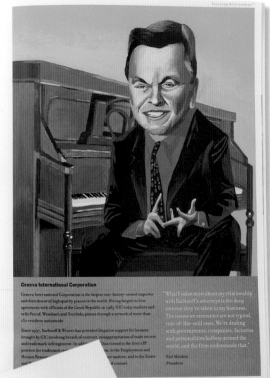

5

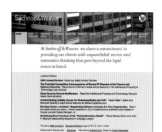

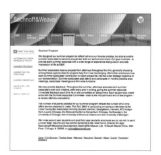

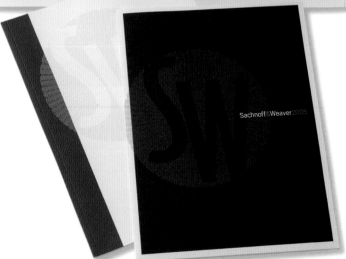

6

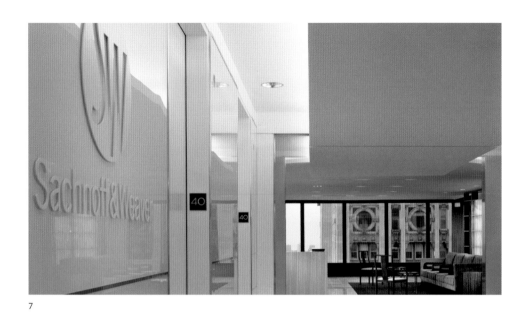

7

7
The identity and branding program is used throughout the company, from the lobby of the corporate offices to the business cards.

8
Crosby chose textured paper and specialty printing techniques to communicate Sachnoff & Weaver's depth and attention to detail.

CLIENT: Sachnoff & Weaver
DESIGN FIRM: Crosby Associates
ART DIRECTOR: Bart Crosby
DESIGNERS: Carl Wolht, Gosia Sobus

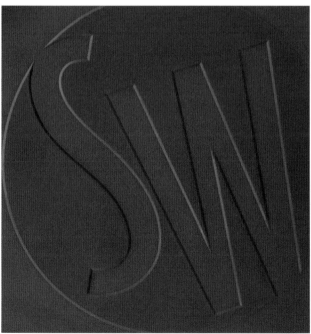

8

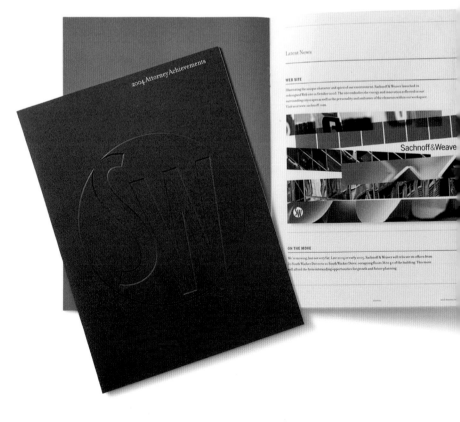

CLIENT:

AMSTERDAM PARTNERS

DESIGN FIRM:

KESSELSKRAMER

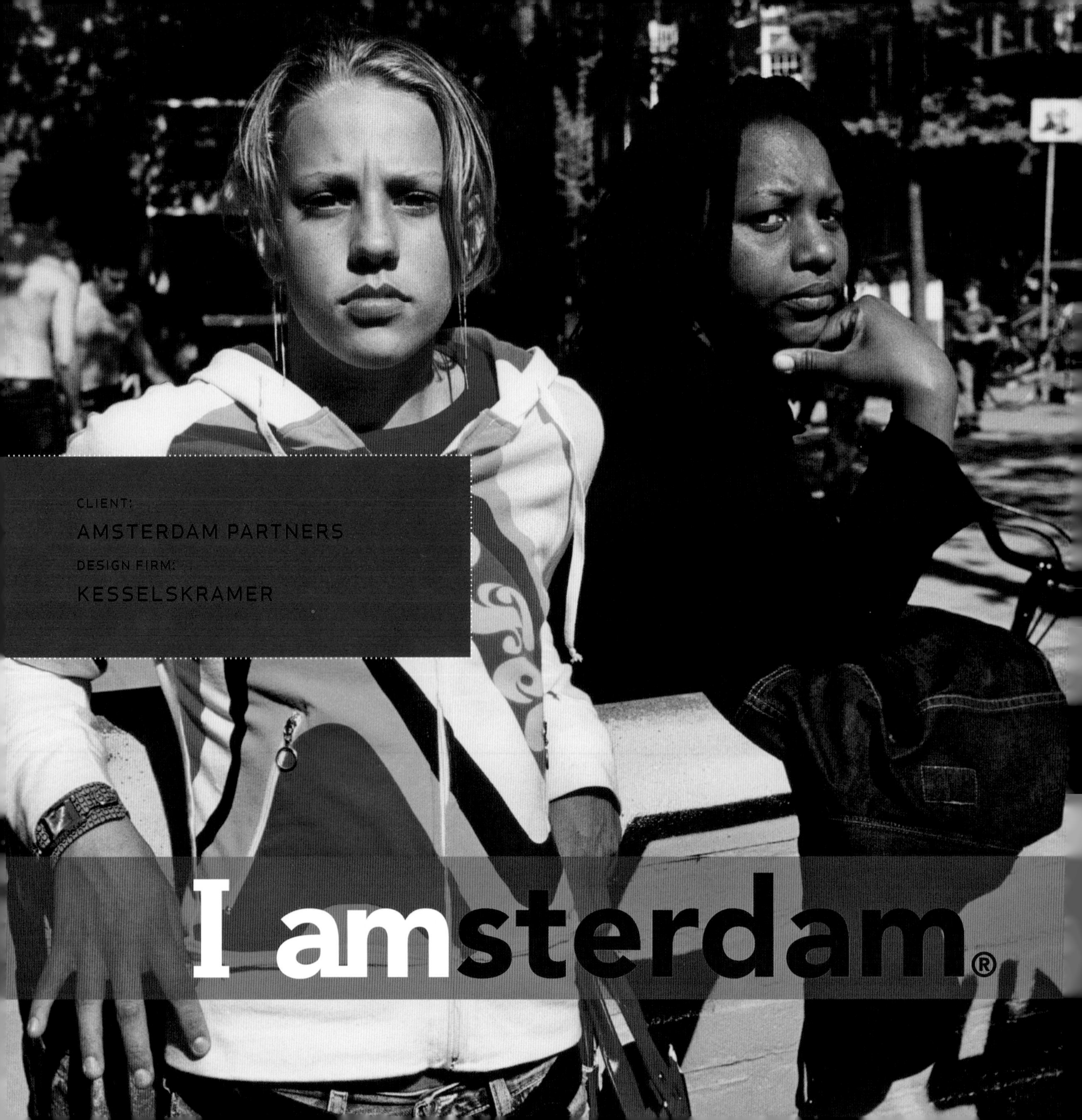

I amsterdam®

DESIGNERS CREATE BRAND PROGRAMS; AUDIENCES CREATE BRANDS. THIS MAKES THE PROCESS OF BRAND DEVELOPMENT BOTH STRATEGIC AND SERENDIPITOUS. DESIGNERS USE COLOR, TEXTURE, SHAPE, AND TEXT TO GUIDE AN AUDIENCE TOWARD PERCEIVING CERTAIN THINGS, BUT THE ULTIMATE INTERPRETATION IS UP TO THEM. HOW PEOPLE INTERPRET A DESIGN DEPENDS ON SEVERAL FACTORS— SOME THAT THE DESIGNERS CAN MANAGE, AND SOME THAT DEPEND ON A PERSON'S OVERALL EXPERIENCE WITH THE PRODUCT, SERVICE, OR COMPANY BEING BRANDED. THE MULTIPLICITY OF FACTORS BRINGS A SURPRISE ELEMENT INTO BRAND CREATION.

I amsterdam.

1

1

I Amsterdam allows the people of Amsterdam to speak for the city.

<<PHOTO: Martijn van de Griendt

This case study showcases a visual system that was designed to harness audience participation in brand development. The client, Amsterdam Partners, engaged KesselsKramer to develop a branding program for the city of Amsterdam. The design solution encourages open and varied interpretations of what Amsterdam represents and how best to express the essence of the city.

CLIENT Amsterdam has a strong reputation as a hub for international business and a destination for vibrant culture. The region competes with cities such as Barcelona and Berlin for both commerce and tourism. Amsterdam Partners is an initiative comprising government entities, cultural institutions, and local businesses, including Heineken, Philips, and Shell, that works to increase Amsterdam's international appeal.

PROJECT KesselsKramer approached the project by treating the city of Amsterdam like it would any other branding project. The "thing" to be branded in this case happened to be less tangible than a single service or company. While attempting to understand the essence of such a diverse city, KesselsKramer concluded that in the end, a city is its people. From this strategic conclusion, the design team created the central theme for the brand program, I Amsterdam. Deliverables included the I Amsterdam name, a book, photography, an exhibition, and a brand manual directing use for outdoor advertising, posters, merchandise, a website, and co-branded material.

LONG RUN KesselsKramer chose to execute the I Amsterdam concept by letting the people of Amsterdam speak for the city. The design firm

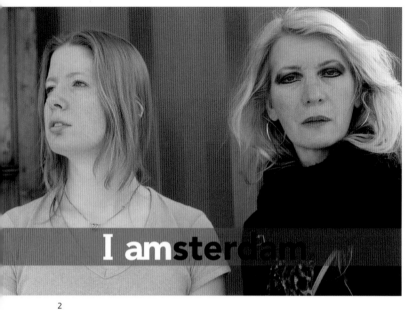

2

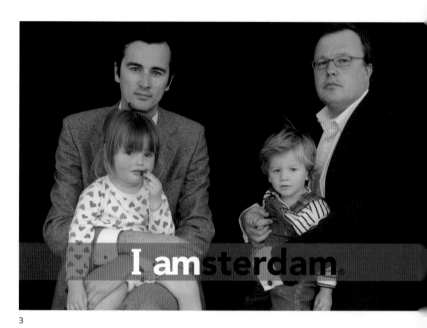

3

commissioned portraits of the city from twenty Amsterdam-based photographers, which became part of a book and an exhibition. The book is sold throughout the world, and the exhibit travels to city museums and international conventions. The book and exhibit provide a compelling solution to the client requirement that the branding program be long lasting and of universal understanding.

FOREIGN LANGUAGE Although the primary language of Amsterdam is Dutch, KesselsKramer chose to communicate the brand message in English. Using English makes the program more universal in scope, and increases the commercial power of both the book and the exhibit. The theme, I Amsterdam, allows both local and international people to define their own experience of the city.

PEOPLE POWER Amsterdam Partners will promote the city internationally using the visual language of I Amsterdam. However, KesselsKramer designed the program to belong primarily to the wider public rather than to the client; I Amsterdam is intentionally left open to interpretation. What it means and how it is used will vary from person to person or company to company. People are free to use the theme for personal or commercial use in whatever settings they choose. The openness of the branding program reflects the diversity and creative spirit that makes Amsterdam such a remarkable and culturally significant city. ∎

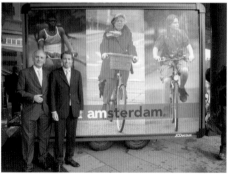

4

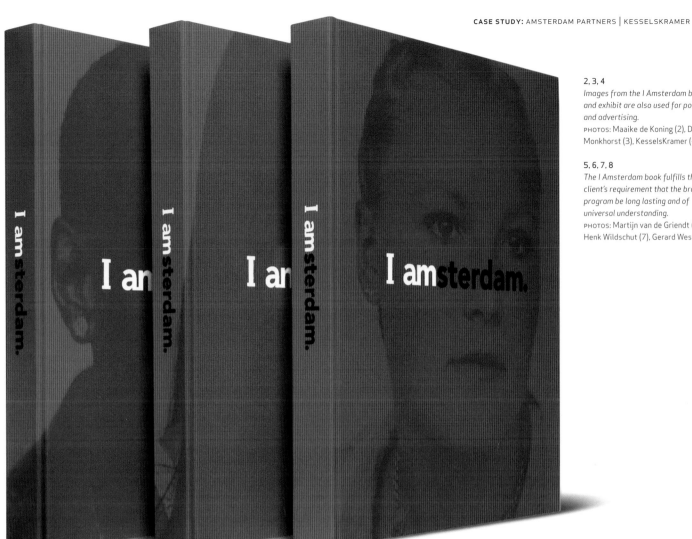

5

2, 3, 4
*Images from the I Amsterdam book
and exhibit are also used for posters
and advertising.*
PHOTOS: Maaike de Koning (2), Diana
Monkhorst (3), KesselsKramer (4)

5, 6, 7, 8
*The I Amsterdam book fulfills the
client's requirement that the branding
program be long lasting and of
universal understanding.*
PHOTOS: Martijn van de Griendt (6),
Henk Wildschut (7), Gerard Wessel (8)

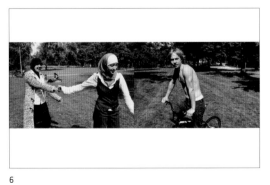

6

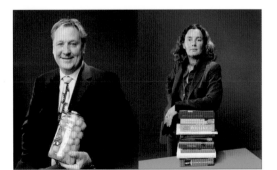

7

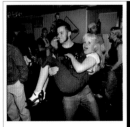

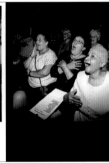

8

9

I Amsterdam is meant to be defined by—and belong to—the wider public.
PHOTO: Peter Verduin

10

The brand manual helps ensure consistency. This is particularly important since the brand program will be executed by several different government agencies and businesses.

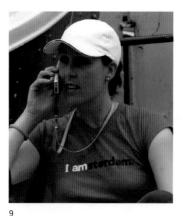

9

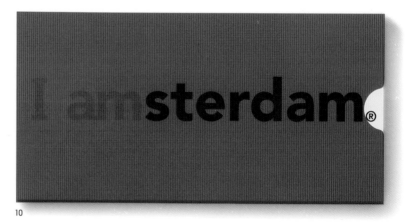

10

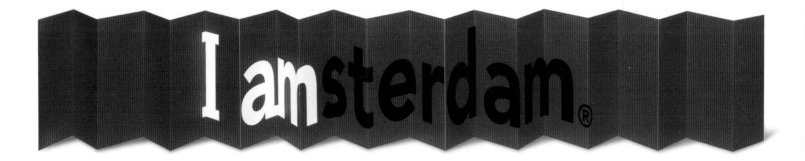

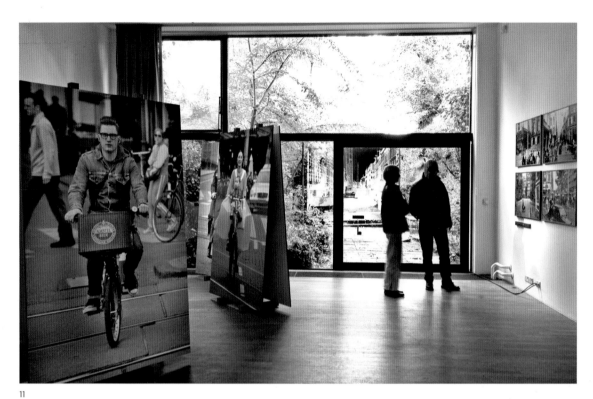

11

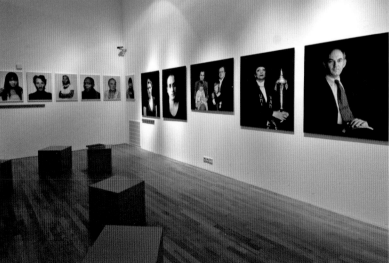

12

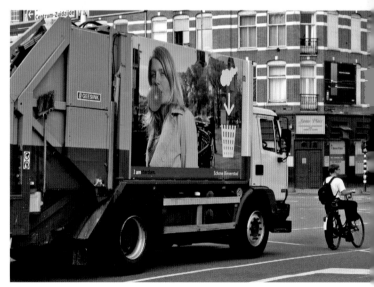

13

11, 12
The I Amsterdam exhibit launched the campaign and travels internationally to conventions and museums to promote the city and region.
PHOTOS: KesselsKramer

13
The I Amsterdam campaign found expression on city vehicles and in other municipal venues.
PHOTO: Peter Verduin

14, 16
The giant 3D version of the logo is used throughout the city, encouraging people to interact with the brand program.
PHOTOS: Peter Verduin (14), Matthijs de Jongh (16)

15
I Amsterdam applies not only to the people, but also to the cultural institutions of the city.
PHOTO: Peter Verduin

CLIENT: Amsterdam Partners
DESIGN FIRM: KesselsKramer

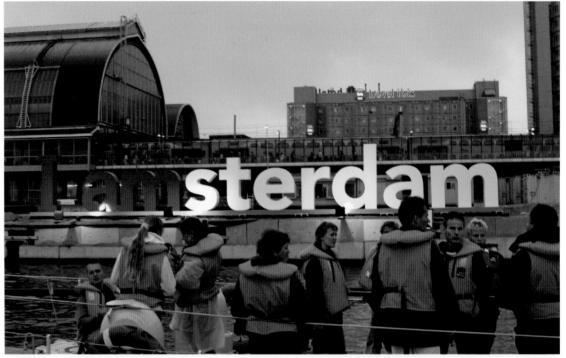

14

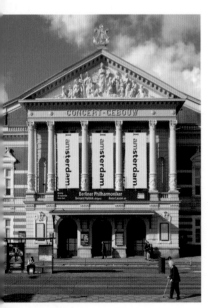

15

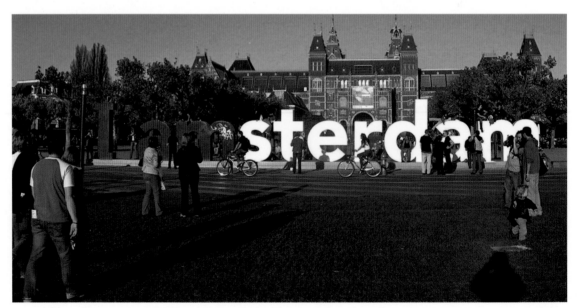

16

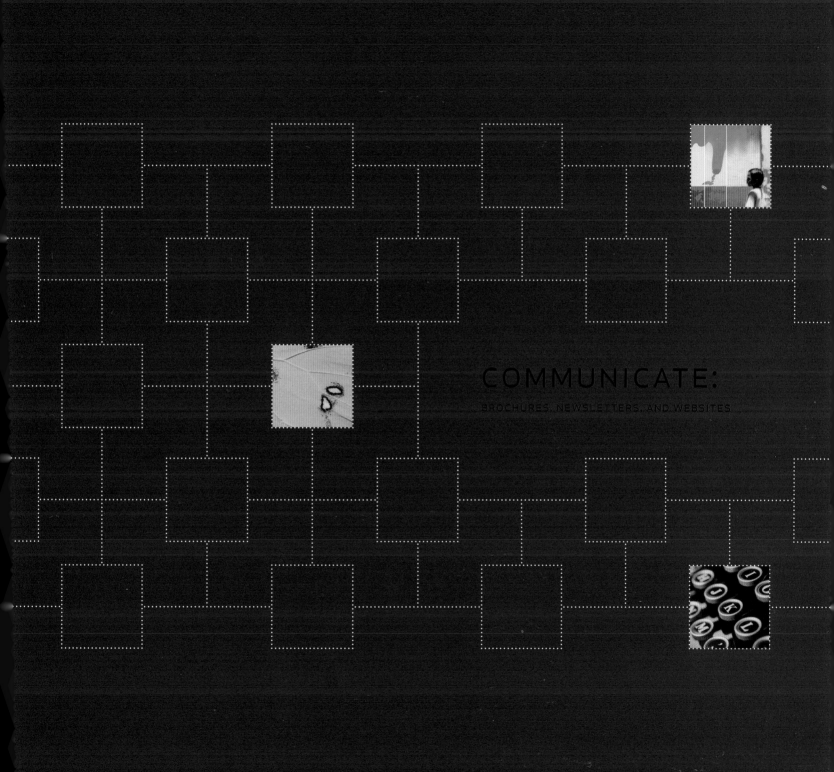

COMMUNICATE:

BROCHURES, NEWSLETTERS, AND WEBSITES

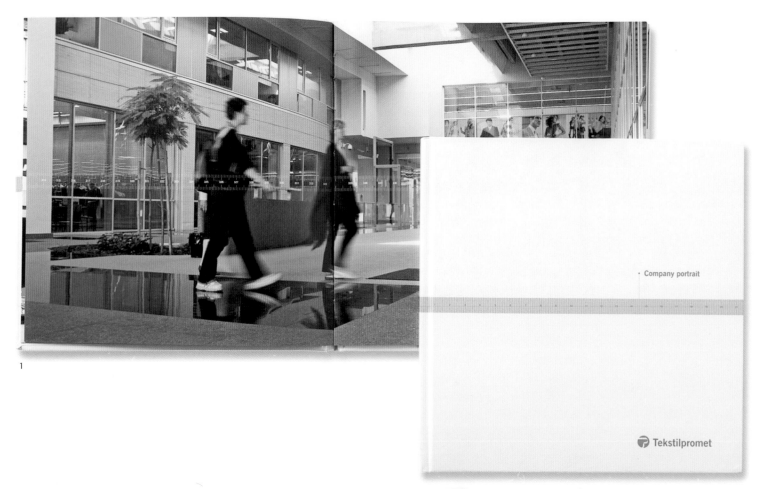

1

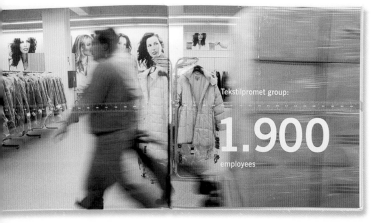

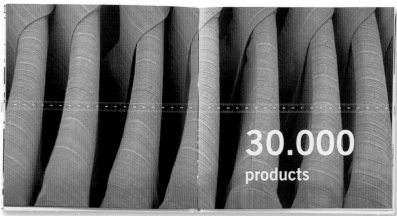

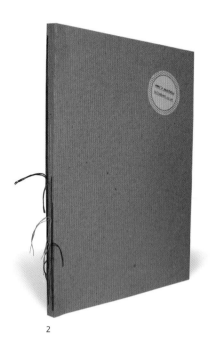

2

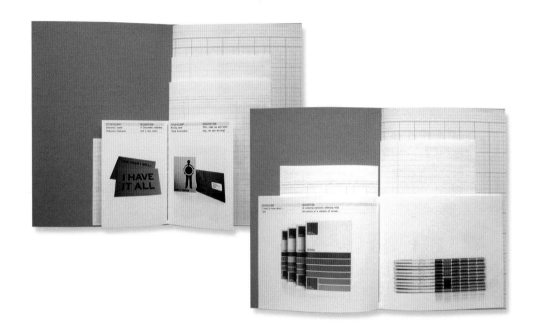

1
CLIENT: Tekstilpromet
DESIGN FIRM: Brandoctor

2
CLIENT: Emmi Salonen
DESIGN FIRM: Emmi Salonen

3
CLIENT: OrangeSeed Design
DESIGN FIRM: OrangeSeed Design

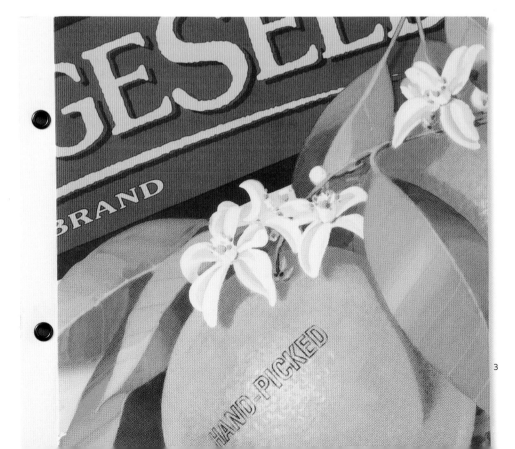

3

4
CLIENT: Step Wines Australia
DESIGN FIRM: Voice

5
CLIENT: Alexander, Berkey, Williams
& Weather, LLP
DESIGN FIRM: Stoller Design Group

6
CLIENT: Ian Kelly Landscaping
DESIGN FIRM: Spark Studio

7
CLIENT: Sorrento Hotel
DESIGN FIRM: urbanINFLUENCE
Design Studio

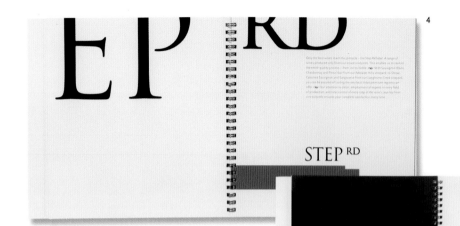

4

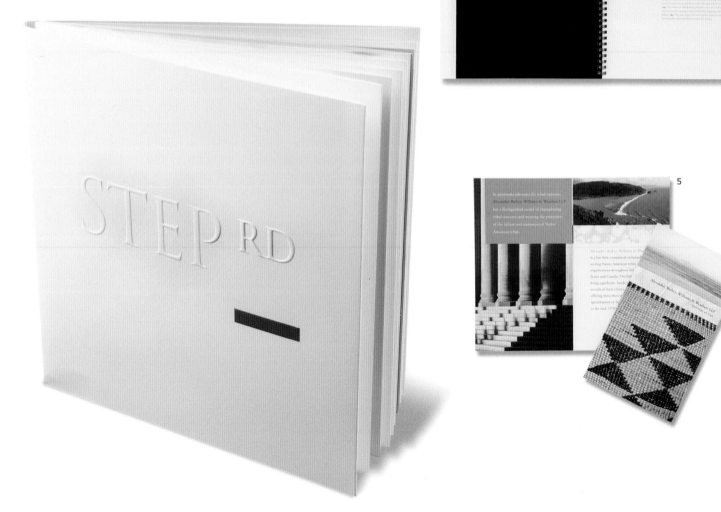

5

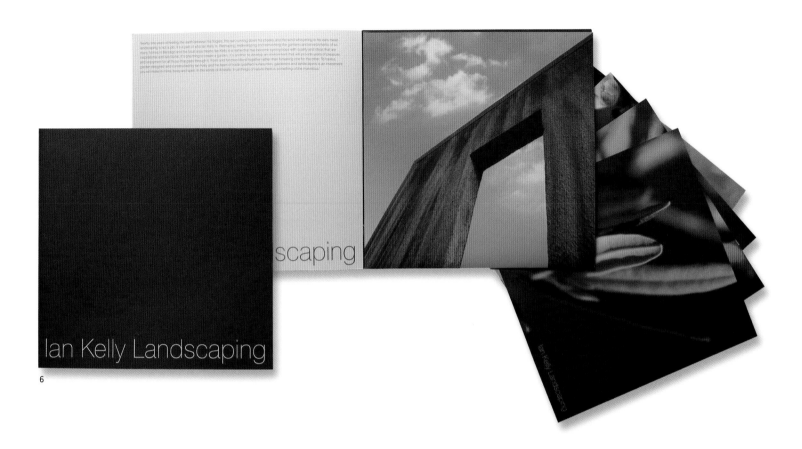

6

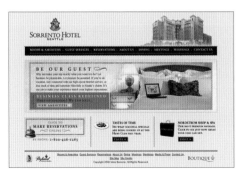
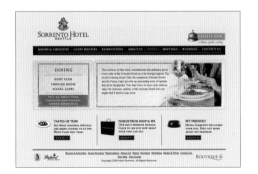
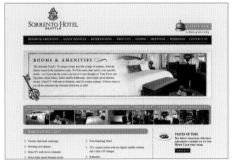

7

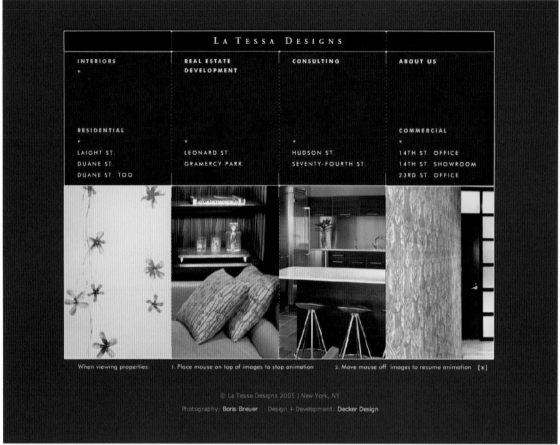

8

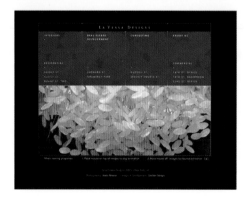

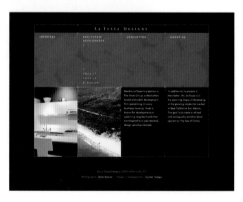

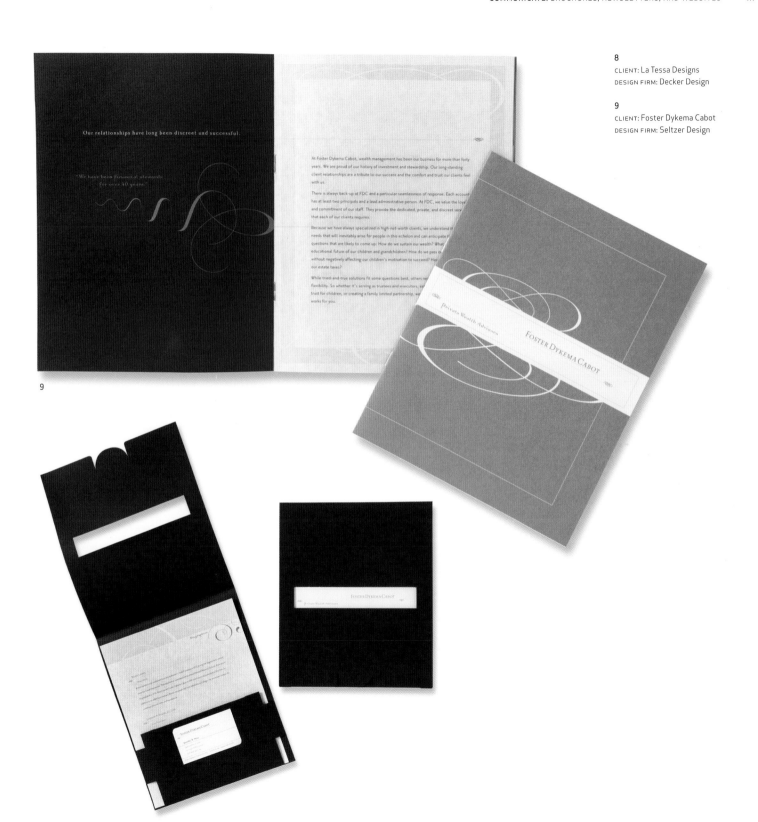

9

8
CLIENT: La Tessa Designs
DESIGN FIRM: Decker Design

9
CLIENT: Foster Dykema Cabot
DESIGN FIRM: Seltzer Design

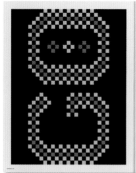

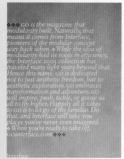

◆◆◆ GO is the magazine that modularity built. Naturally, that means it comes from Interface, pioneers of the modular concept way back when. ◆ While the idea of modularity had its roots in efficiency, the Interface 2005 collection has traveled many light years beyond that. Hence this name. GO is dedicated not to just aesthetic freedom, but to aesthetic exploration. GO embraces transformation and adventure. GO will inspire, push, tickle, or goose us all to fly higher. Happily all it takes to GO is to let go of the familiar. Do that, and Interface will take you places you've never even imagined. ◆ When you're ready to take off, GOinterface.com ◆◆◆

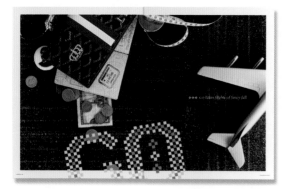

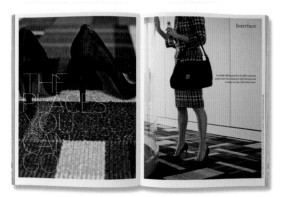

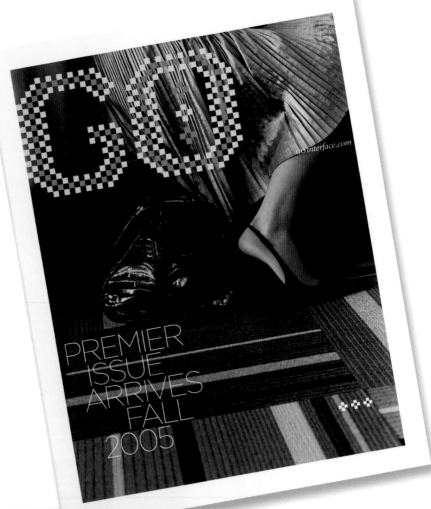

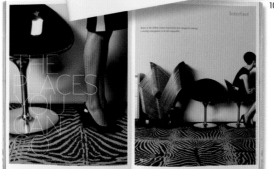

GOinterface.com

PREMIER
ISSUE
ARRIVES
FALL
2005

10

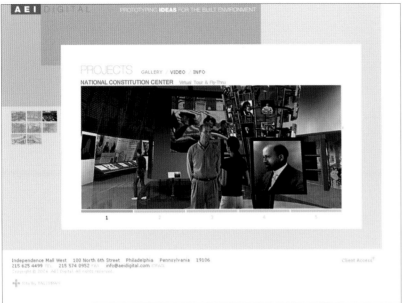

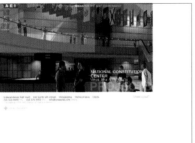

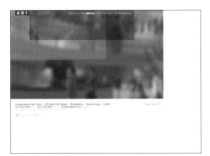

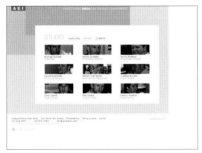

11

10
CLIENT: Interface
DESIGN FIRM: The Valentine Group

11
CLIENT: AEI Digital
DESIGN FIRM: Talisman Interactive

12
CLIENT: Film Visions Funding, L.L.C.
DESIGN FIRM: Lain Livingston
Marketing Studio

12

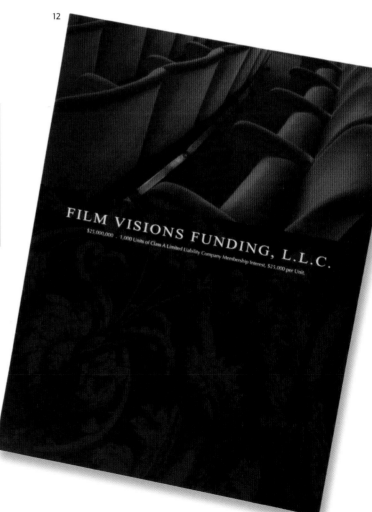

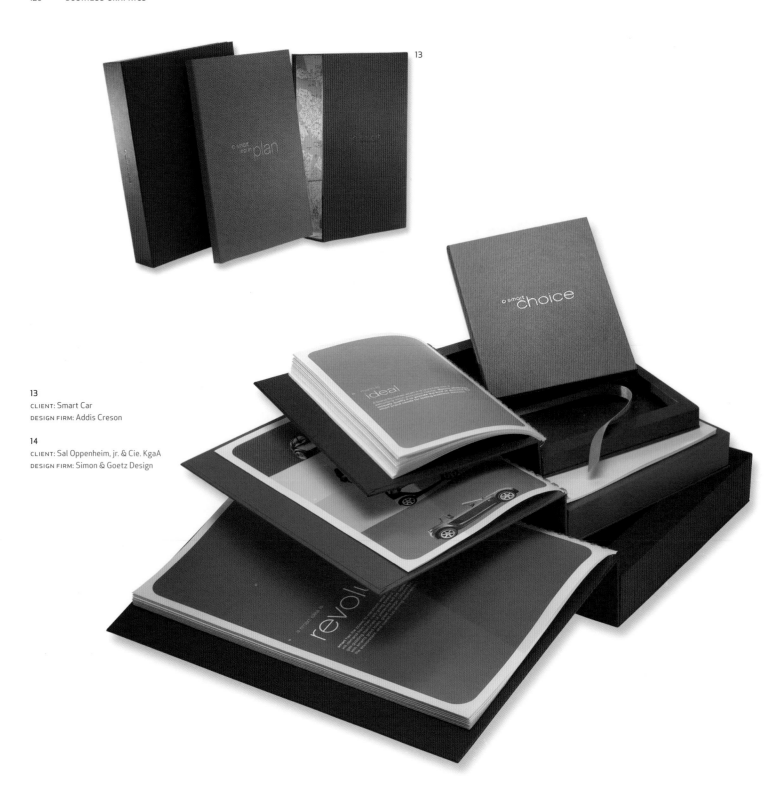

13
CLIENT: Smart Car
DESIGN FIRM: Addis Creson

14
CLIENT: Sal Oppenheim, jr. & Cie. KgaA
DESIGN FIRM: Simon & Goetz Design

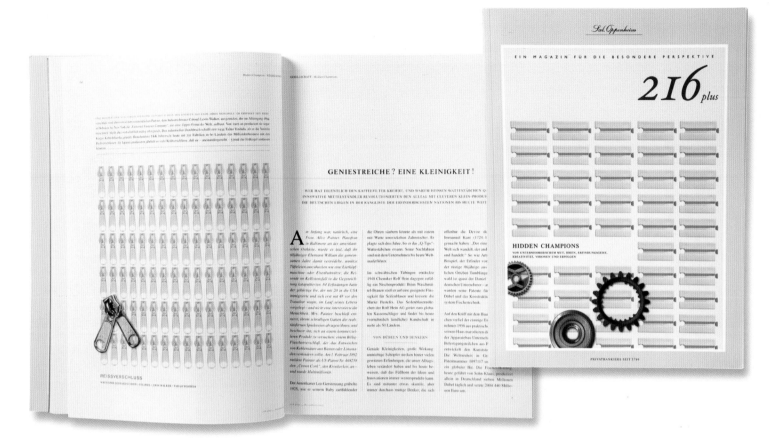

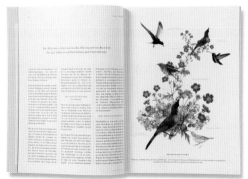

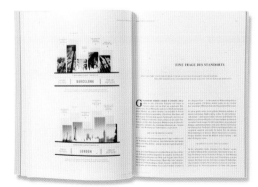

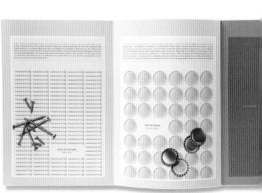

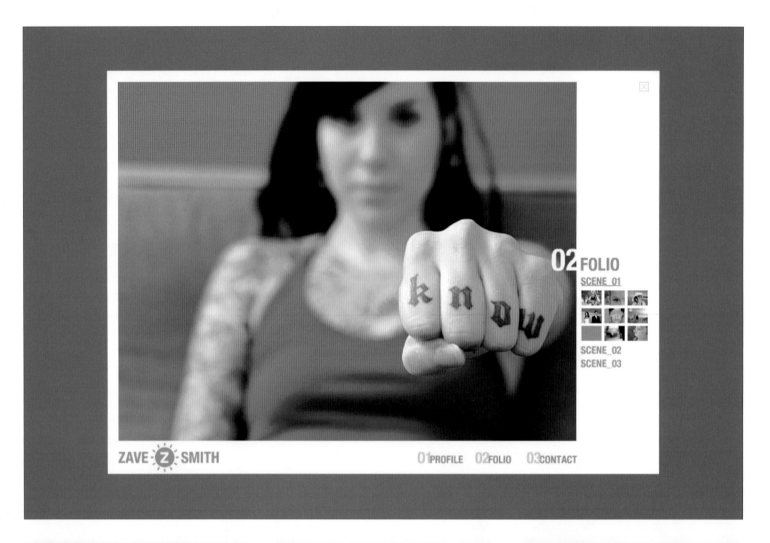

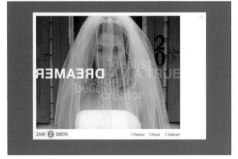

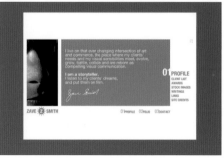

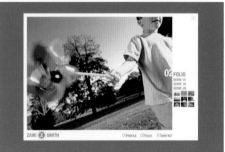

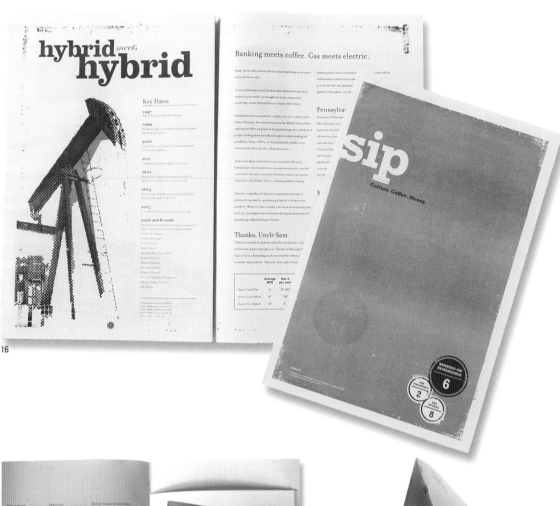

16

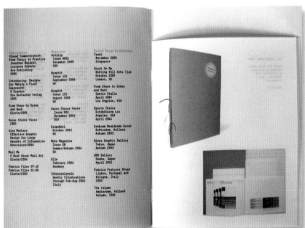

17

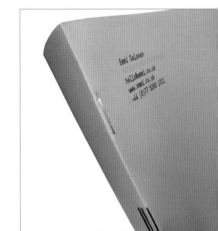

15
CLIENT: Zave Smith Photography
DESIGN FIRM: Talisman Interactive

16
CLIENT: Gold Cafe
DESIGN FIRM: Go Welsh

17
CLIENT: Emmi Salonen
DESIGN FIRM: Emmi Salonen

18
CLIENT: Health Net
DESIGN FIRM: The Valentine Group

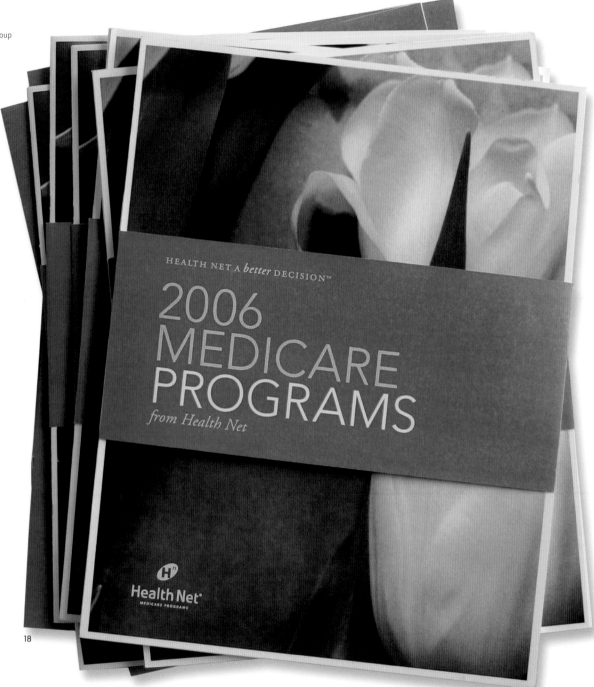

18

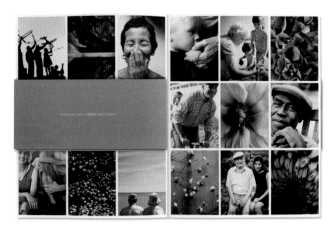

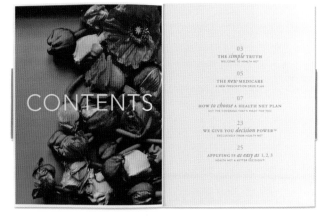

CONTENTS

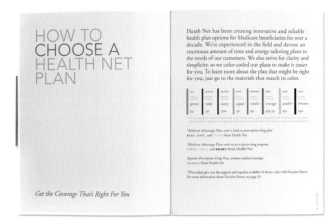

HOW TO CHOOSE A HEALTH NET PLAN

Heath Net has been creating innovative and reliable health plan options for Medicare beneficiaries for over a decade. We're experienced in the field and devote an enormous amount of time and energy tailoring plans to the needs of our customers. We also strive for clarity and simplicity, so we color-coded our plans to make it easier for you. To learn more about the plan that might be right for you, just go to the materials that match its color.

Get the Coverage That's Right For You

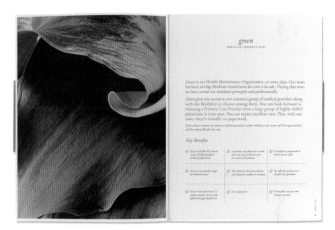

green
(HEALTH NET SENIORITY PLUS)

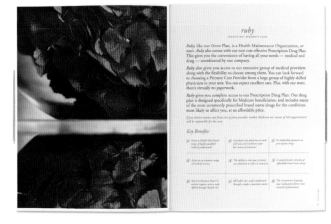

ruby
(HEALTH NET SENIORITY PLUS)

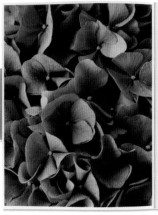

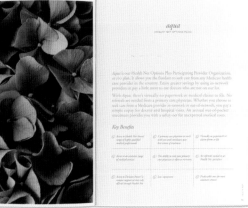

aqua
(HEALTH NET OPTIONS PLUS)

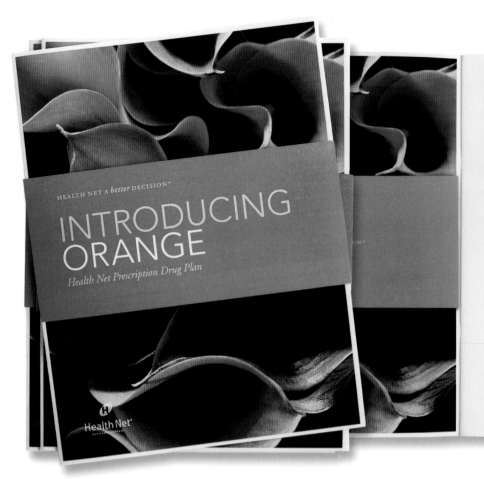

THE PLAN
THAT AFFORDS
YOU MORE

If you're shopping for a separate prescription drug coverage, then *Orange,* the Prescription Drug Plan from Health Net, is just for you. And if you're comparing drug pricing for a Prescription Drug Plan, then you'll find Health Net to be one of the least expensive.

One of the most critical components of good health care is a common sense Prescription Drug Plan that's tailored to your needs — a plan that's reasonably priced and easy to use. That's why thousands of people have chosen Health Net Medicare plans. We've based our business on the specific needs of the individuals we serve. Plus, our vast network of nationwide pharmacies means you can probably get your prescriptions filled at your neighborhood drug store.

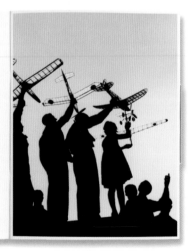

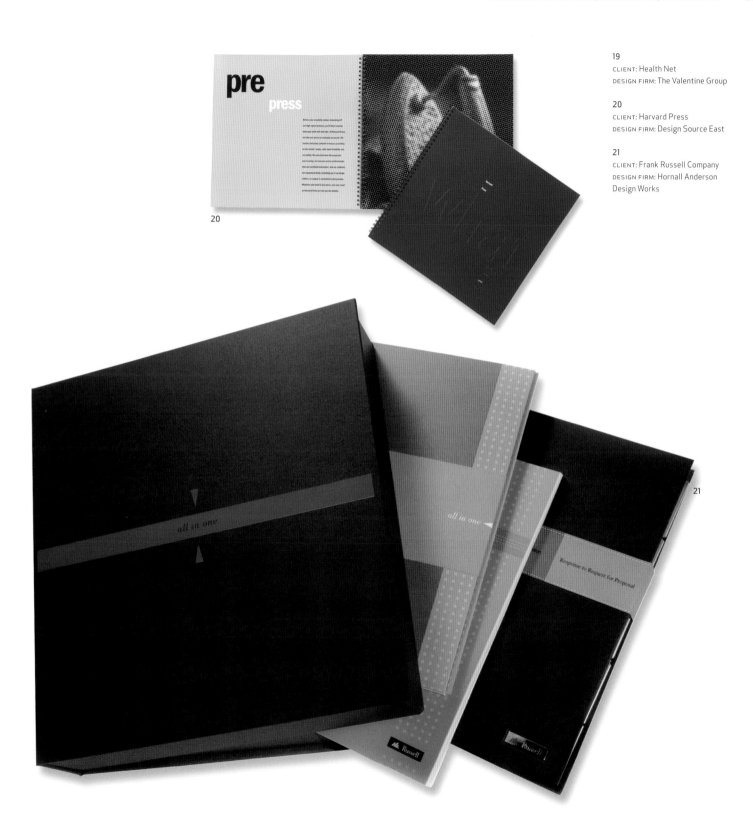

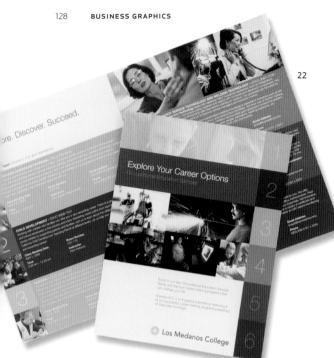

22

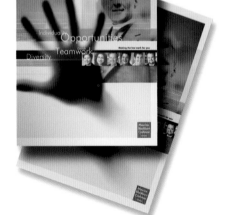

23

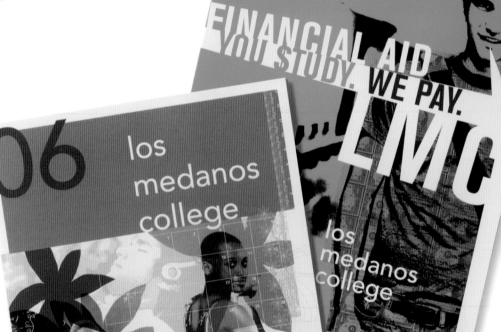

24

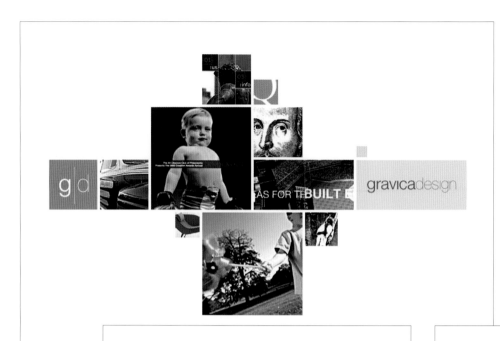

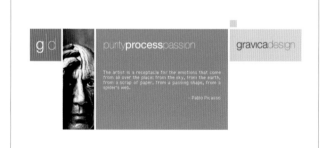

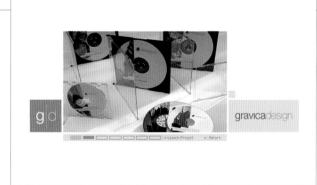

25

22
CLIENT: Los Medanos College
DESIGN FIRM: Stoller Design Group

23
CLIENT: Maurice Blackburn Cashman
DESIGN FIRM: Octavo Design/
Spark Studio

24
CLIENT: Los Medanos College
DESIGN FIRM: Stoller Design Group

25
CLIENT: Gravica Design
DESIGN FIRM: Talisman Interactive

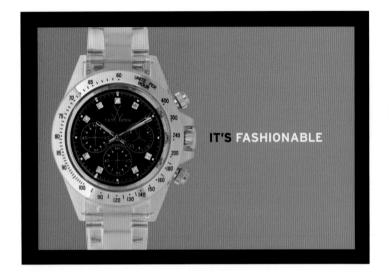

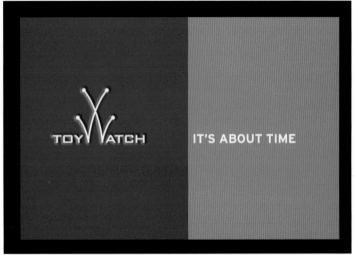

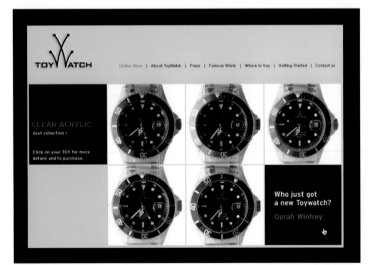

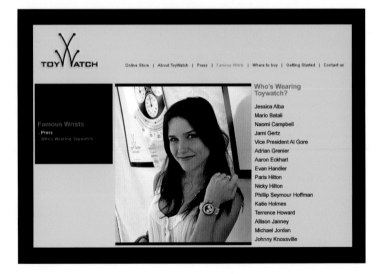

27

Foundation seeks to improve education.
Looking for leading-edge thinkers to
collaborate on solutions to tough questions.

Help Wanted

26
CLIENT: ToyWatch USA
DESIGN FIRM: Liska + Associates

27
CLIENT: The Spencer Foundation
DESIGN FIRM: Kym Abrams Design

28
CLIENT: Australian Ballet School
DESIGN FIRM: Spark Studio

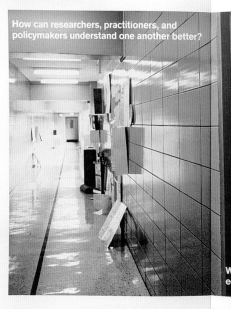

How can researchers, practitioners, and
policymakers understand one another better?

What can help them collaborate to produce
educational improvements?

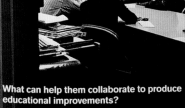

An exquisite evening
of fine dining and superb entertainment

28

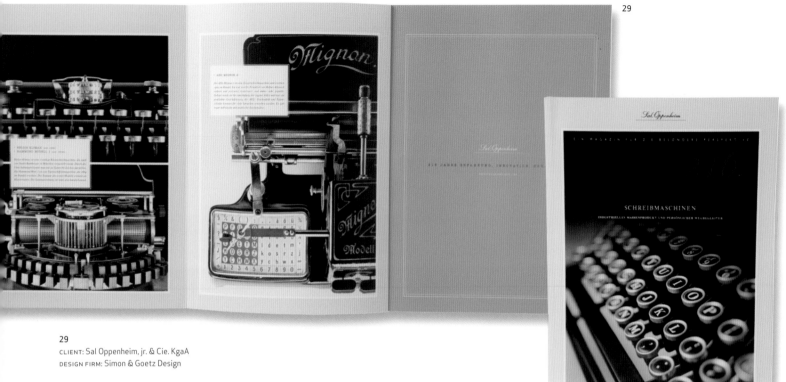

29

29
CLIENT: Sal Oppenheim, jr. & Cie. KgaA
DESIGN FIRM: Simon & Goetz Design

30
CLIENT: Postspeed
DESIGN FIRM: Spark Studio

31
CLIENT: Target Commercial Interiors
DESIGN FIRM: Sussner Design Company

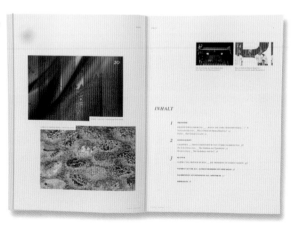

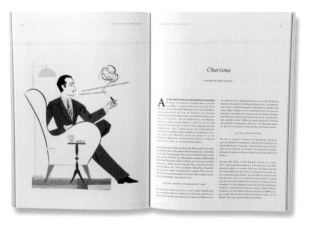

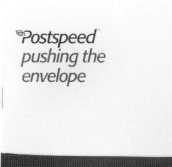

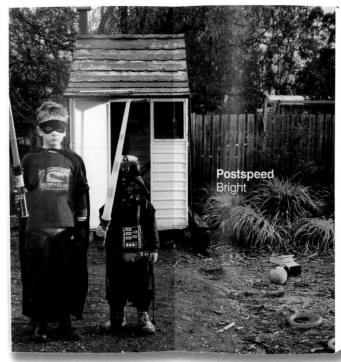

30

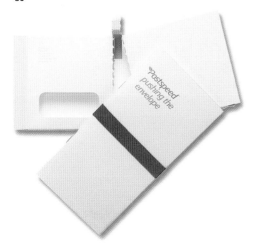

31

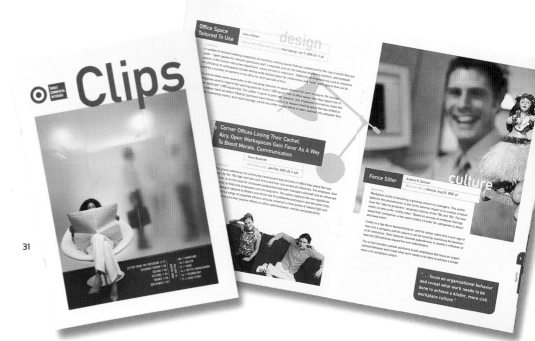

32
CLIENT: The Buzz Company
DESIGN FIRM: Faust Associates

33
CLIENT: Swanson, Martin & Bell
DESIGN FIRM: Liska + Associates

34
CLIENT: California Council for Humanities
DESIGN FIRM: Stoller Design Group

Hey, The Buzz Company desperately wants you to work with them.

Really. For crying out loud, just talk to them. What would it hurt you?

Or maybe you do, but really don't care. Well, it's time to take notice. The Buzz Company is only the pluckiest, most dedicated (let's not forget handsome) and, frankly, the best darn temp/full/part time creative placement firm on Huron in Chicago. And, if that wasn't enough, they're comprised of terribly interesting people with riveting personal stories about their obsession with George Foreman Grill recipes.

32

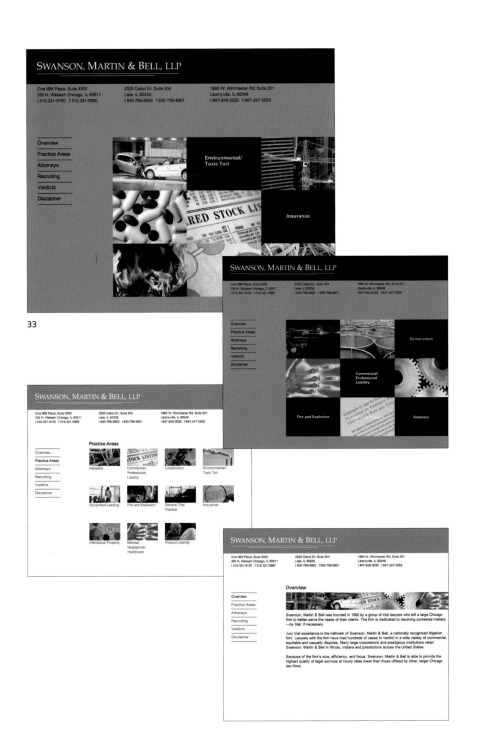

33

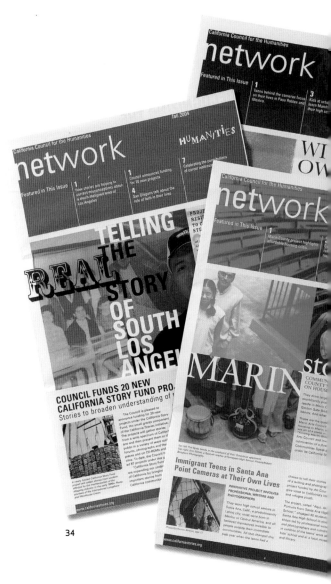

34

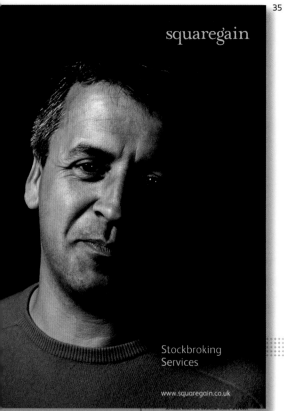

35

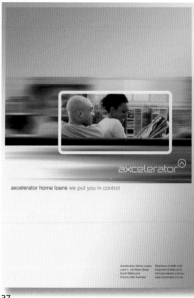

36

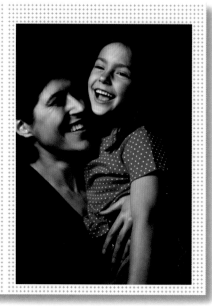

37

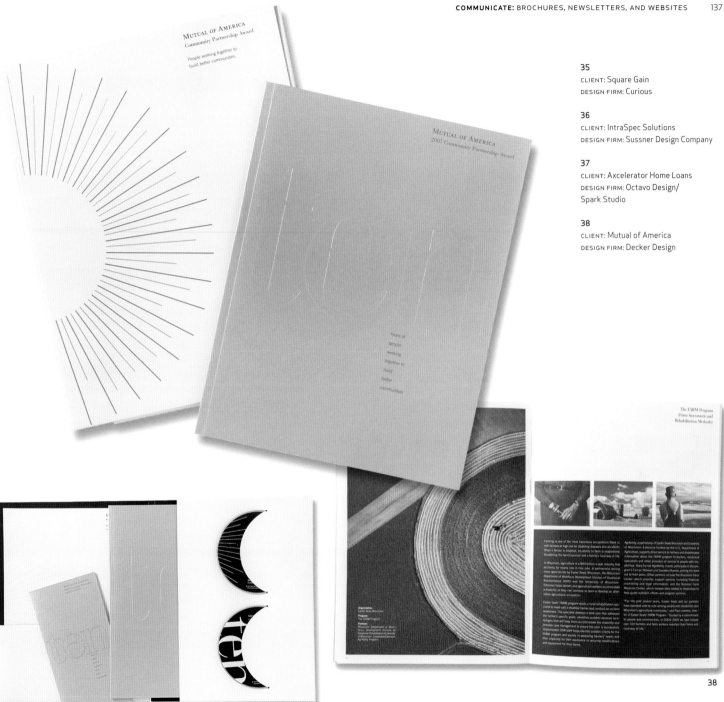

35
CLIENT: Square Gain
DESIGN FIRM: Curious

36
CLIENT: IntraSpec Solutions
DESIGN FIRM: Sussner Design Company

37
CLIENT: Axcelerator Home Loans
DESIGN FIRM: Octavo Design/
Spark Studio

38
CLIENT: Mutual of America
DESIGN FIRM: Decker Design

38

39
CLIENT: City Bay Developers
DESIGN FIRM: Design Source East

40
CLIENT: Skanska USA Building, Inc.
DESIGN FIRM: Design Source East

41
CLIENT: Oxiana Limited
DESIGN FIRM: Octavo Design/
Spark Studio

42
CLIENT: Martin Architectural
DESIGN FIRM: Front Media Studio

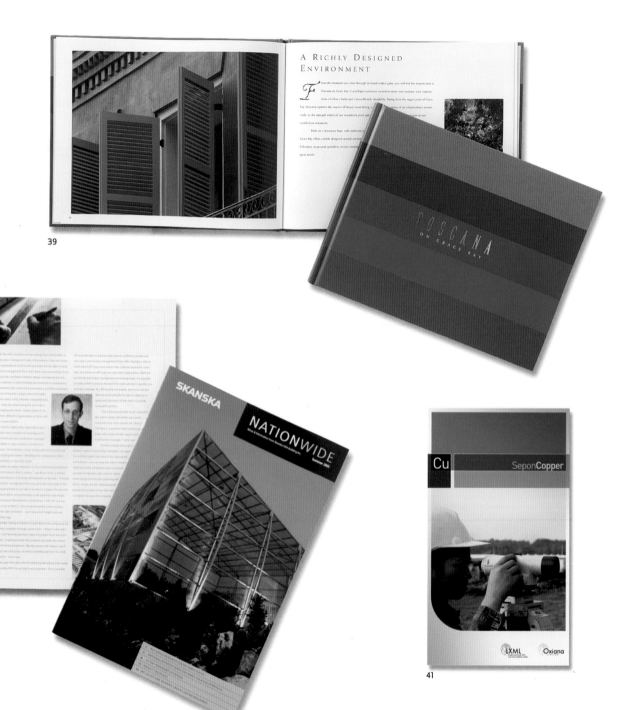

39

40

41

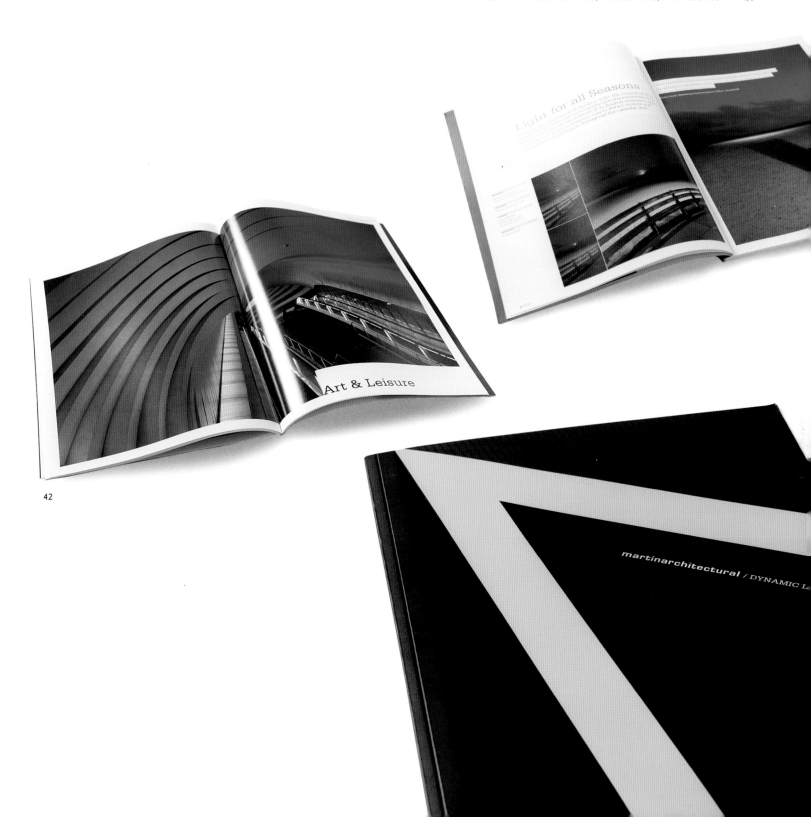

43
CLIENT: Seva Foundation
DESIGN FIRM: Stoller Design Group

44
CLIENT: Continental Warranty
DESIGN FIRM: urbanINFLUENCE
Design Studio

45
CLIENT: America Abroad Media
DESIGN FIRM: Matthew Schwartz
Design Studio

43

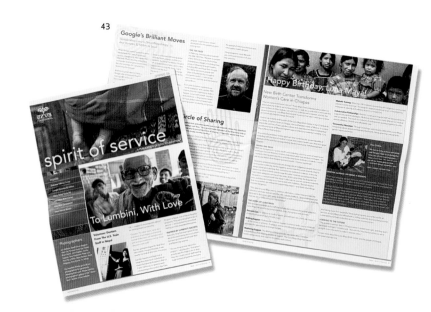

44

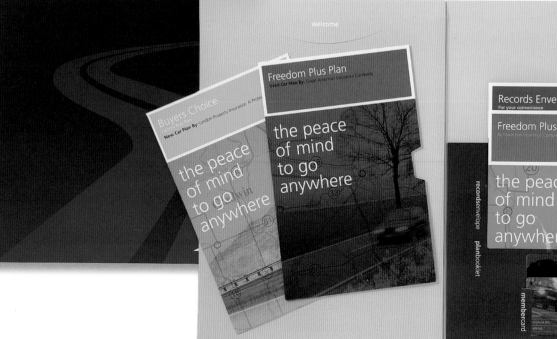

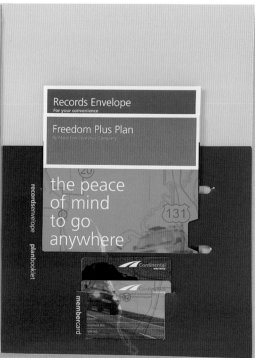

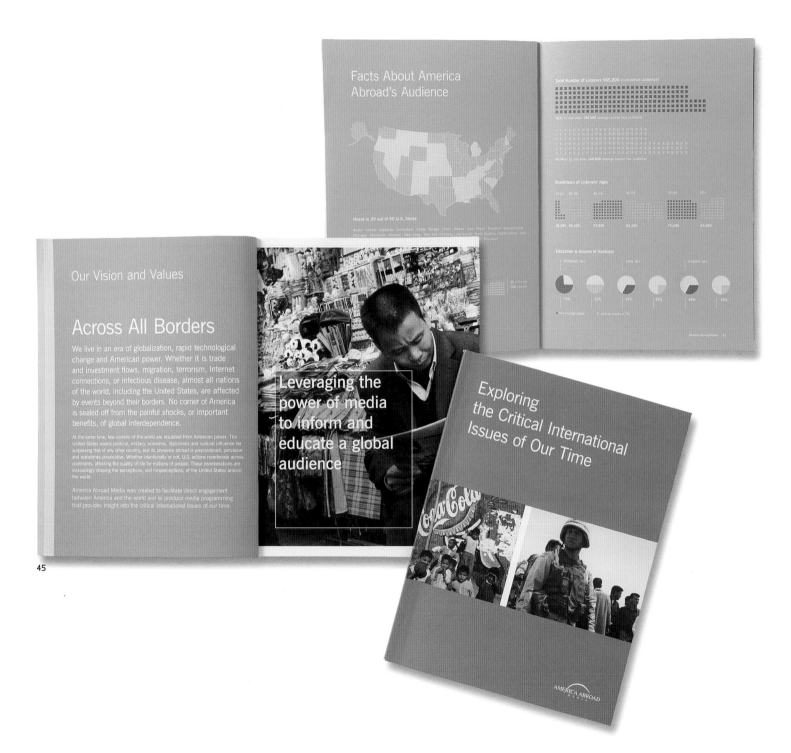

Facts About America
Abroad's Audience

Heard in 29 out of 50 U.S. States

Total Number of Listeners 565,200 (cumulative audience)

Breakdown of Listeners' Ages

Education & Income of Audience

Our Vision and Values

Across All Borders

We live in an era of globalization, rapid technological change and American power. Whether it is trade and investment flows, migration, terrorism, Internet connections, or infectious disease, almost all nations of the world, including the United States, are affected by events beyond their borders. No corner of America is sealed off from the painful shocks, or important benefits, of global interdependence.

At the same time, few corners of the world are insulated from American power. The United States wields political, military, economic, diplomatic and cultural influence far surpassing that of any other country, and its presence abroad is preponderant, pervasive and sometimes provocative. Whether intentionally or not, U.S. actions reverberate across continents, affecting the quality of life for millions of people. These reverberations are increasingly shaping the perceptions, and misperceptions, of the United States around the world.

America Abroad Media was created to facilitate direct engagement between America and the world and to produce media programming that provides insight into the critical international issues of our time.

Leveraging the power of media to inform and educate a global audience

Exploring the Critical International Issues of Our Time

AMERICA ABROAD

45

46
CLIENT: International Wall Designs
DESIGN FIRM: Sussner Design Company

47
CLIENT: Dual Immobiliare
DESIGN FIRM: Fluid Design Lab

48
CLIENT: GFa, Architects
DESIGN FIRM: TD2, Identity & Strategic
Design Consultants

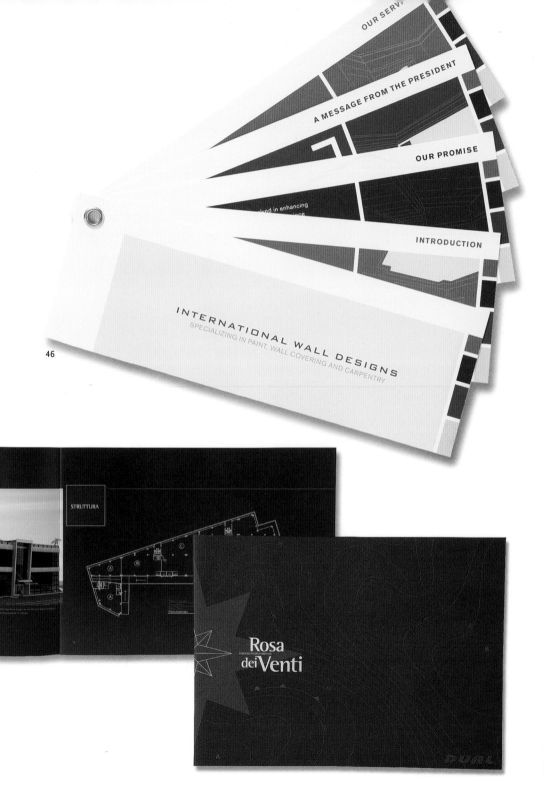

46

47

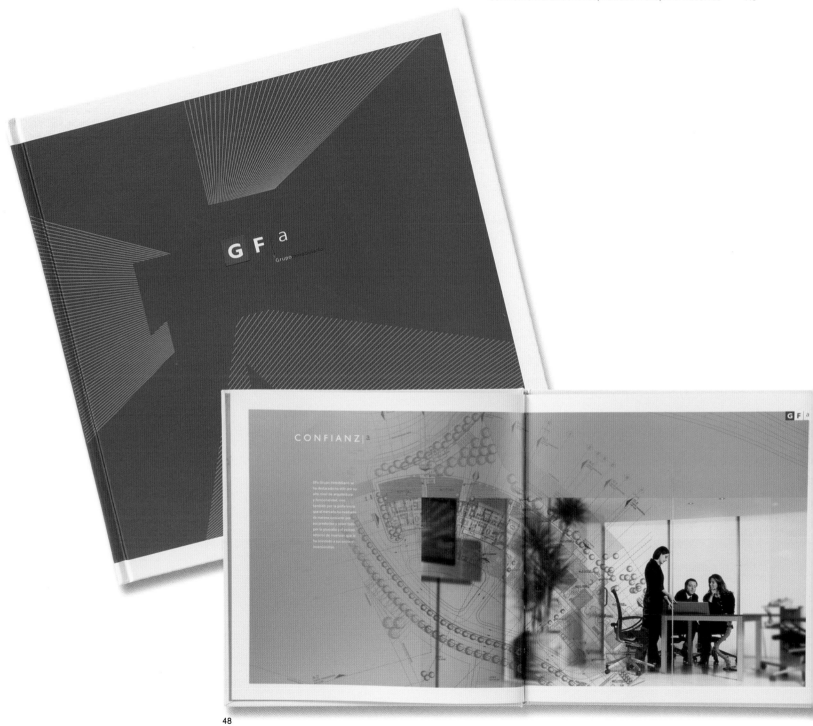

48

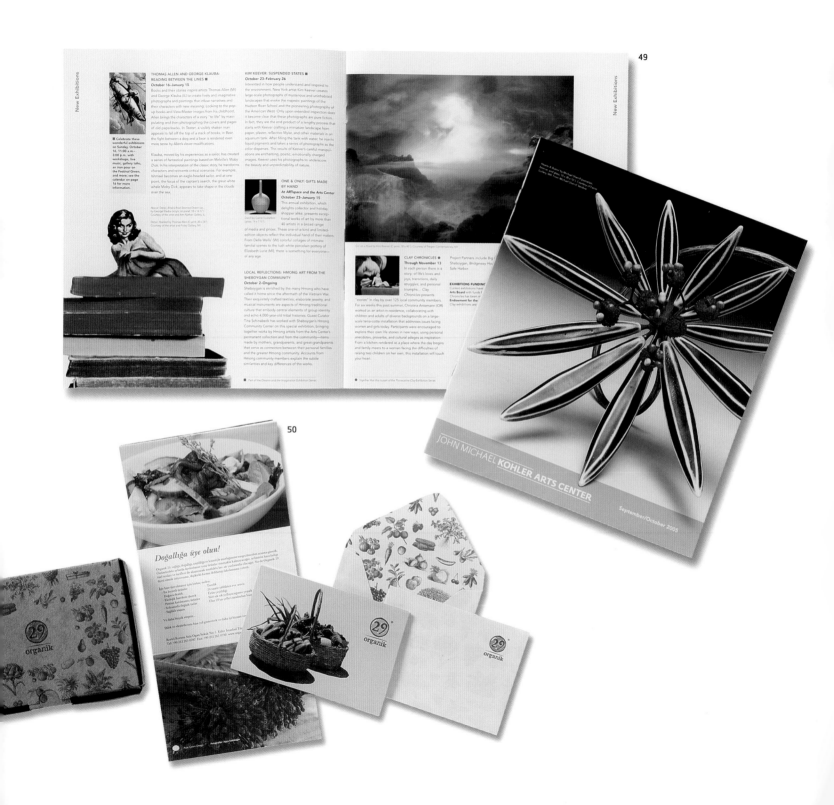

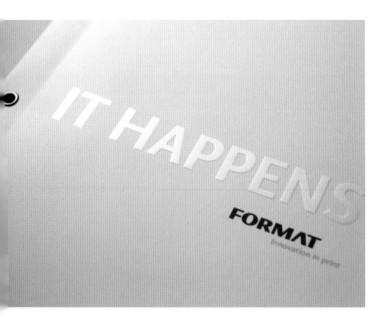

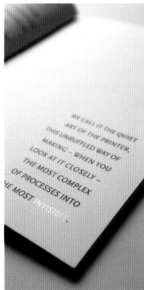

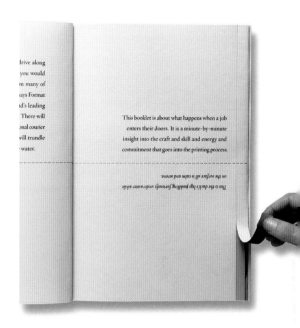

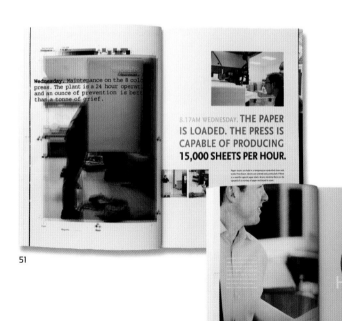

51

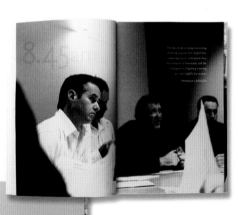

49
CLIENT: John Michael Kohler Arts Center
DESIGN FIRM: Liska + Associates

50
CLIENT: Organik 29
DESIGN FIRM: Ayse Celem Design

51
CLIENT: FORMAT Printers
DESIGN FIRM: Clemenger BBDO

52
CLIENT: Marge Casey + Associates
DESIGN FIRM: Liska + Associates

53
CLIENT: Fluent
DESIGN FIRM: Monderer Design

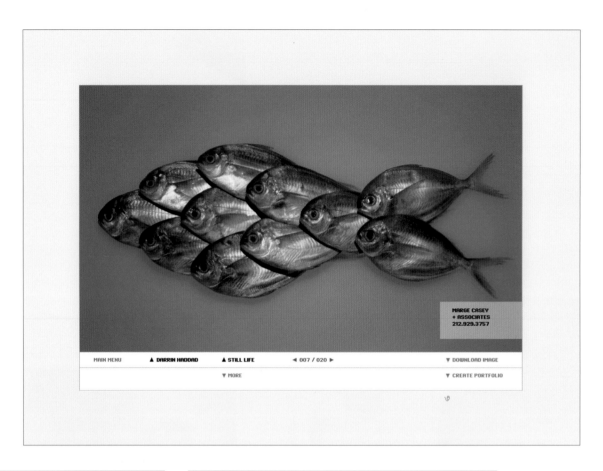

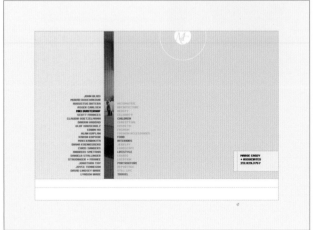

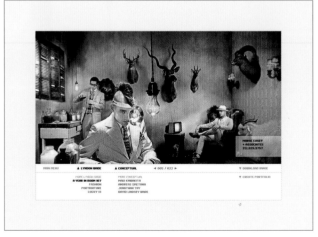

52

53

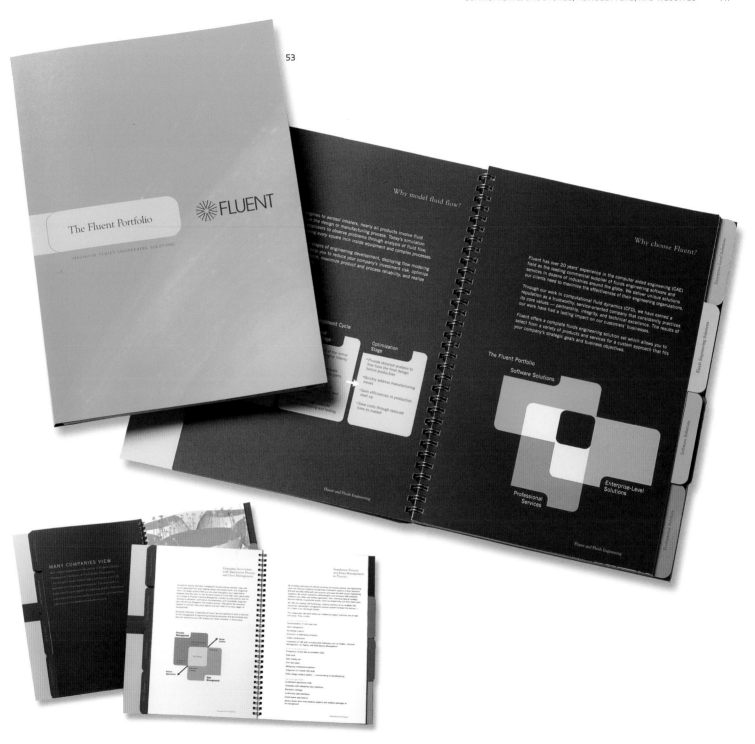

54
CLIENT: Mainland
DESIGN FIRM: Clemenger BBDO

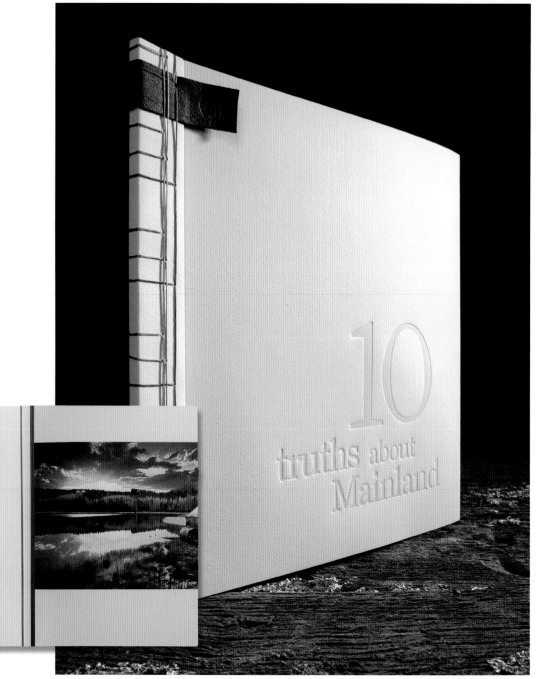

A Brand needs to come from somewhere, stand for something and have a story to tell.

54

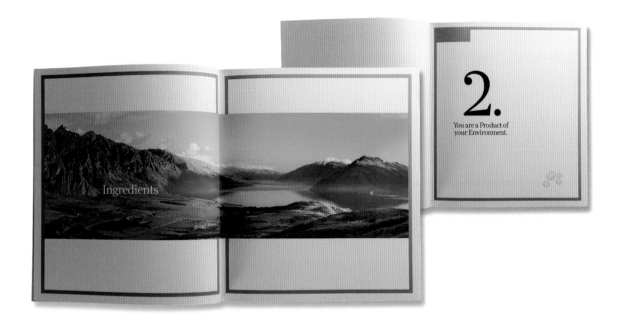

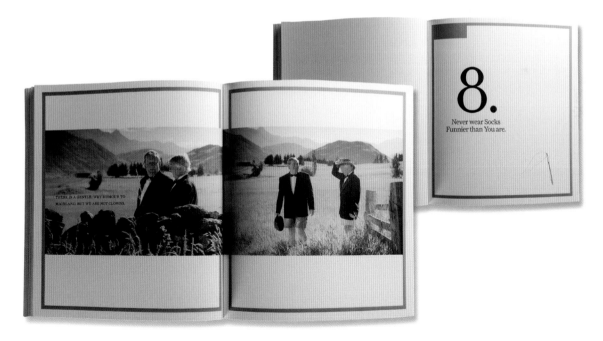

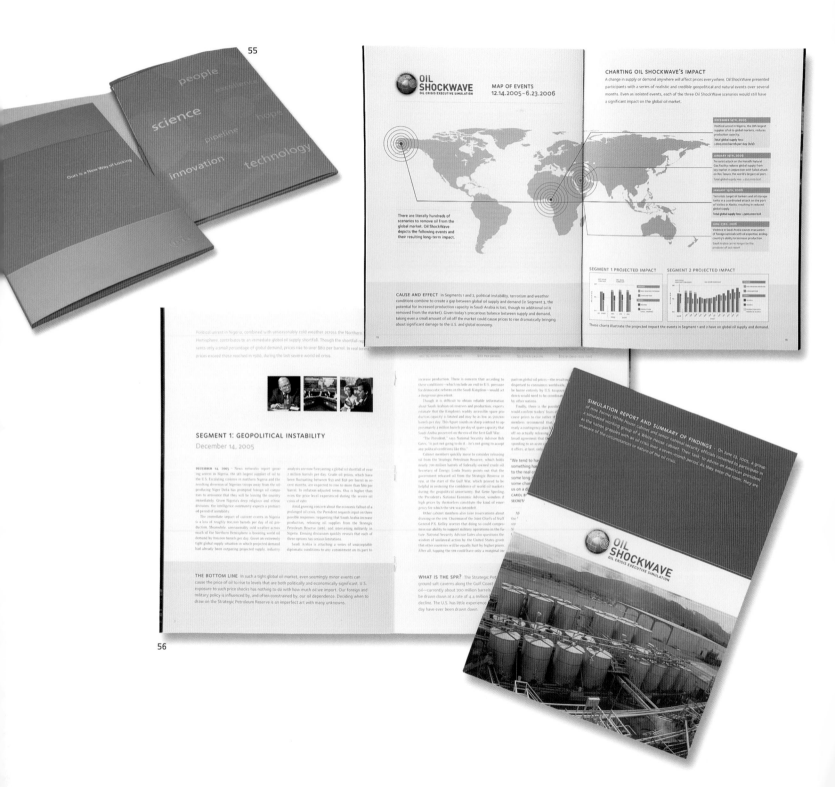

55

56

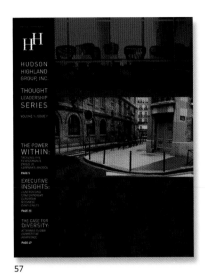

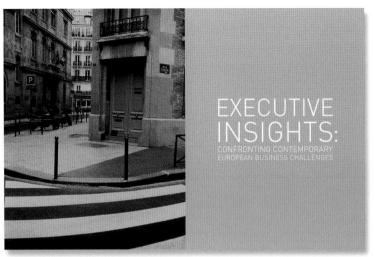

57

55
CLIENT: PIC
DESIGN FIRM: Jason and Jason

56
CLIENT: Securing America's
Future Energy
DESIGN FIRM: Matthew Schwartz
Design Studio

57
CLIENT: Hudson Highland
DESIGN FIRM: Lowercase, Inc

58
CLIENT: Davies Collision Cave
DESIGN FIRM: Davidson Design

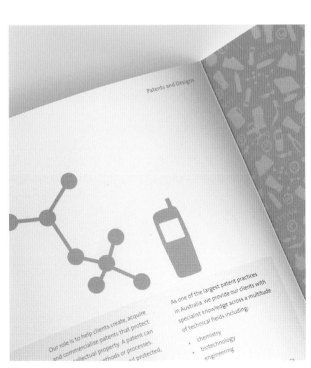

58

59
CLIENT: Gilon
DESIGN FIRM: Jason and Jason

60
CLIENT: Sappi Fine Paper Europe
DESIGN FIRM: Curious

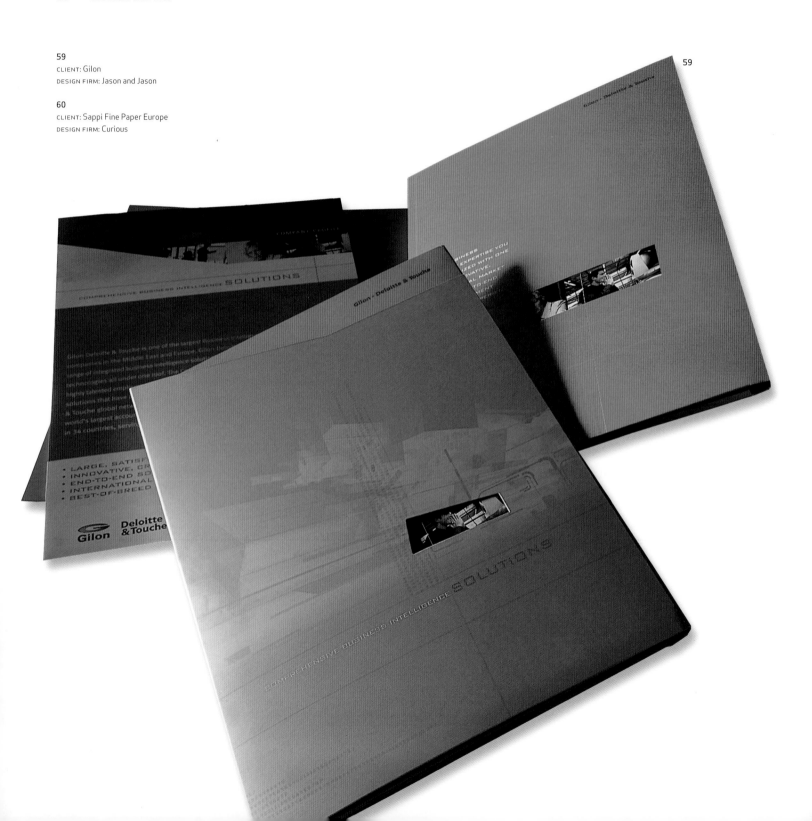

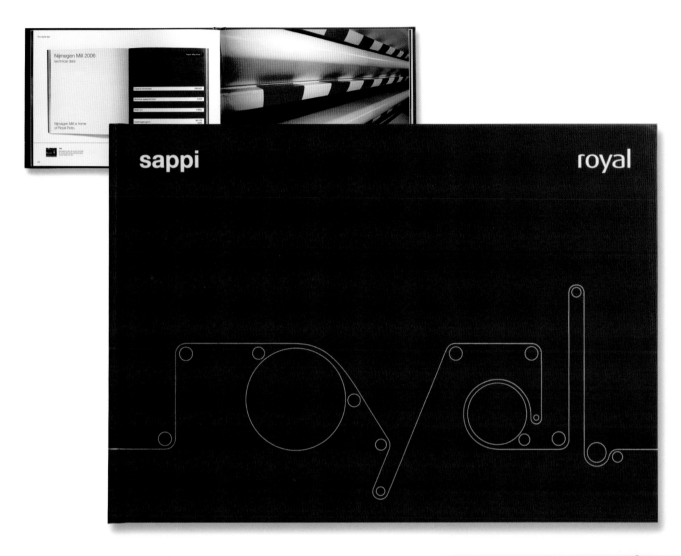

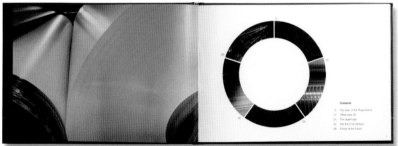

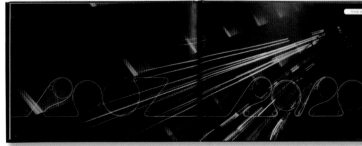

61
CLIENT: Motorola
DESIGN FIRM: Liska + Associates

62
CLIENT: Sydney College of the Arts
DESIGN FIRM: Boccalatte

63
CLIENT: Cooper, Robertson & Partners
DESIGN FIRM: Poulin + Morris Inc.

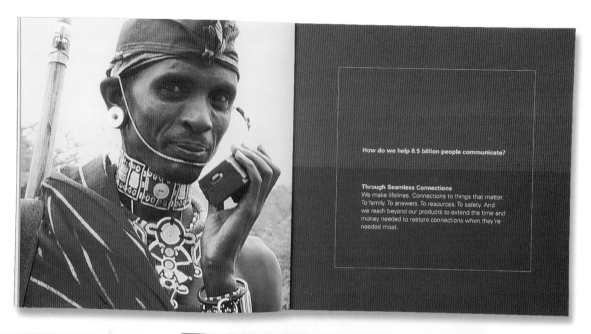

How do we help 6.5 billion people communicate?

Through Seamless Connections
We make lifelines. Connections to things that matter.
To family. To answers. To resources. To safety. And
we reach beyond our products to extend the time and
money needed to restore connections when they're
needed most.

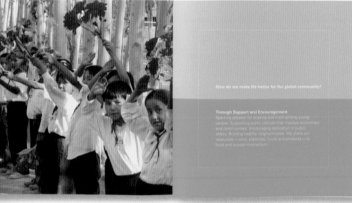

How do we make life better for the global community?

Through Support and Encouragement

61

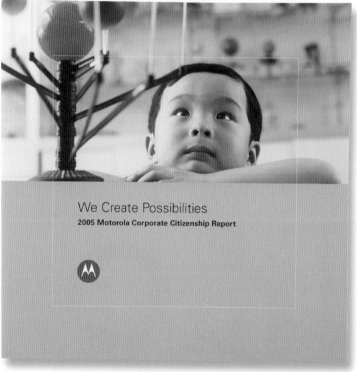

We Create Possibilities
2005 Motorola Corporate Citizenship Report

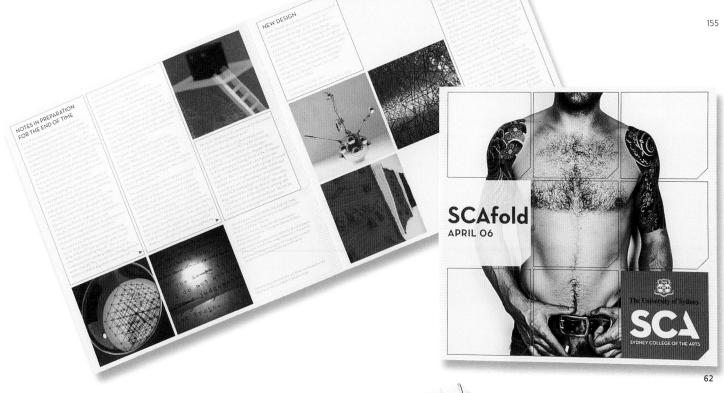

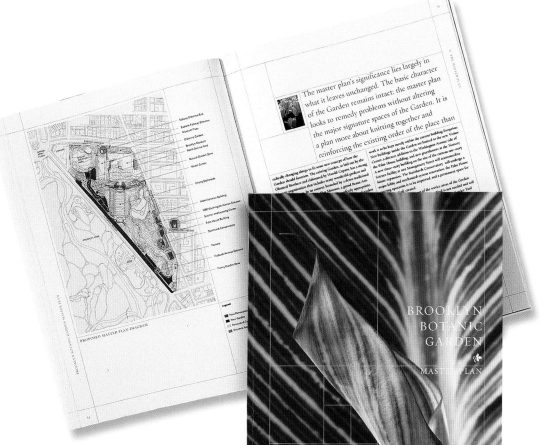

64
CLIENT: Adobe
DESIGN FIRM: AdamsMorioka

65
CLIENT: Brininstool + Lynch
DESIGN FIRM: Liska + Associates

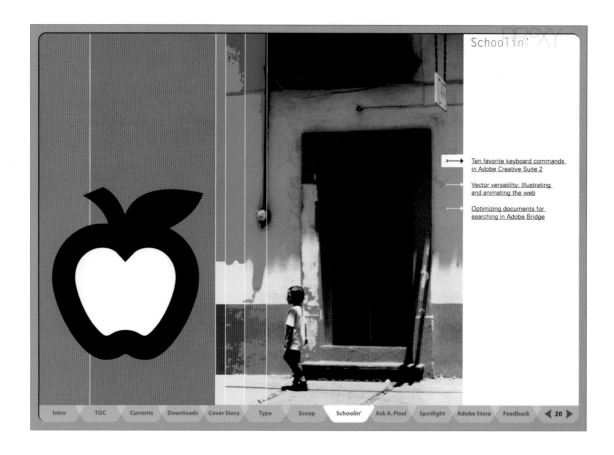

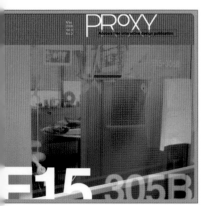

64

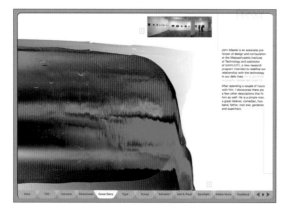

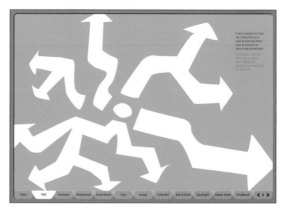

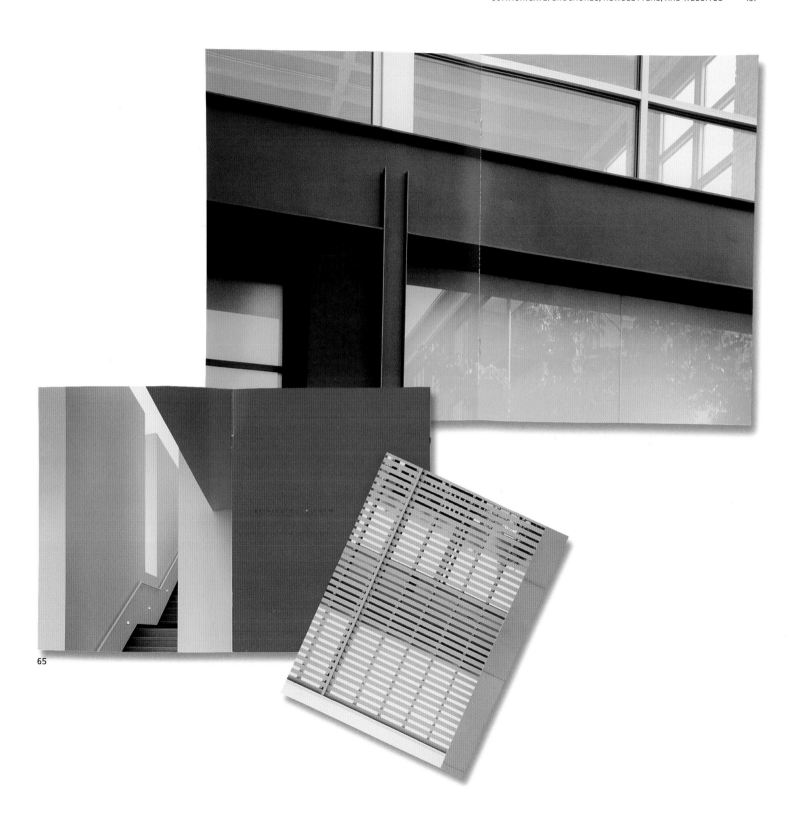

65

66
CLIENT: The McKay Foundation
DESIGN FIRM: Hollis Brand
Communications

67
CLIENT: Portland Opera
DESIGN FIRM: Sockeye Creative

68
CLIENT: American Tap Foundation
DESIGN FIRM: AS|D Labs, Inc.

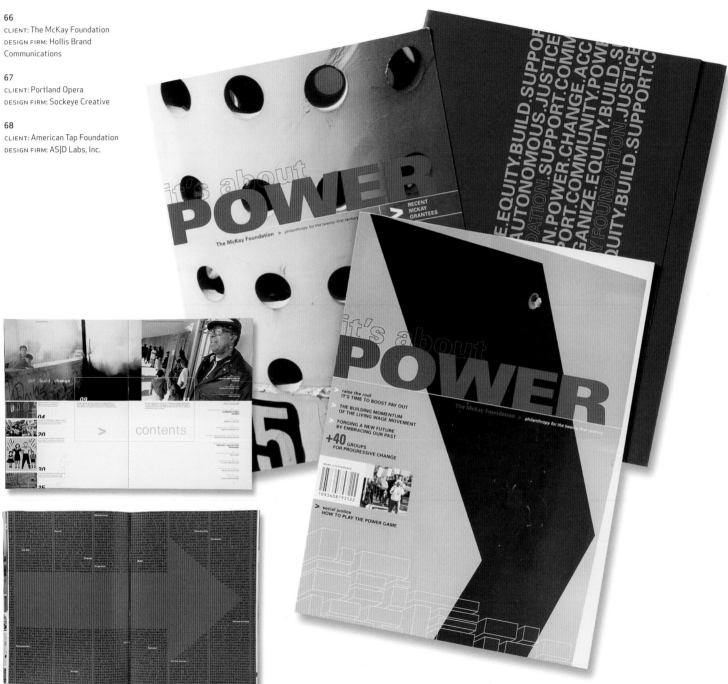

66

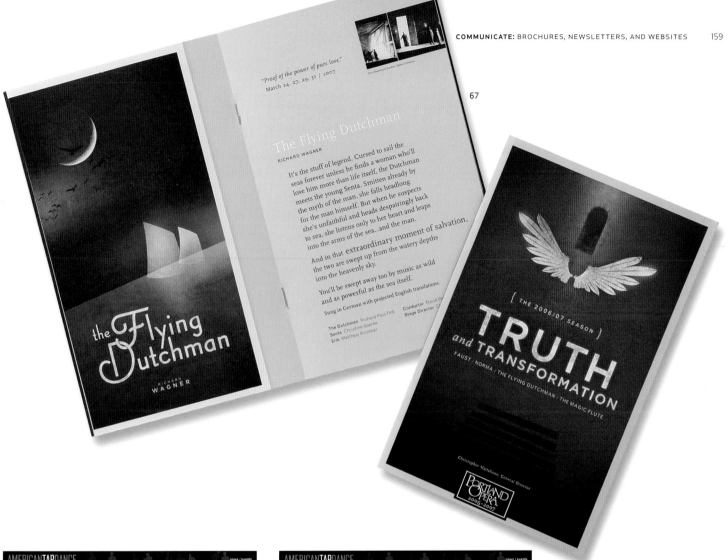

67

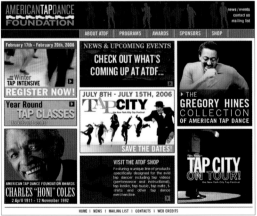

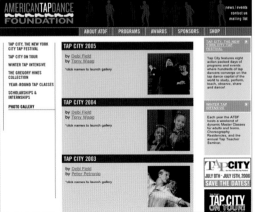

68

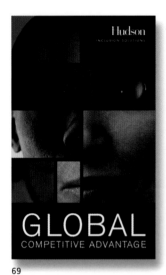

69

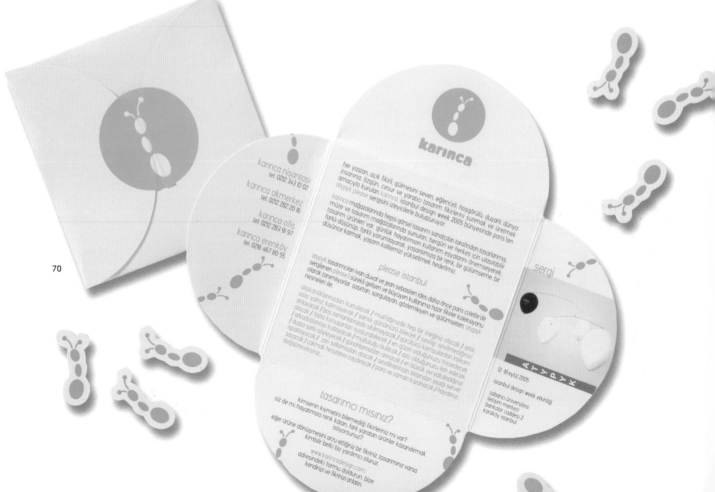

70

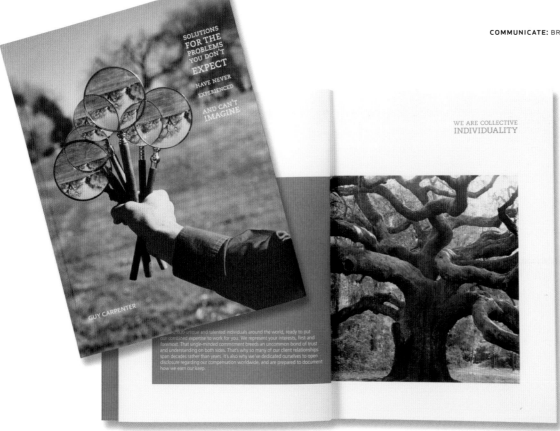

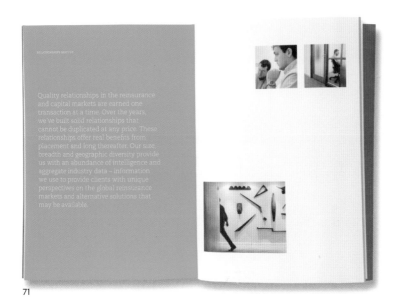

71

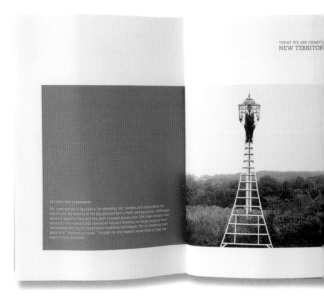

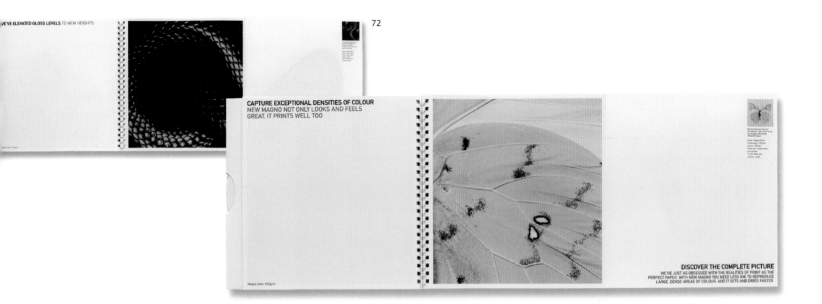

WE'VE ELEVATED GLOSS LEVELS TO NEW HEIGHTS

72

CAPTURE EXCEPTIONAL DENSITIES OF COLOUR
NEW MAGNO NOT ONLY LOOKS AND FEELS
GREAT, IT PRINTS WELL TOO

DISCOVER THE COMPLETE PICTURE
WE'RE JUST AS OBSESSED WITH THE REALITIES OF PRINT AS THE
PERFECT PAPER. WITH NEW MAGNO YOU NEED LESS INK TO REPRODUCE
LARGE, DENSE AREAS OF COLOUR. AND IT SETS AND DRIES FASTER.

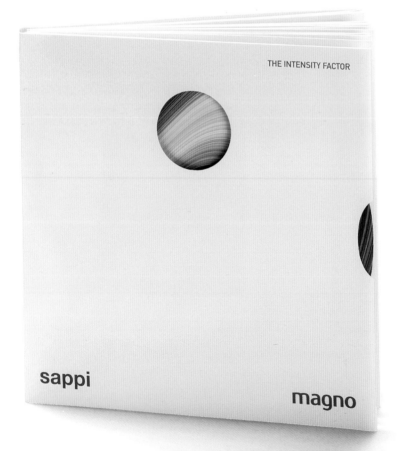

THE INTENSITY FACTOR

sappi

magno

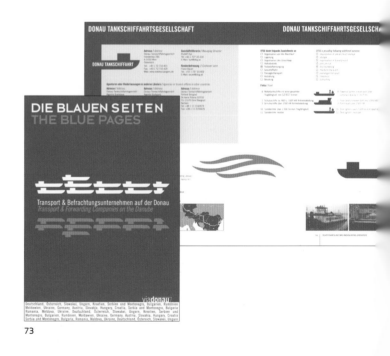

DIE BLAUEN SEITEN
THE BLUE PAGES

73

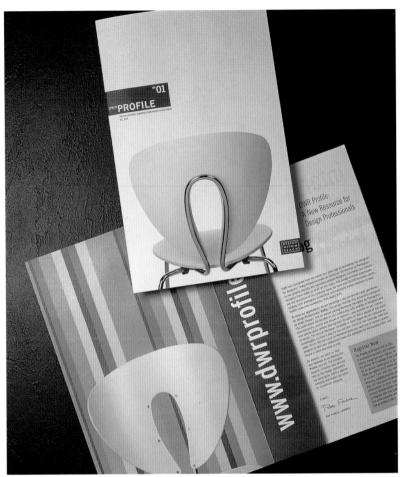

74

72
CLIENT: Sappi Fine Paper Europe
DESIGN FIRM: Curious

73
CLIENT: Via Donau
DESIGN FIRM: KASHI_design

74
CLIENT: Design Within Reach
DESIGN FIRM: Morla Design, Inc.

75
CLIENT: Vovovod-Kanalizacija, Ljubljana
DESIGN FIRM: KROG, Ljubljana

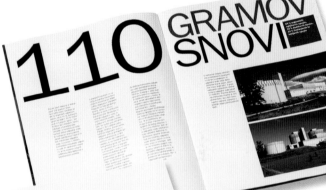

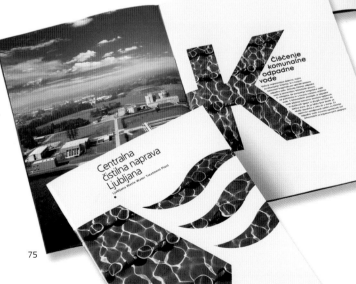

75

76
CLIENT: o.n – G.D. Review
DESIGN FIRM: Carrè Noir Roma

77
CLIENT: Zilio Ecologia
DESIGN FIRM: Fluid Design Lab

78
CLIENT: Harinera Beleño
DESIGN FIRM: Diseño Dos Asociados

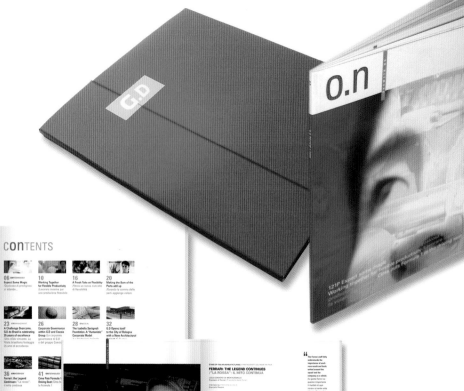

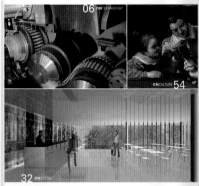

CONTENTS

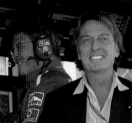
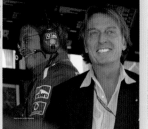
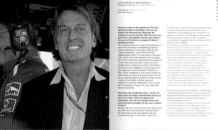

FERRARI: THE LEGEND CONTINUES "LA ROSSA": IL MITO CONTINUA

An exhibition of paintings by a leading late-Renaissance painter opens in Bologna and in Rome. The exhibition will feature a wide selection of works from some of the most important galleries in Italy and around the world
In mostra a Bologna e a Roma i dipinti di uno dei protagonisti dell'arte europea del tardo Rinascimento. Un'ampia selezione di opere provenienti dalle più importanti raccolte d'Italia e del mondo

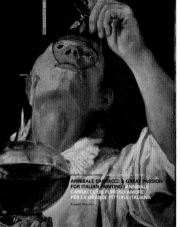

ANNIBALE CARRACCI: A GREAT PASSION FOR ITALIAN PAINTING / ANNIBALE CARRACCI UN FURIOSO AMORE PER LA GRANDE PITTURA ITALIANA

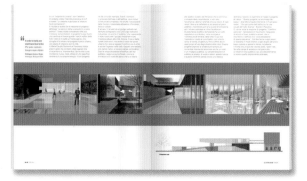

EOLICA
WIND

Perchè?

L'uomo ha imparato a volare, ha applicato le leggi della fisica, ha capito che l'aria ed il vento possono essere al suo servizio, traendo da esse molteplici benefici. Basta pensare all'aviazione civile e militare o ad uno Shuttle in orbita alla Terra, o lo sfruttamento energetico della forza che sprigiona.

Questo grazie al fatto che l'atmosfera genera un carico sulla superficie terrestre chiamato pressione atmosferica. Questa pressione può essere più o meno forte e creare degli spostamenti dell'aria da zone ad alta pressione a zone a bassa pressione dove il carico è minore. Il Vento è uno spostamento d'aria tra punti in condizioni di pressione differenti.

Le particelle dell'aria del vento, essendo esse in movimento, generano energia di tipo cinetico. La captazione dell'energia del vento avviene mediante l'utilizzo di tecnologia eolica, sviluppata dall'uomo nel corso dei secoli. Chi dimentica i mulini a vento o il Don Chisciotte?

Why?

Mankind has learned to fly, apply the laws of physics, has understood that the air and wind may be enlisted in his service and that he may extract many benefits from them. Just think of civil and military aviation or the space shuttle that orbits the Earth, not to mention exploitation of the energy released by the force of the wind.

That exploitation is possible thanks to the fact that the atmosphere generates a change on the surface of the Earth known as atmospheric pressure. The pressure may be stronger or weaker and creates movement of air from high pressure to low-pressure areas, where the charge is less. The wind is a movement of air between points where the atmospheric pressure is different.

The particles of air in the wind, which are in movement, generate kinetic energy. The energy of the wind captured thro...

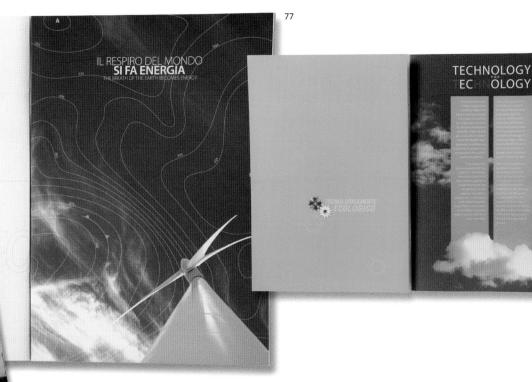

IL RESPIRO DEL MONDO
SI FA ENERGIA
THE BREATH OF THE EARTH BECOMES ENERGY

TECHNOLOGY
FOR
TECHNOLOGY

77

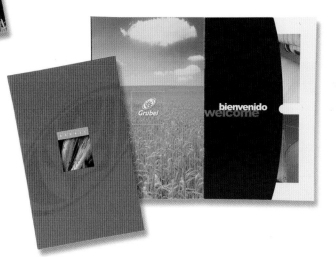

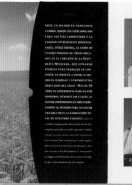

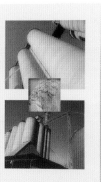

78

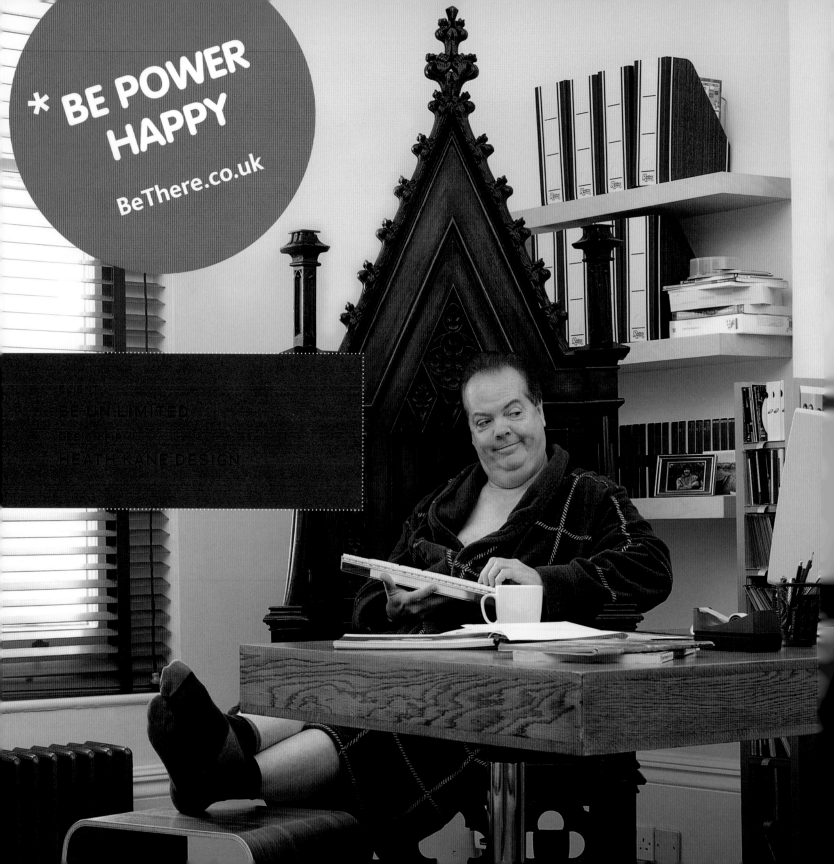

CLIENT

BE UN LIMITED

DESIGN FIRM

HEATH KANE DESIGN

BE UN LIMITED (BE) OFFERS AN EXAMPLE OF BUSINESS DESIGN THAT COMMUNICATES THROUGH UNEXPECTED IMAGES AND VOICE. THE VISUAL SYSTEM DESCRIBES A HIGHLY TECHNICAL PRODUCT IN A FRIENDLY WAY THAT FOCUSES ON END-USER BENEFITS. THE BRAND COMMUNICATES PROFESSIONALISM, COMPETENCY, AND QUALITY IN A MORE INVIGORATING AND CLEVER WAY THAN MOST COMPANIES DO. THE RESULT IS A DIFFERENTIATED AND UNMISTAKABLE BRAND IDENTITY.

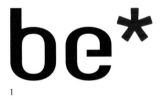

1

1
The asterisk is part of Be's logo and acts as a metaphor representing connotation and connection (e.g. Be* Online, Be* Active, Be* Informed, Be* Entertained).

CLIENT Founded in 2004, Be was the UK's first Internet Service Provider (ISP) to harness the latest ADSL2+ technology and maximize phone line capacity at a highly competitive price. Be grew rapidly—from zero to 10,000 customers in little more than a year—and was acquired in 2006 by a larger telecom, 02.

Be understood the benefit of strategic design from the very beginning. Heath Kane helped Be define and communicate the company's values in a branded way. Using the name as a lead-in, they articulated the values: Be challenging, Be efficient, Be inspirational, Be the best, and Be cool. The brand attributes derived from the values include engineered, clever, invigorating, and responsive.

PROJECT In addition to naming the company, deliverables for Be included all internal and external communication design and collateral:

advertising (print, radio, and online), direct marketing, Web and online media, display and exhibition design, packaging, presentation and corporate branding.

FOCUSED VISION Big-picture vision often comes across as "we want to reach everyone and be the best at everything." Laudable as that may be, a broad scope makes it difficult to deliver a clear message to anyone about anything in particular. Heath Kane developed a series of short-term and long-term advertising objectives that focused initial advertising and marketing efforts on specific market segments. As the brand became more established and the company had a successful story to tell, the message was extended to additional audiences.

JUXTAPOSE Heath Kane helped define the initial target market as predominantly male, well-educated, early-technology adopters,

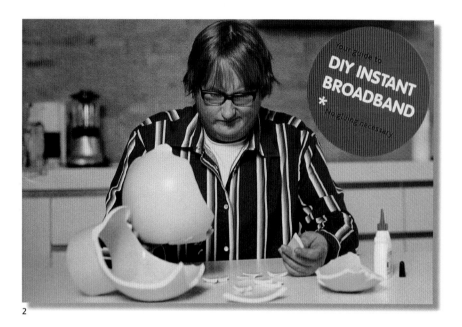

Your guide to
DIY INSTANT BROADBAND
*
No gluing necessary

2

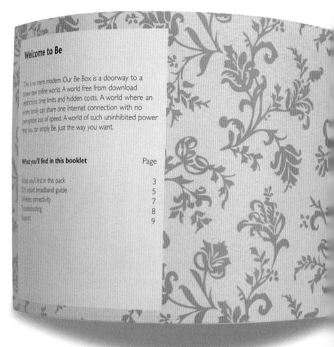

Welcome to Be

This is no mere modem. Our Be Box is a doorway to a brave new online world. A world free from download restrictions, time limits and hidden costs. A world where an entire family can share one Internet connection with no perceptible loss of speed. A world of such uninhibited power that you can simply Be. Just the way you want.

What you'll find in this booklet	Page
What you'll find in this pack	3
DIY instant broadband guide	5
Wireless connectivity	7
Troubleshooting	8
Support	9

and peer-influenced. The last color that may come to mind when imagining what appeals to this audience is pink—the exact color Heath Kane chose as the backbone of the Be brand. However, pink works perfectly well with the company values and brand attributes. It vastly differentiates Be from the dozens of competing telecom companies and contributed to Be becoming a widely recognizable brand almost overnight. ■

3

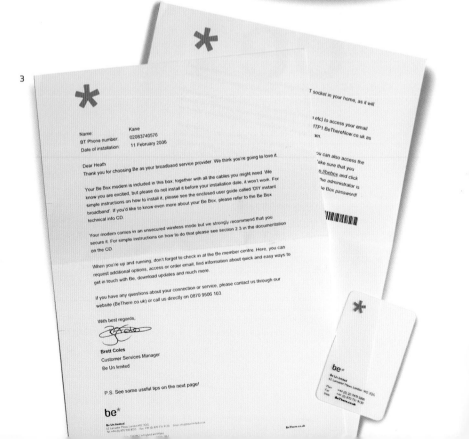

Name: Kane
BT Phone number: 02083740576
Date of installation: 11 February 2006

Dear Heath

Thank you for choosing Be as your broadband service provider. We think you're going to love it.

Your Be Box modem is included in this box, together with all the cables you might need. We know you are excited, but please do not install it before your installation date, it won't work. For simple instructions on how to install it, please see the enclosed user guide called 'DIY instant broadband'. If you'd like to know even more about your Be Box, please refer to the Be Box technical info CD.

Your modem comes in an unsecured wireless mode but we strongly recommend that you secure it. For simple instructions on how to do that please see section 2.3 in the documentation on the CD.

When you're up and running, don't forget to check in at the Be member centre. Here, you can request additional options, access or order email, find information about quick and easy ways to get in touch with Be, download updates and much more.

If you have any questions about your connection or service, please contact us through our website (BeThere.co.uk) or call us directly on 0870 9506 103.

With best regards,

Brett Coles
Customer Services Manager
Be Un limited

P.S. See some useful tips on the next page!

be*

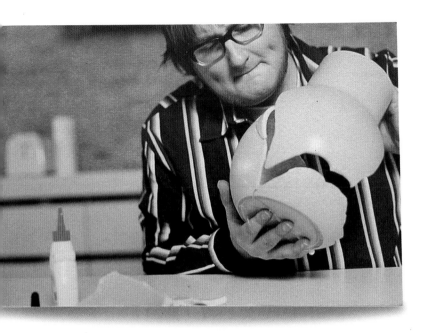

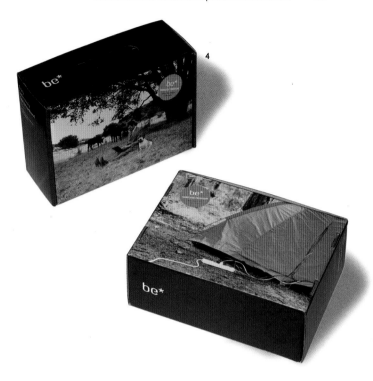

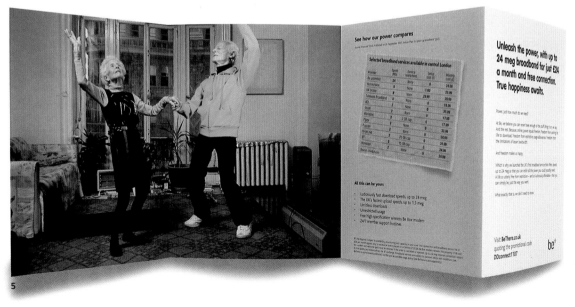

2

Even the instruction manual received branding attention. Friendly, helpful, and entertaining, it clearly differentiates Be from other telecom companies.

3

The asterisk at the top, anchored by the logo at the bottom, communicates that Be is transparent and straight-forward, without small print or unwelcome clauses.

4

The welcome pack is the familiar size of a lunch-box and includes everything the user needs to get online.

5

Direct mail pieces need to have visual stopping power. This piece uses Be's quirky, unexpected style to capture attention and engage the reader.

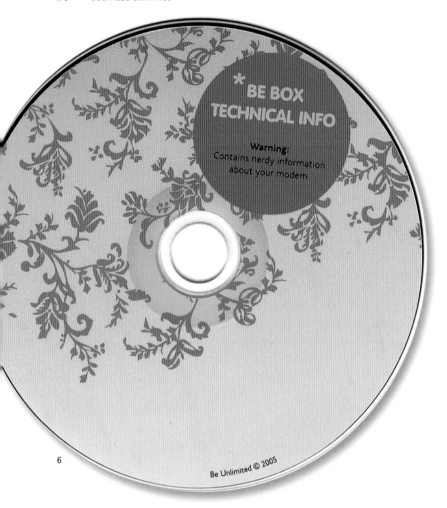

6

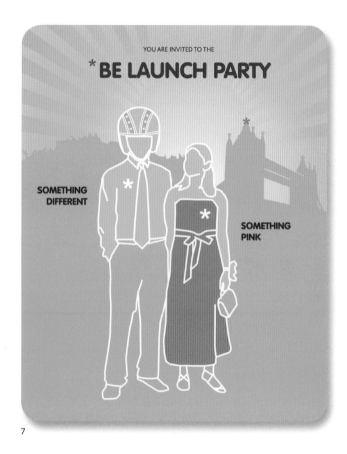

7

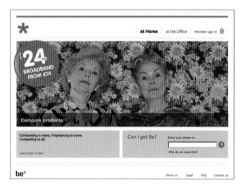

8

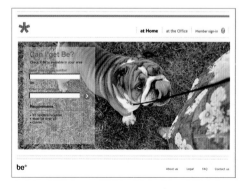

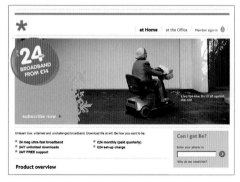

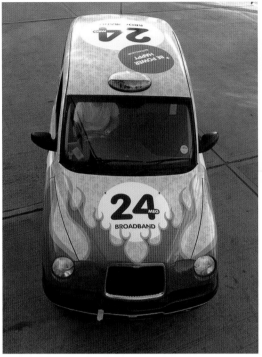

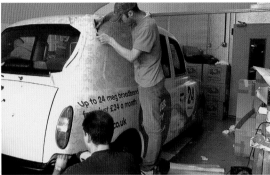

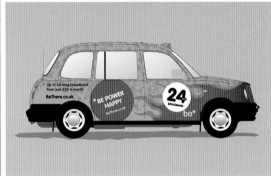

9

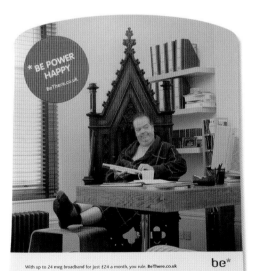

10

6

The CD-ROM containing technical information reflects the Be brand. The label reads: "Warning: Contains nerdy information about your modem."

7

The launch party reinforced the idea that Be is a different kind of communication company. The theme was "Something Different, Something Pink."

8

The website avoids typical clichés and opts for vibrant, witty images of people being liberated and inspired by the potential of online capabilities.

9

More than fifty pink Be branded taxis hit the streets of London in 2005, helping to make the company an instantly recognizable brand.

10

In addition to branding livery exteriors, designers created branded messages that were placed on the backs of taxi cab seats.

CLIENT: Be Un Limited
DESIGN FIRM: Heath Kane Design
ART DIRECTOR: Heath Kane
DESIGNER: Heath Kane

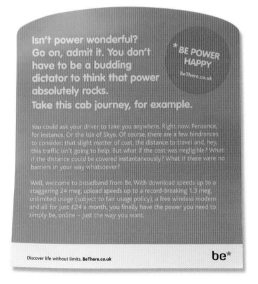

THE MOST EFFECTIVE DESIGN COMES FROM A STRATEGIC AND METHODICAL APPROACH. THIS CASE STUDY PROVIDES A BRILLIANT EXAMPLE OF THE DIFFERENCE IT MAKES WHEN DESIGN FIRMS TAKE TIME TO LOOK STRATEGICALLY INTO THEIR CLIENT'S BUSINESS AND CREATE VISUAL SYSTEMS THAT FUNCTION AS BUSINESS COMMUNICATION SOLUTIONS. IN THIS CASE STUDY, LANDINI ASSOCIATES DEVELOPED A BRAND IDENTITY THAT REFLECTS CLEARLY THE BUSINESS STRATEGY OF ITS CLIENT, **MACQUARIE TELECOM**.

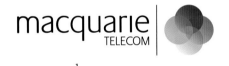

1

CLIENT Macquarie Telecom provides information and communications technology for business and government clients throughout Australia and Singapore. The company develops and implements a range of voice, mobile, and data networks, as well as hosting and security products. Macquarie is the challenger to the top two telecom providers in their market. The company positions itself as a "business only" telecom, pursuing medium- to large-scale businesses and not serving consumer markets.

PROJECT Landini approached the project by taking a strategic look at Macquarie's business. Designers developed a logo to reflect the four key business areas and overlayed them to show the client's expertise in convergent communications systems. Project deliverables included the brand platform, identity and identity

guidelines for all customer touch points, a launch party, and third-party-sponsored branding guidelines.

LOGO AT WORK The logo is designed to work as a visual communication tool for several communication pieces. Each of the four atoms represents a key business area: voice, data, mobile, and hosting. The four business areas often converge and are connected by account-able service and a high level of security.

By designing the logo to reflect Macquarie's business strategy, the logo serves as a visual cue for employees and customers. Employees can use the logo as a talking point to describe their key business functions to customers. Then, when customers see the logo, they experience a visual reminder of Macquarie's business areas

1
The logo represents Macquarie's four key business areas; the overlay shows their convergence within the brand.

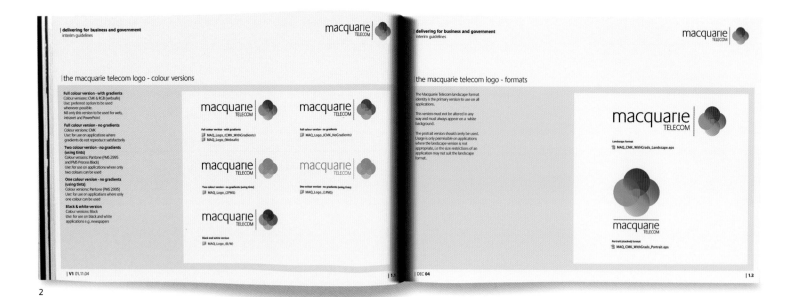

2

and attributes. The strategic design also works as a versatile visual reference within several communication pieces.

NICE APPROACH A strategic approach to design involves studying the attributes that differentiate clients from their competitors. It also involves asking questions about any communication barriers faced by the client. The designer then has the challenge of developing a visual system that addresses each of these (and other) issues.

Landini learned that Macquarie has a surprisingly approachable nature. This approachability clearly differentiated Macquarie from its competitors and addressed a major obstacle for customers. That is, most people assume that telecom companies are high-tech and low-touch; that telecoms speak another language, and are neither easy to communicate with nor friendly.

Landini designed the visual system to reflect accurately the client's approachable nature and commitment to providing highly accountable service. The designers did this through the four overlaid atoms, rounded typeface, and with added attention to the website design. To counter the perception of telecom businesses as unapproachable and difficult to communicate with, Landini designed the website to be very easy to navigate and to reflect the core attributes of the company: approachable, secure, and highly accountable.

ADDED DIMENSION Corporate offices provide tremendous opportunities to reinforce brand identity among employees and customers. Landini extended the reach of the brand identity to the Macquarie corporate office in Sydney, providing depth and dimension through reception signage, wayfinding, and ambient art pieces. ■

3

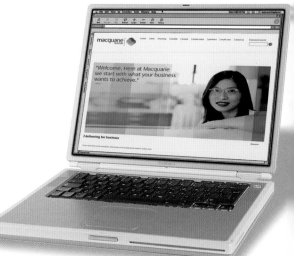

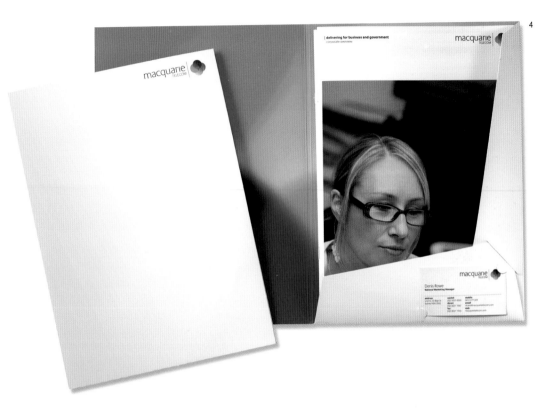

2
Style manuals help internal staff and external contractors support the brand values effectively and consistently.

3
The website communicates Macquarie's core attribute of being a surprisingly approachable technology company.

4
The corporate brochure gives internal staff and customers an overview of the brand elements, key messages, and company products and services.

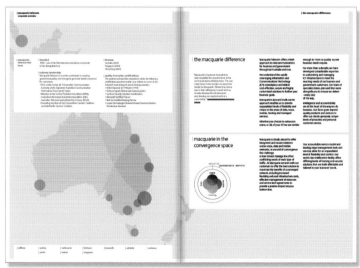

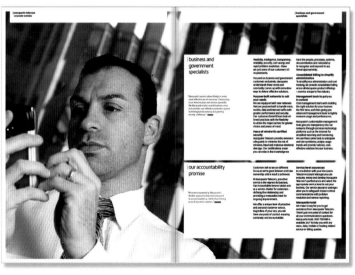

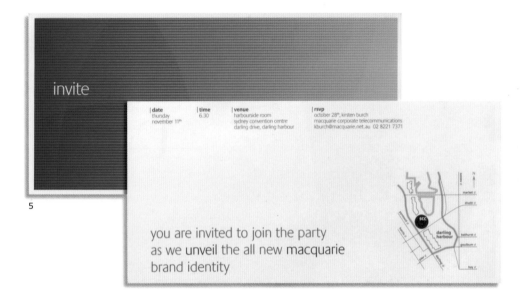

invite

date	time	venue	rsvp
thursday	6.30	harbourside room	october 28th, kirsten burch
november 11th		sydney convention centre	macquarie corporate telecommunications
		darling drive, darling harbour	kburch@macquarie.net.au 02 8221 7371

you are invited to join the party
as we unveil the all new **macquarie**
brand identity

5

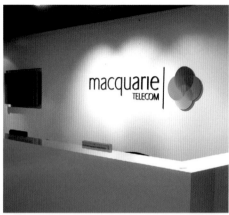

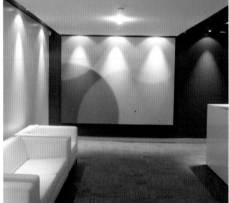

6

5

*Macquarie hosted a launch party for
key staff and customers to introduce
the new brand.*

6

*Corporate offices provide an
opportunity to extend the brand
with added depth and dimension.*

7

*Landini set up digital, in-house
printing to be consistent with
preprinted material.*

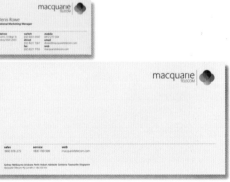

7

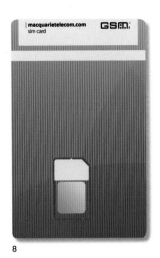

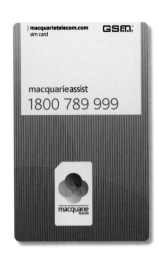

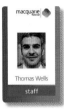

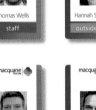

8

8

Landini reinforced the brand by adding the logo to a variety of products and business items.

CLIENT: Macquarie Telecom
DESIGN FIRM: Landini Associates
ART DIRECTOR: Mark Landini
DESIGNER: Clayton Andrews

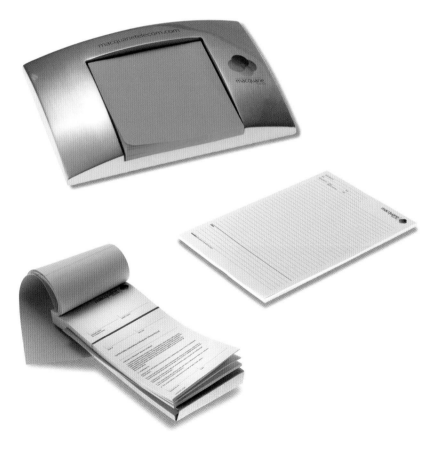

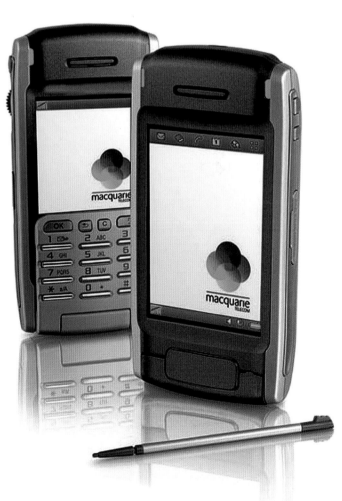

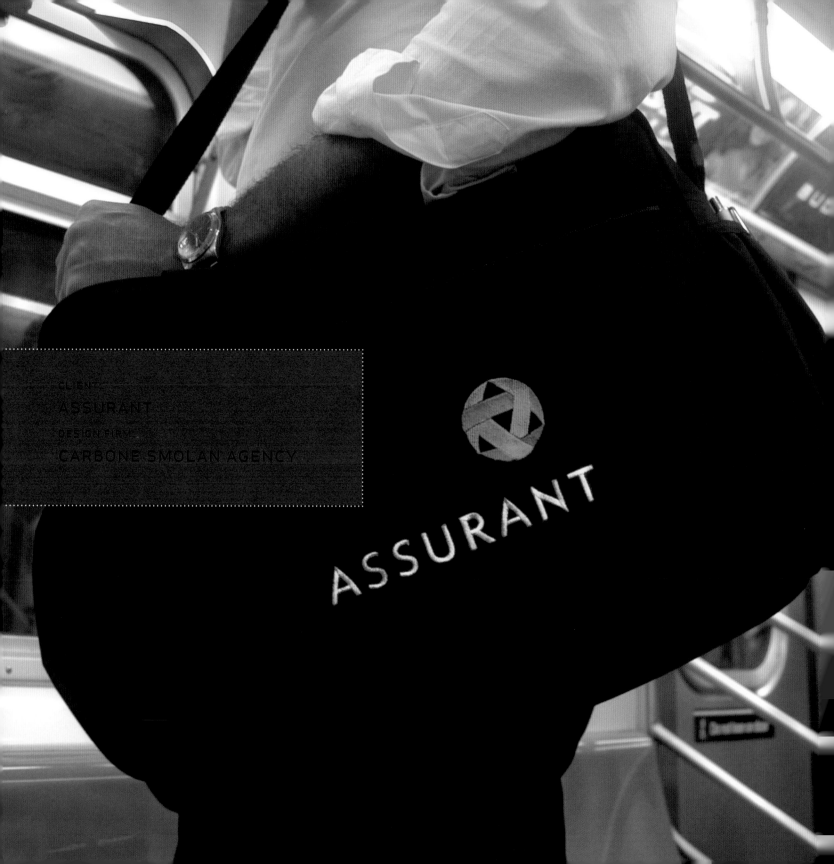

CLIENT
ASSURANT
DESIGN FIRM
CARBONE SMOLAN AGENCY

ASSURANT

DESIGNERS USE AESTHETICS TO HELP BUSINESSES SOLVE COMMUNICATION ISSUES. THROUGH STRATEGIC COMBINATION OF ELEMENTS SUCH AS COLOR, SHAPE, TEXTURE, PHOTOGRAPHY, ILLUSTRATION, AND ANIMATION, THEY DEVELOP VISUAL AND VERBAL SYSTEMS THAT COMMUNICATE THE ATTRIBUTES AND BENEFITS OF A PRODUCT, SERVICE, OR COMPANY. THIS CASE STUDY FEATURES A VISUAL SYSTEM THAT HELPS **ASSURANT** COMMUNICATE ITS ABILITY TO BRING CLARITY TO THE INCREDIBLY COMPLEX BUSINESS OF SPECIALTY INSURANCE.

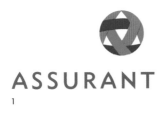

ASSURANT
1

1
The loosely woven symbol and use of three colors in the logo represent the integration of Assurant's three key business areas.

CLIENT Assurant, a Fortune 500 company, provides specialty insurance and insurance-related services through five subsidiaries: Assurant Employee Benefits, Assurant Health, Assurant Preneed, Assurant Solutions, and Assurant Specialty Property. The company prides itself on communicating complicated ideas in accessible and understandable ways.

PROJECT Fortis changed its name to Assurant to coincide with the company's initial public offering (IPO). Company officials engaged Carbone Smolan Agency (CSA) to develop a new identity system to support the name change. CSA worked in tandem with Assurant's in-house communications team to develop the brand. Deliverables included brand identity, a stationery system, advertising, and a style guide.

GOOD TIMING By launching a branding program simultaneously with its IPO, Assurant was able to capitalize on the press coverage already garnered by the IPO. The branding program provided Assurant with a visual tool with which they could discuss the attributes that differentiate it from competitors.

DEFINING IDENTITY CSA designed Assurant's brand identity to communicate two key concepts. First, the use of three colors illustrates Assurant's three key businesses: risk management, customized technology, and long-term partnerships. Second, the logo demonstrates that the three are interwoven to provide a rich range of integrated services.

SAME BUT DIFFERENT Assurant needed to develop an identity that allowed subsidiaries to retain independence while also creating a unified brand presence. The design solution involved maintaining the various subsidiary names and treating them with a shared logo and typeface.

2
The ad campaign used simple and familiar items such as a kite and a yo-yo to communicate Assurant's ability to bring clarity to complex issues.

3
Strategic branded items included USB drives and luggage tags.

4
The use of brilliant color makes Assurant stand out from competitors in the more traditional and conservative insurance industry.

CLIENT: Assurant
DESIGN FIRM: Carbone Smolan Agency
ART DIRECTOR: Ken Carbone

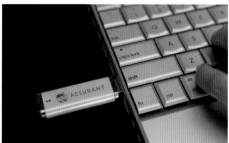

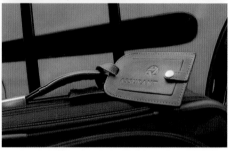

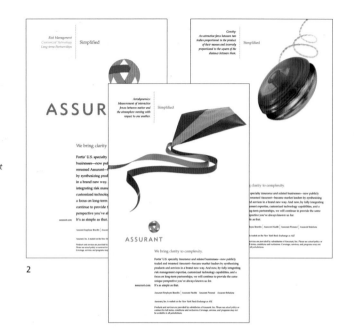

2

3

DIFFERENT TYPE Designers chose brilliant colors for the loosely woven logo sphere. The colors communicate vibrancy, dynamism, and inter-connection. The colors help Assurant stand out in an industry dominated by conservative, corporate "suits." The rounded type follows the spherical shape of the logo and communicates approachability and warmth, suggesting that Assurant is a different type of insurance company.

OBJECT LESSON Full-page ads introduced the new name and brand identity. In each ad, a simple image connects with a complex idea to commu-nicate the core strengths of the company. For example, the design team used the symbol of a kite to illustrate aerodynamics and interrela-tionships. Another ad features the logo sphere to express the company's attributes. The campaign demonstrates Assurant's ability to communicate complex concepts in clear ways. ■

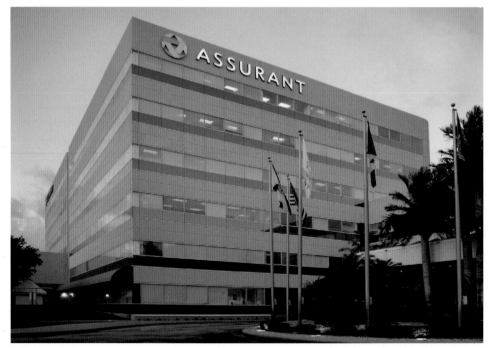

4

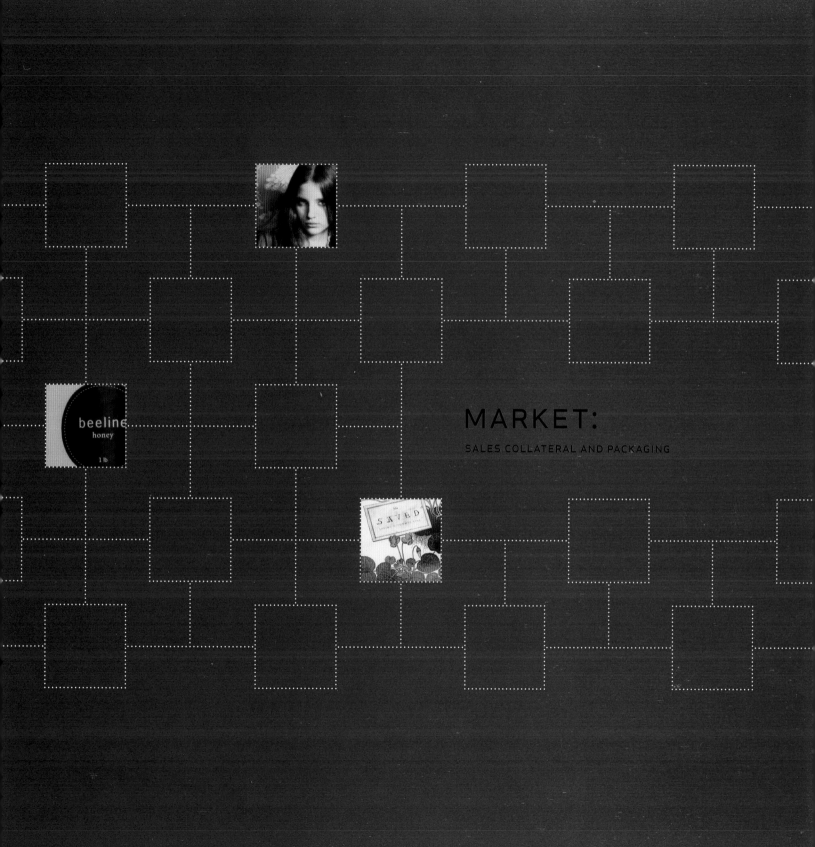

MARKET:

SALES COLLATERAL AND PACKAGING

1
CLIENT: The Vesta Group
DESIGN FIRM: Decker Design

2
CLIENT: Saved Gallery of Art & Craft
DESIGN FIRM: Nothing: Something: NY

3
CLIENT: Martin Architectural
DESIGN FIRM: Frontmedia Studio

1

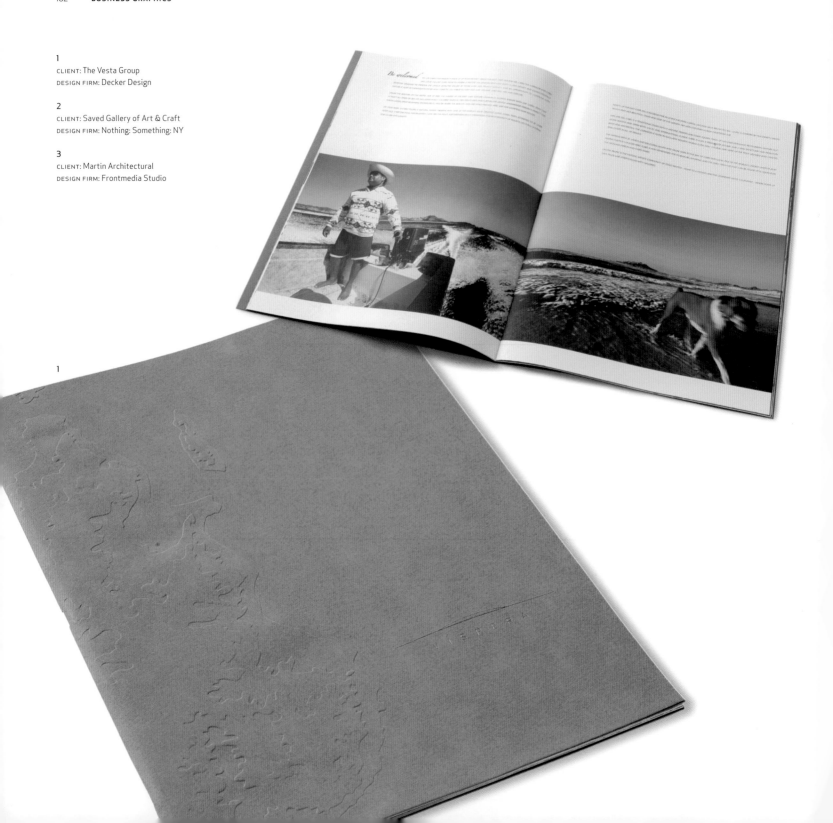

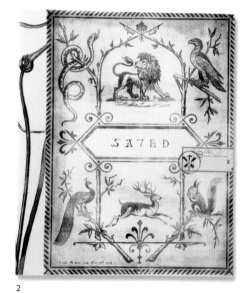

2

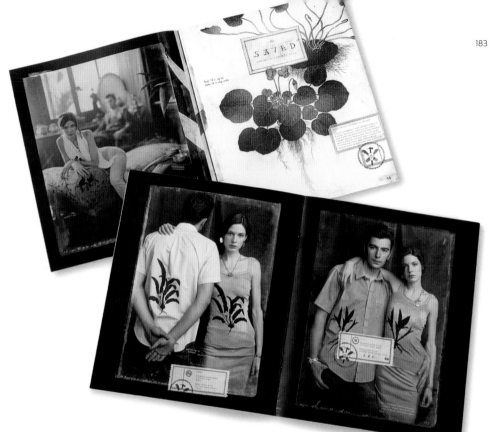

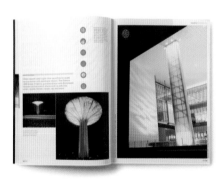

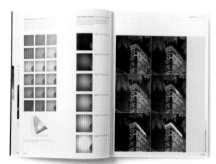

3

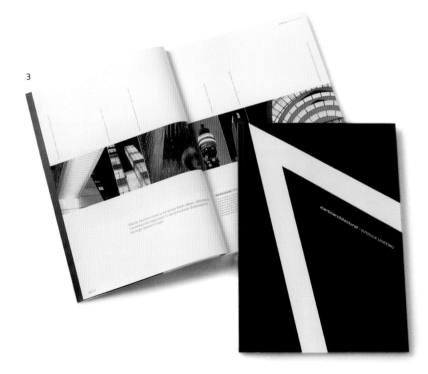

4
CLIENT: Essenciale
DESIGN FIRM: Hardy Design

5
CLIENT: Wong Co Co (Jubes)
DESIGN FIRM: Kinetic

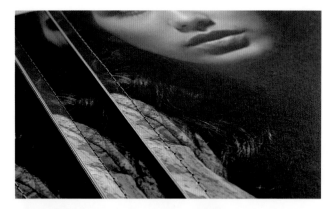

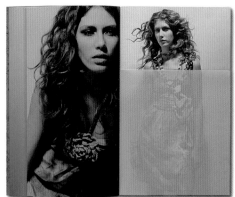

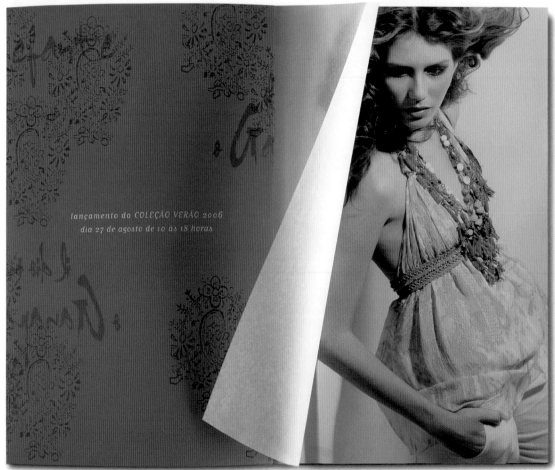

4

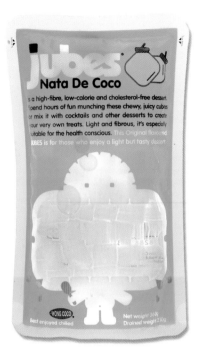

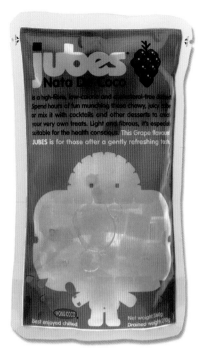

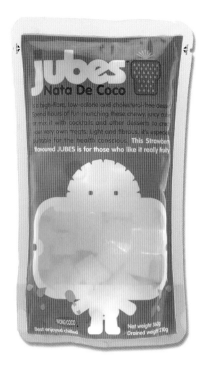

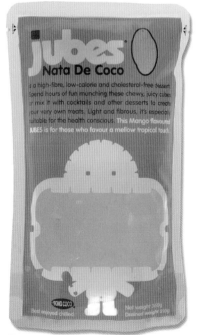

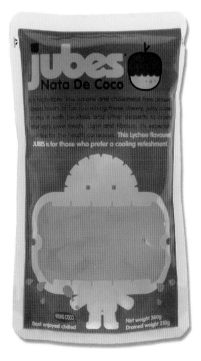

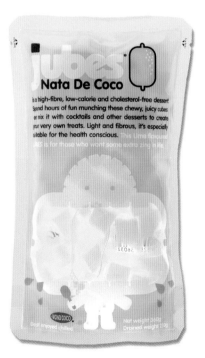

5

6

CLIENT: Montville Sales
DESIGN FIRM: Sussner Design Company

7

CLIENT: Made Her Think
DESIGN FIRM: Nothing: Something: NY

8

CLIENT: Robert K. Futterman
& Associates (RKF)
DESIGN FIRM: Liska + Associates

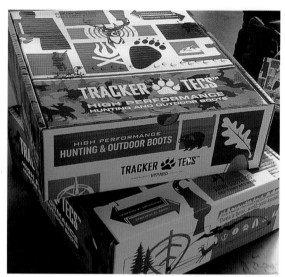

6

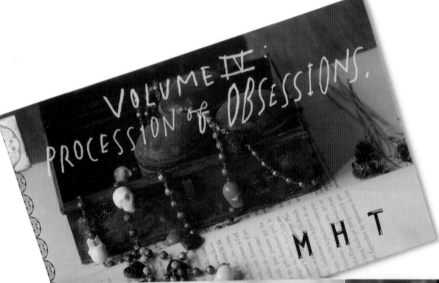

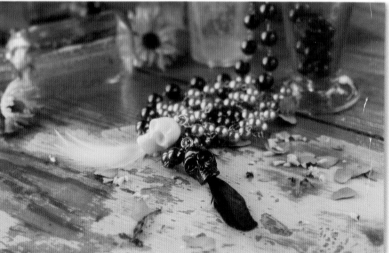

7

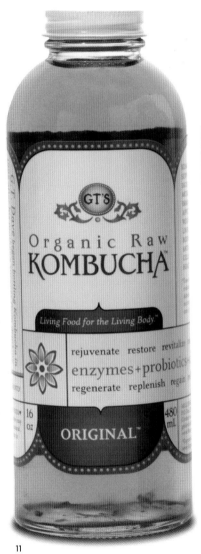
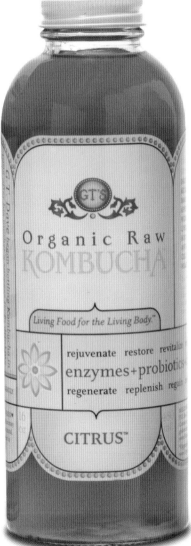
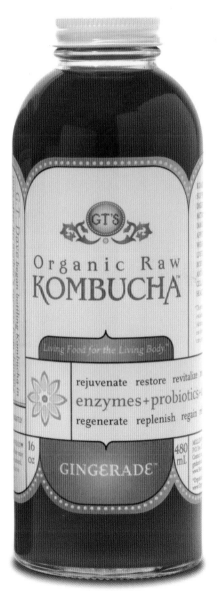

11

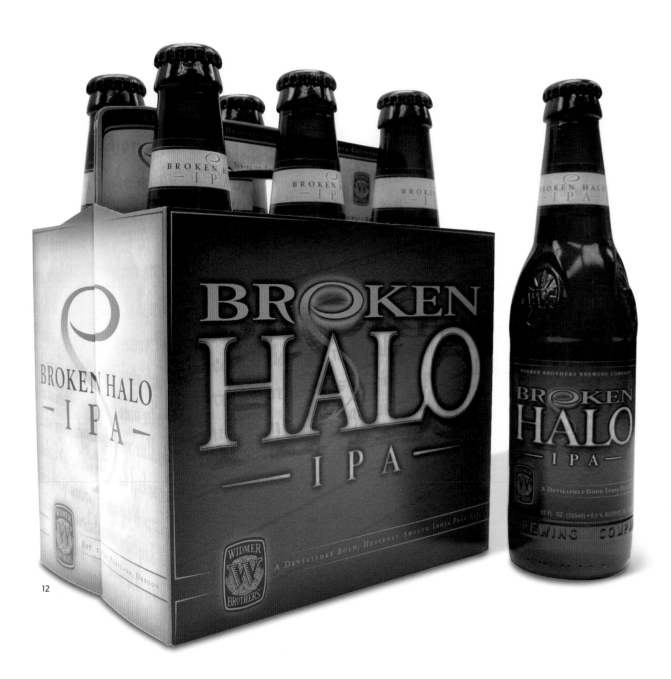

12

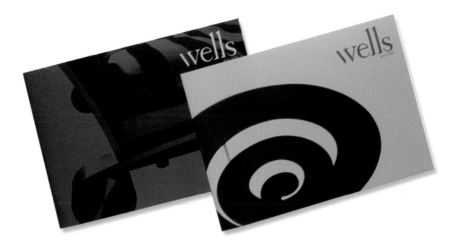

12
CLIENT: Widmer Brothers Brewery
DESIGN FIRM: Hornall Anderson
Design Works

13
CLIENT: Wells
DESIGN FIRM: Curious

Hibernate: Bedding and linen We look for value – whether it's a polycotton sheet or Egyptian cotton percale sheet; wool blanket or bedspread; man-made pillow (for allergy sufferers) or Hungarian goose down duvet. Our linen workshop can also make most things to most sizes. Our range includes bathrobes and towels.

Manufacturers include: Brinkhaus, Designers Guild, Peter Reed and Yves Delorme, Kenzo and Pierre Frey. Shown opposite: Brinkhaus fine duvets and pillows in natural materials.

20

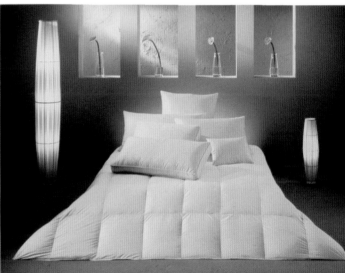

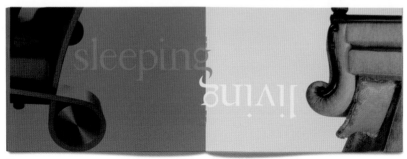

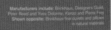

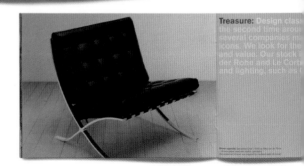

Treasure: Design classics the second time around. Several companies make icons. We look for the and value. Our stock der Rohe and Le Corbu and lighting, such as t

13

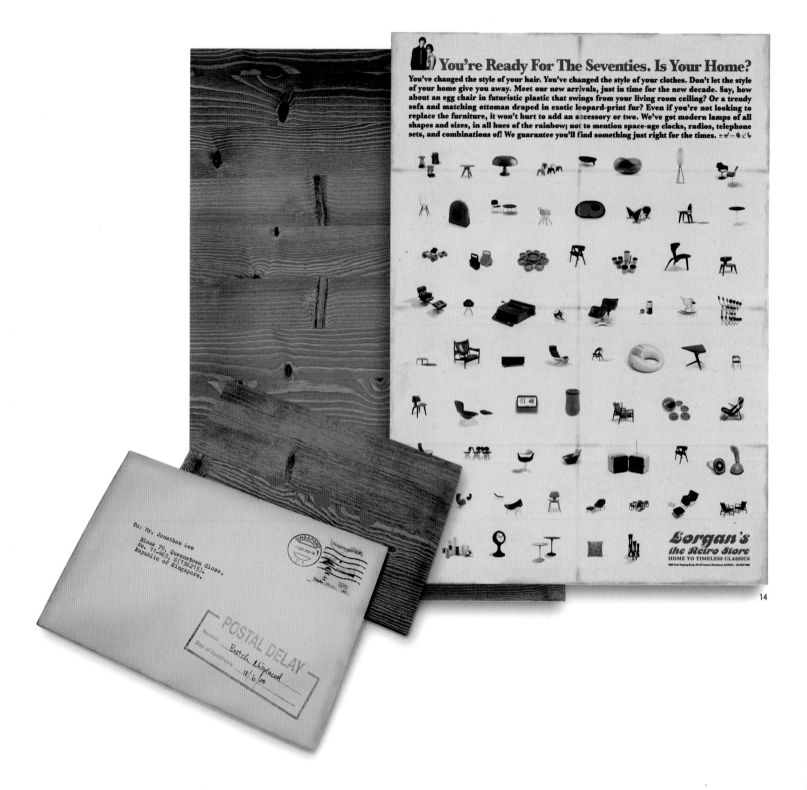

14

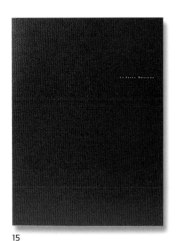

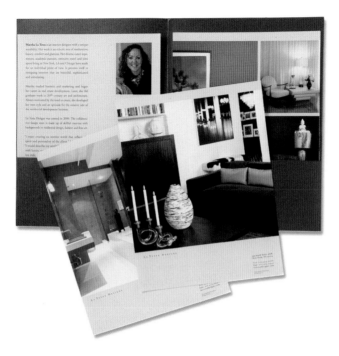

15

14
CLIENT: Lorgan
DESIGN FIRM: Kinetic

15
CLIENT: La Tessa Designs
DESIGN FIRM: Decker Design

16
CLIENT: OC Tanner
DESIGN FIRM: Hornall Anderson
Design Works

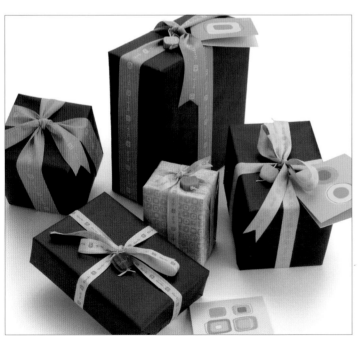

16

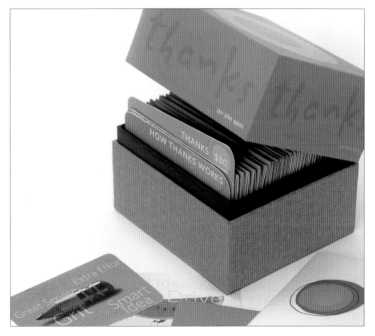

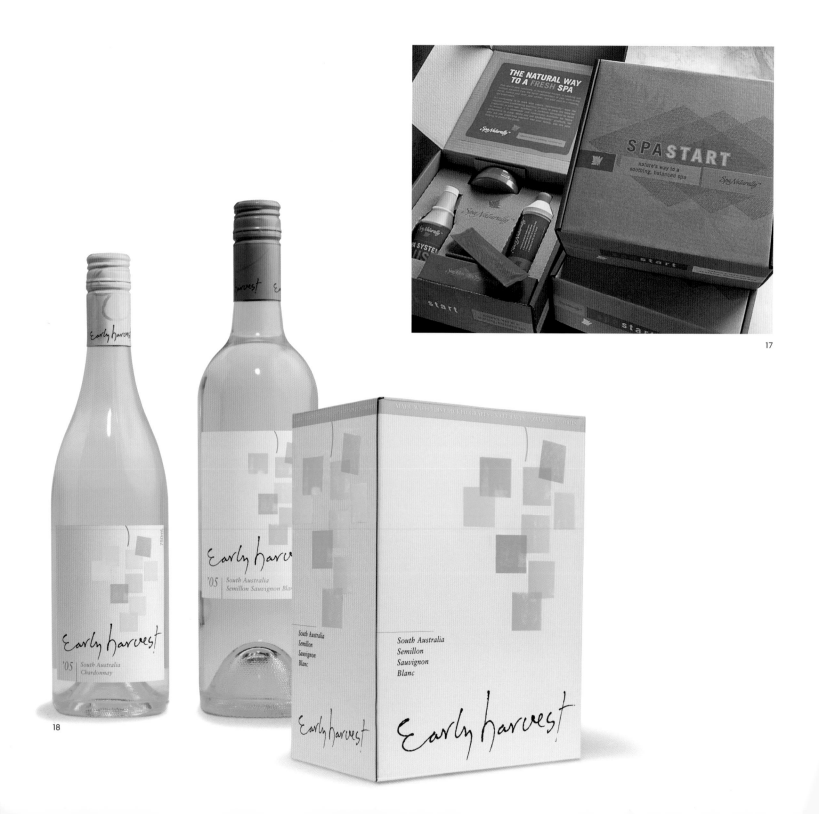

17

18

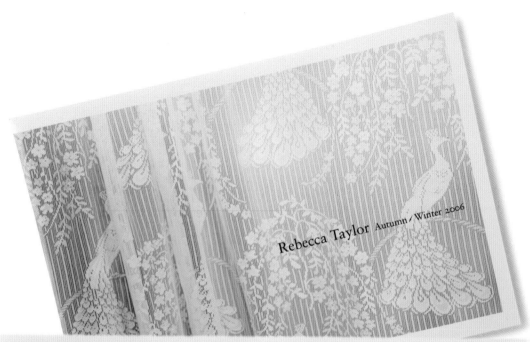

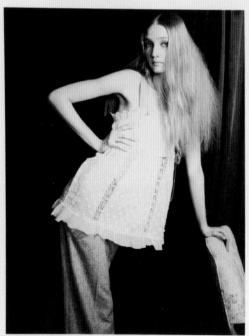
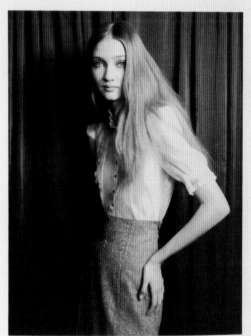
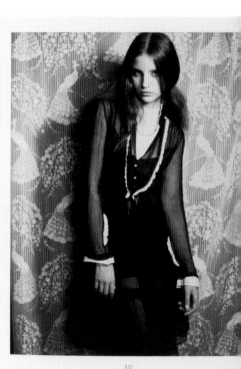

17
CLIENT: Spa Naturally
DESIGN FIRM: Sussner Design Company

18
CLIENT: Foster's Australia
DESIGN FIRM: Davidson Design

19
CLIENT: Rebecca Taylor
DESIGN FIRM: Liska + Associates

19

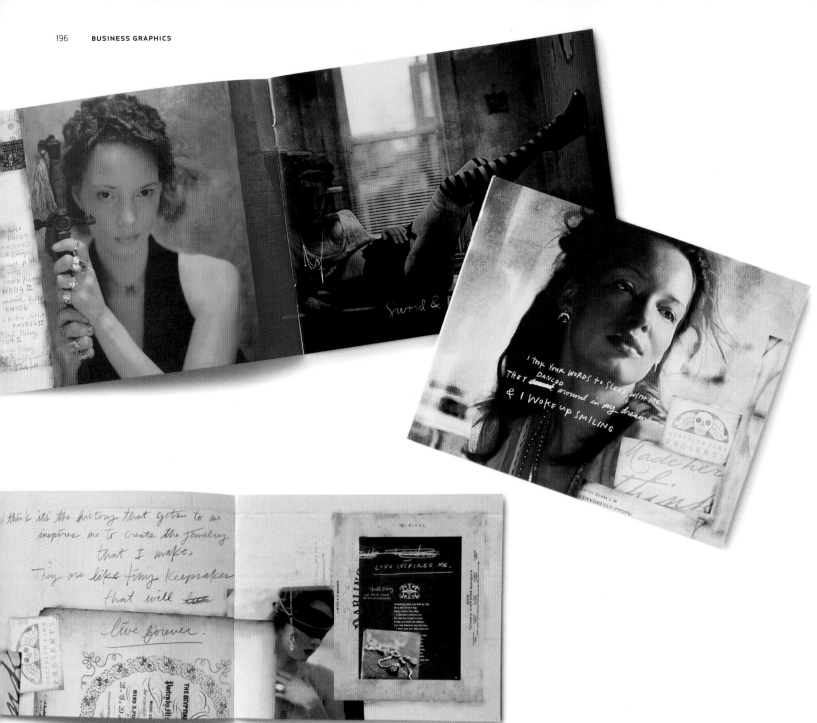

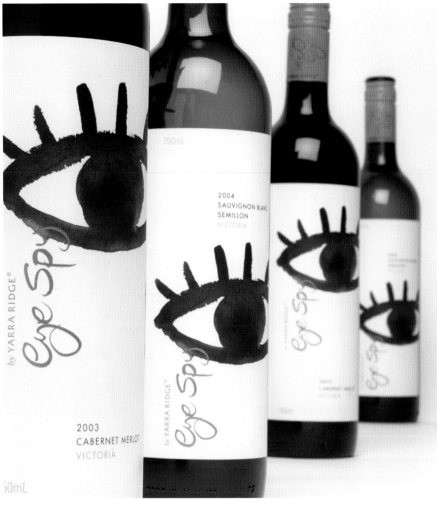

21

20
CLIENT: Made Her Think
DESIGN FIRM: Nothing: Something: NY

21
CLIENT: Beringer Blass Wine Estates
DESIGN FIRM: Davidson Design

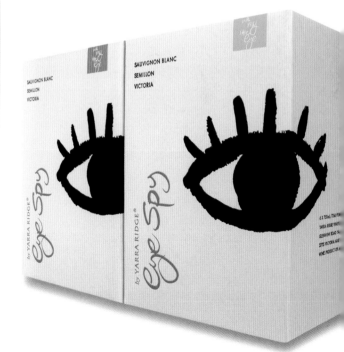

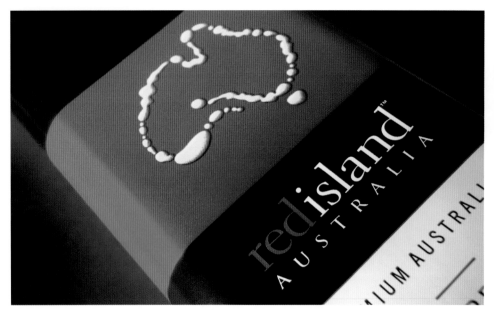

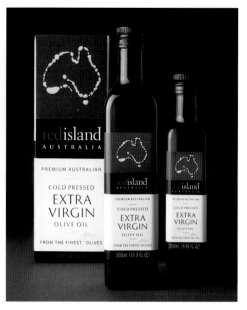

22

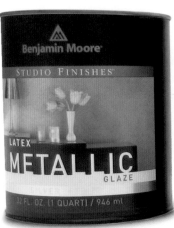
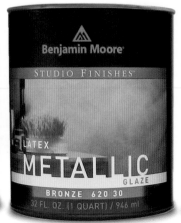
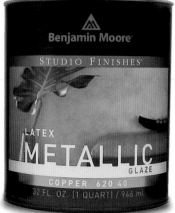
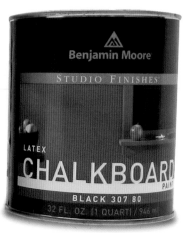

23

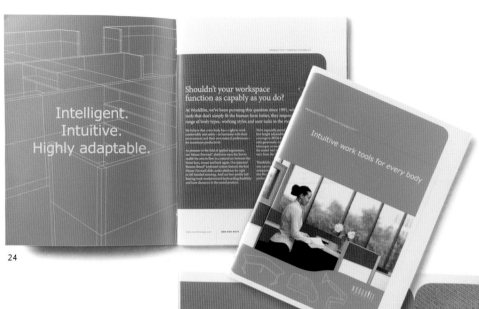

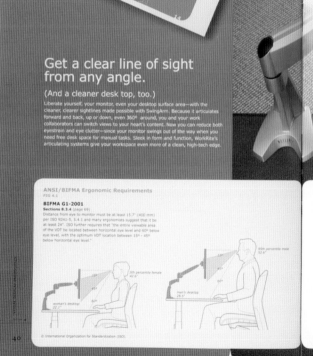

22
CLIENT: Piquant Blue
DESIGN FIRM: Perks Design Partners

23
CLIENT: Benjamin Moore
DESIGN FIRM: Hornall Anderson
Design Works

24
CLIENT: WorkRite Ergonomics
DESIGN FIRM: Wages Design

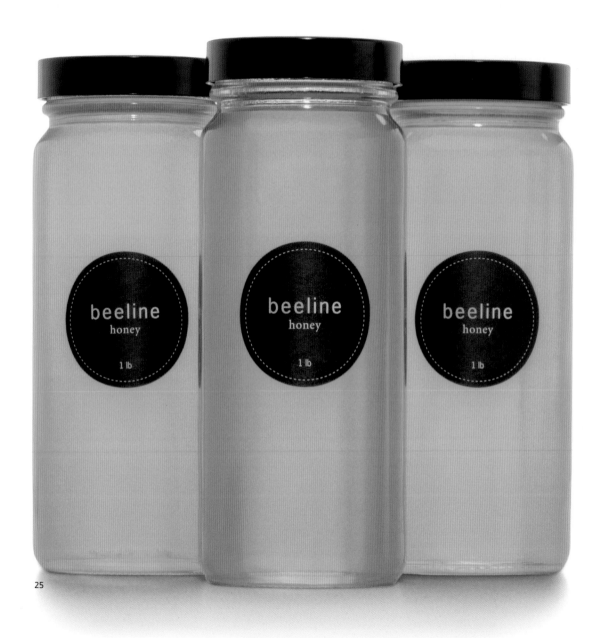

25

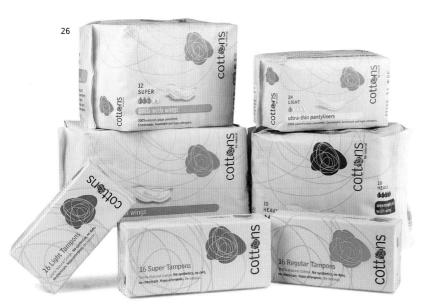

25
CLIENT: North Lawndale
Employment Network
DESIGN FIRM: Kym Abrams Design

26, 27
CLIENT: Cottons, Feminine
Hygiene Products
DESIGN FIRM: Spark Studio

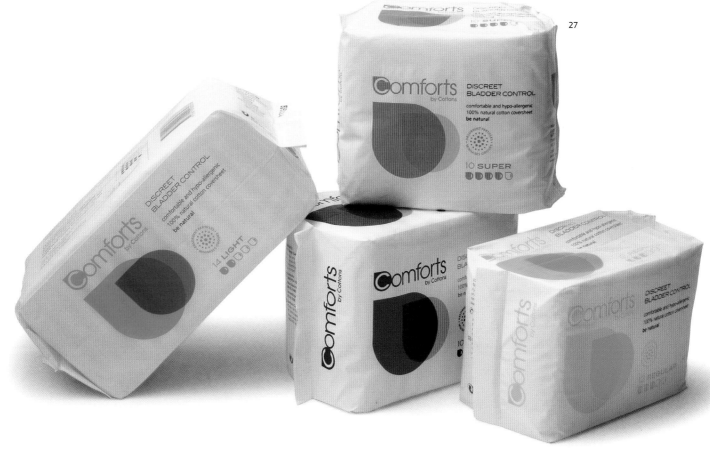

28
CLIENT: Reflections
DESIGN FIRM: Sussner Design Company

29
CLIENT: Bally's
DESIGN FIRM: Addis Creson

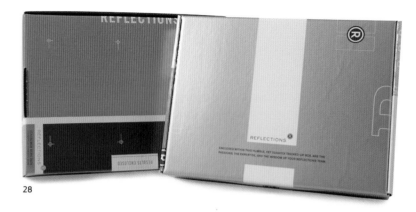

28

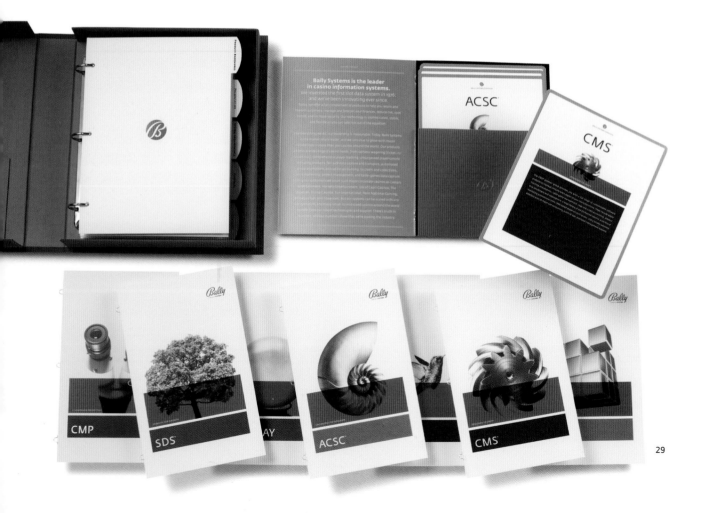

29

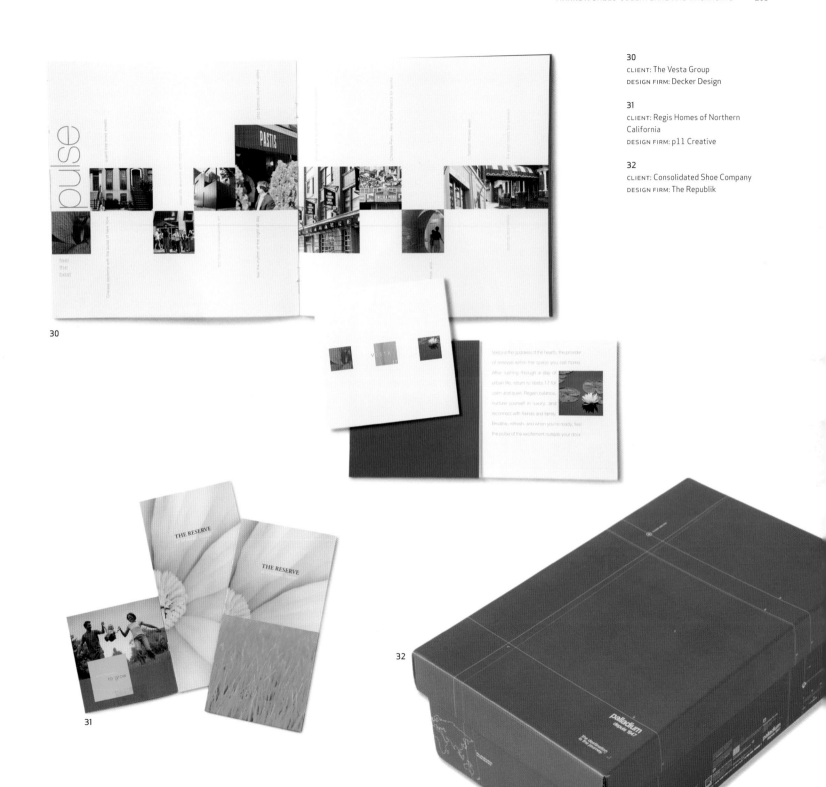

30

31

32

33
CLIENT: Wingara Wine Group
DESIGN FIRM: Perks Design Partners

34
CLIENT: Centex Homes
DESIGN FIRM: p11 Creative

35
CLIENT: Ryco Filters
DESIGN FIRM: Octavo Design/
Spark Studio

36
CLIENT: Posestvo Črni kos, Rošpoh
DESIGN FIRM: KROG, Ljubljana

37
CLIENT: Ljubljanski grad
DESIGN FIRM: KROG, Ljubljana

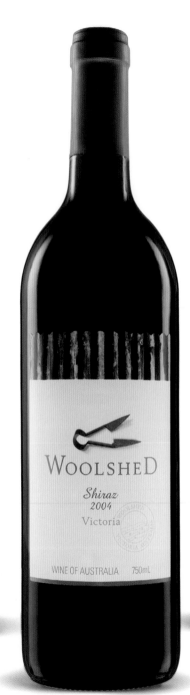
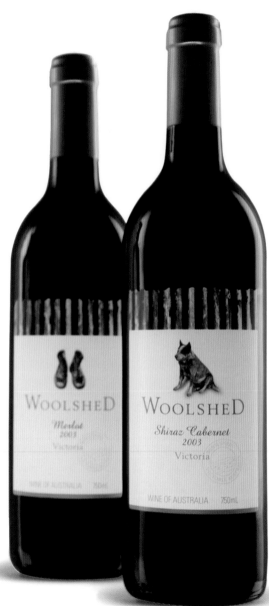

33

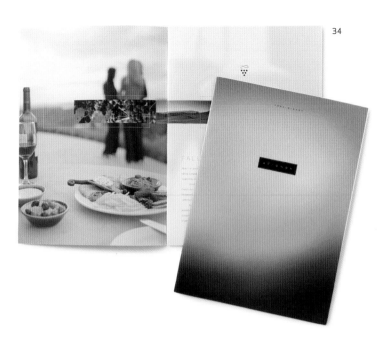

34

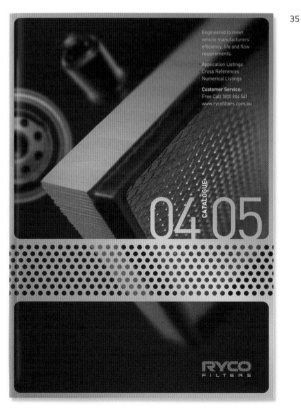

35

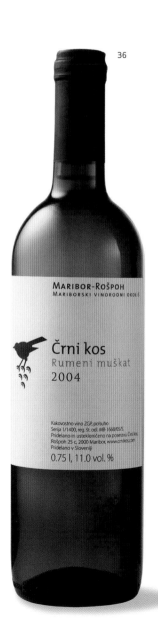

36

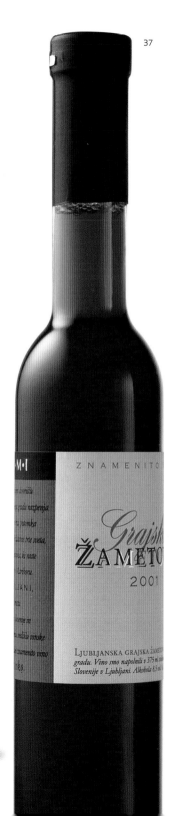

37

38
CLIENT: J. Boag & Son
DESIGN FIRM: Perks Design Partners

39
CLIENT: Cold Standard
DESIGN FIRM: Hornall Anderson
Design Works

40
CLIENT: Bing Bang
DESIGN FIRM: Nothing: Something: NY

41
CLIENT: Lyon Capital Ventures
DESIGN FIRM: p11 Creative

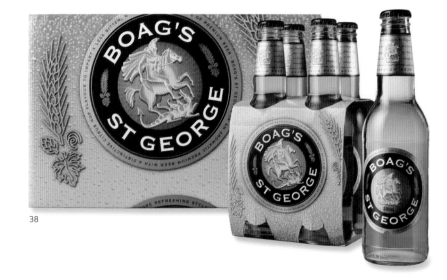

38

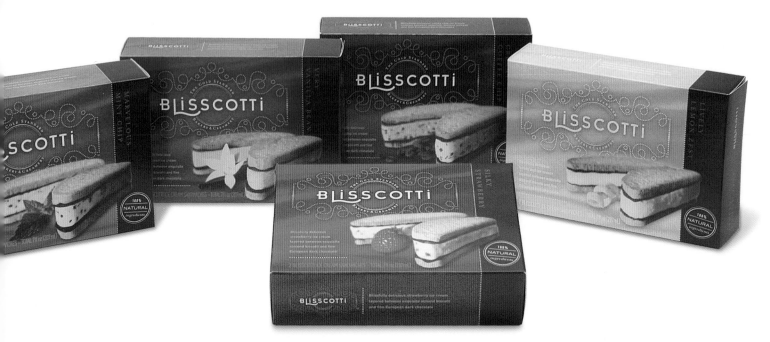

39

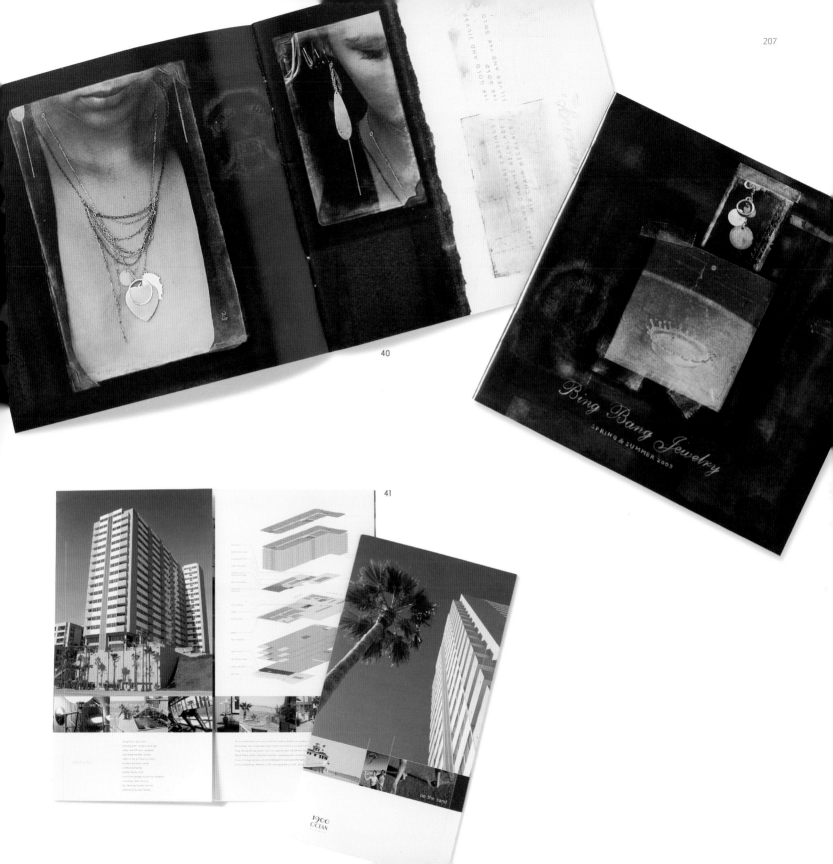

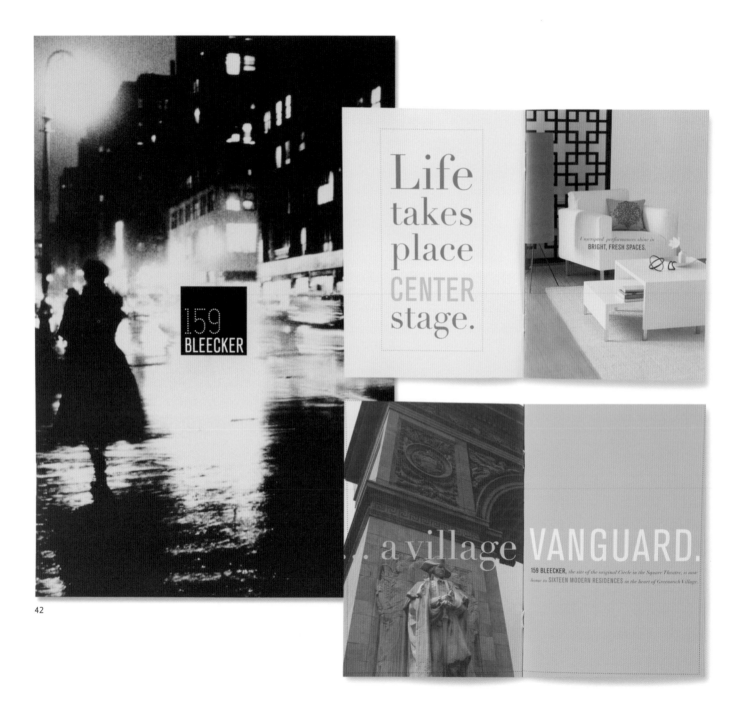

42

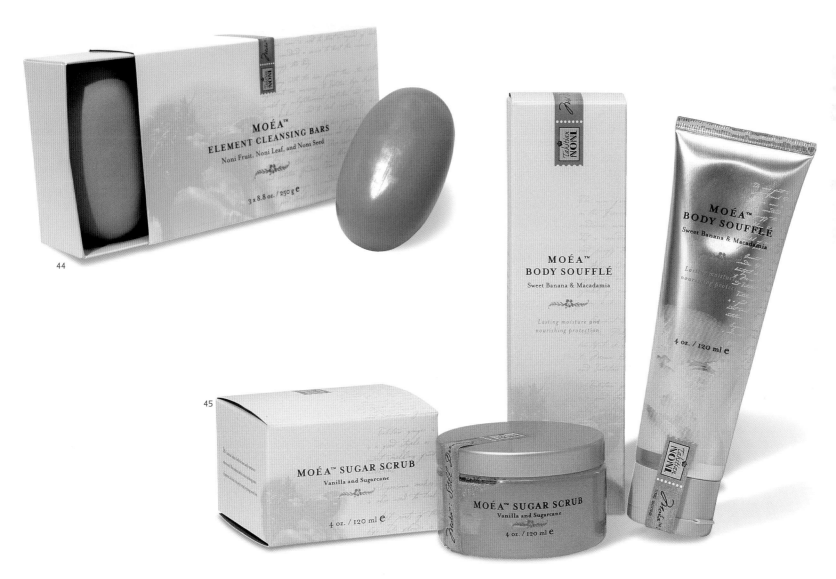
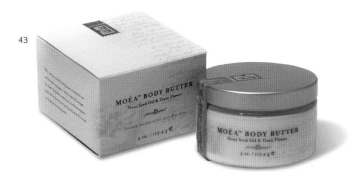

42
CLIENT: Coldwell Banker Hunt Kennedy
DESIGN FIRM: Liska + Associates

43, 44, 45
CLIENT: Tahitian Noni
DESIGN FIRM: Hornall Anderson
Design Works

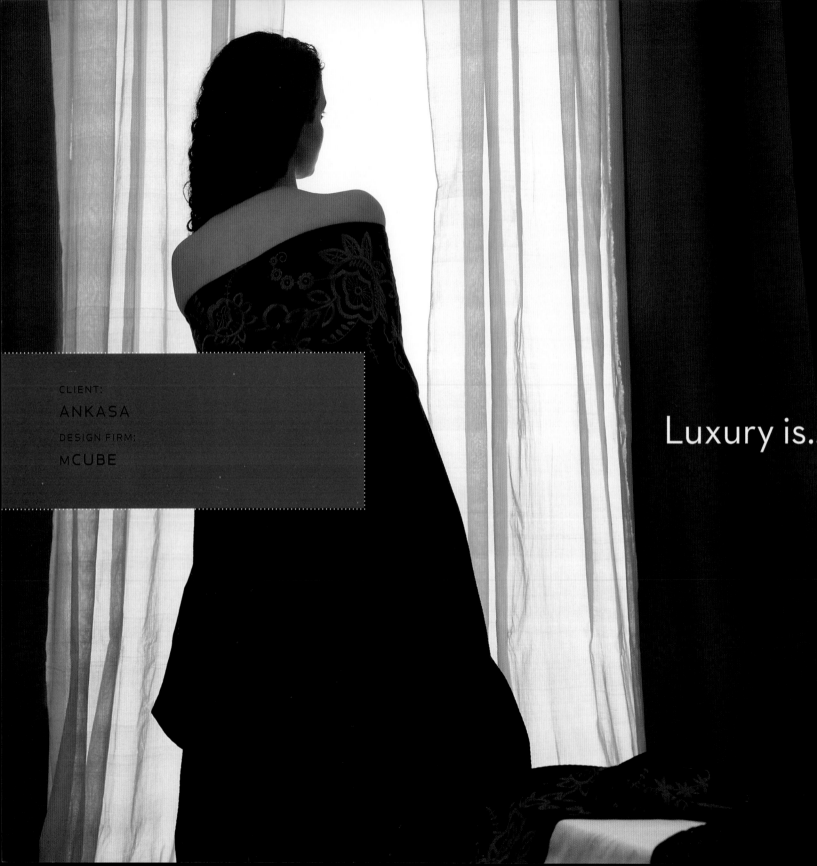

CLIENT:

ANKASA

DESIGN FIRM:

MCUBE

Luxury is.

THE MOST IMPORTANT COMPONENT OF THE DESIGN PROCESS TAKES PLACE
BEFORE ANY SKETCHING BEGINS. THE WORK OF INTERVIEWING THE CLIENT,
ASSESSING THE EXISTING BRAND PROGRAM, RESEARCHING THE INDUSTRY,
AND UNDERSTANDING THE COMPETITION ESTABLISHES AND DEFINES THE
BRANDING STRATEGY FOR BOTH THE DESIGN TEAM AND THE CLIENT.
THIS CASE STUDY SHOWS HOW THE INITIAL WORK HAD AN IMPACT ON THE
PROJECT SCOPE AND RESULTED IN A VISUAL SYSTEM THAT REFLECTS
ANKASA'S CORE ATTRIBUTES AND PRODUCT BENEFITS.

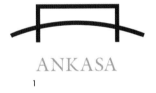

ANKASA

1

1
*The symbol for the logo represents
a softened, stylized letter A and hints
at a piece of furniture.*

CLIENT Based in New York and Mumbai, India, Ankasa designs and manufactures high-end, luxurious home-furnishing couture collections. Its sister company, ANK International, sources, designs, and manufactures fabrics and rare finishes for fashion designers including Oscar de la Renta, Armani, and Escada.

PROJECT The designers at mCube developed a visual system that reflects and highlights the luxurious quality of the Ankasa brand. Wherever the design interacted with the product line (either physically or through imagery), the designers chose to keep design elements to a minimum and let the product textiles, patterns, and textures speak for themselves. The use of color and the simplicity of design were particularly valuable for the product tags and packaging, since Ankasa's product line involves multiple colors and continually evolves. Deliverables for the project included a company and industry

analysis, an identity system, a stationery system, a press kit, invoices, tags, invitations, packaging, and website design.

A GOOD FIT Ankasa originally approached mCube to create product tags. When mCube's designers began working with the logo, they realized the mark didn't match the company's brand values or business objectives. As mCube extended its creative review to other branded elements, they found similar discrepancies. mCube approached the client and presented their findings. Ankasa agreed with mCube's analysis and charged them with the larger task of designing a visual system that would differentiate Ankasa from its peers and more clearly reflect the luxury of the product line.

A IS FOR... Ankasa required that the new logo incorporate the letter 'A' from its existing logo. mCube transformed the letter A into a symbol

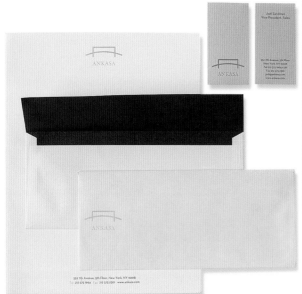

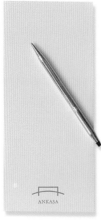

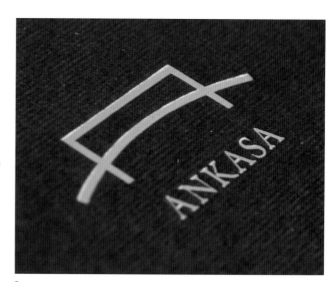

3

2

that references multiple aspects of the company. The logo represents the company name and the home decor industry by hinting at the types of furniture on which Ankasa's products are used. The choice of an earthy brown as the primary logo color reflects the natural source of Ankasa's products.

PRODUCT FEATURES mCube paid particular attention to how the logo and other elements would function with the physical products. The tags, for example, needed to reflect the high-end nature of the products and also work well with a wide variety of colors and textures. mCube chose brown partly because the neutrality works well with the range of product colors. The tags are sewn with silver thread to highlight the richness of the products. Similar thought went into the packaging design. The signature brown strip is large enough to highlight the silver logo and small enough to allow for easy viewing of the package contents. ■

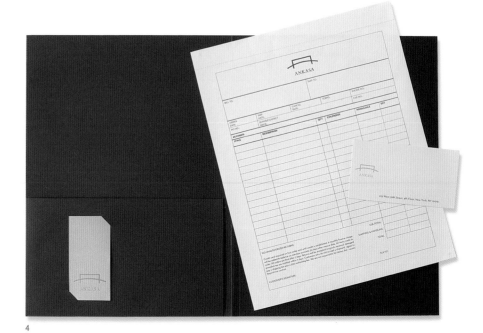

4

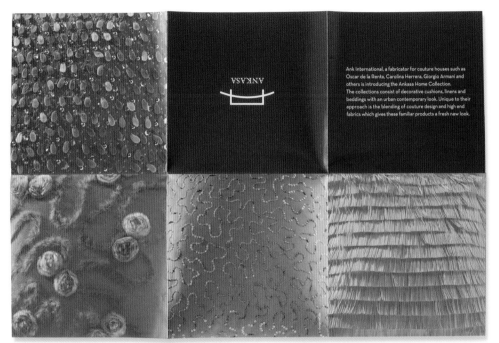

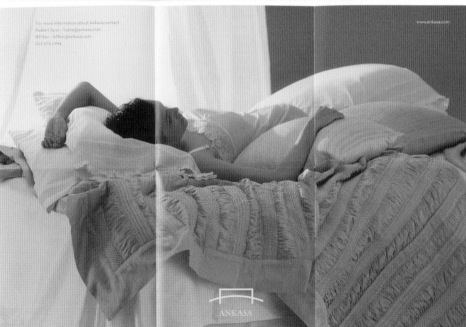

5

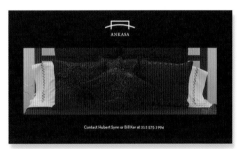

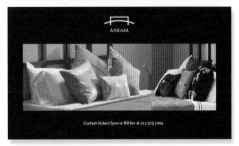

6

2
The stationery system communicates brand attributes of elegance and attention to design detail.

3
In most cases, the logo is foil-stamped in silver against brown to add a distinctive quality and elegance to the brand image.

4
Each element of the business system, including mailing labels and purchase orders, is consistent with the brand standards.

5
The cropped details from textured cushion covers and the lifestyle image communicate attributes of sophistication and luxury.

6
The website follows the simple, elegant, and product-driven strategy.

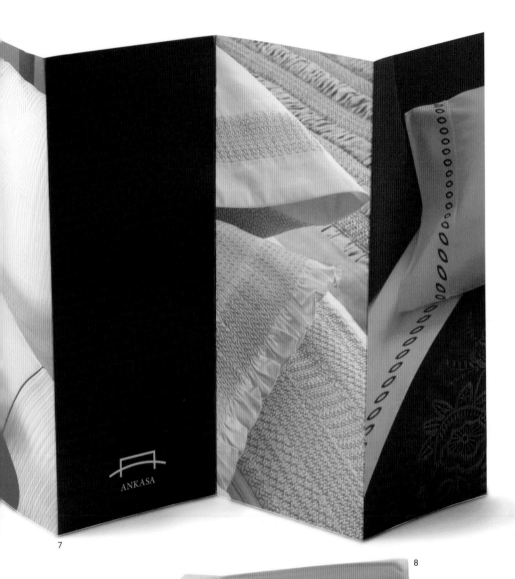

7

8

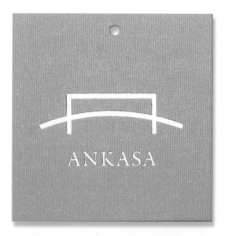

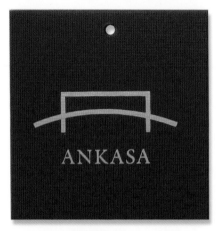

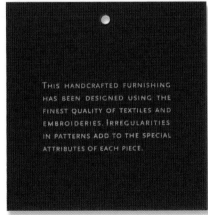

THIS HANDCRAFTED FURNISHING
HAS BEEN DESIGNED USING THE
FINEST QUALITY OF TEXTILES AND
EMBROIDERIES. IRREGULARITIES
IN PATTERNS ADD TO THE SPECIAL
ATTRIBUTES OF EACH PIECE.

9

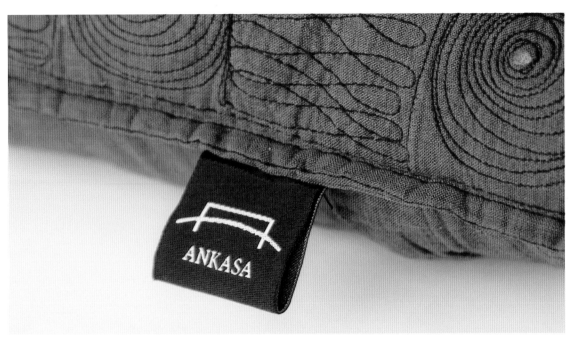

7
Following the overall brand strategy, the trade-show invitation allows the product to speak for itself; text is minimal and doesn't compete with the images.

8
Packaging is designed to showcase the beauty of the products.

9
Consistent with the other brand collateral, the paper tags are square with the logo foil-stamped in silver.

10
The neutral brown product tags fit well with a wide variety of textiles and patterns.

11
The launch invitation gives a feeling of unveiling and invites the reader to learn more about Ankasa.

CLIENT: Ankasa
DESIGN FIRM: mCube
ART DIRECTOR: Rachana Shah
DESIGNER: Neha Mehta

10

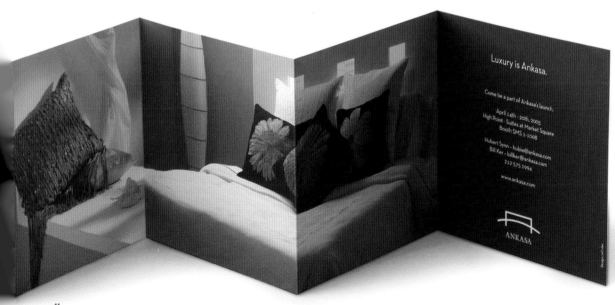

Luxury is Ankasa.

Come be a part of Ankasa's launch.

April 14th - 20th, 2005
High Point - Suites at Market Square
Booth SMS 1-1008

Hubert Symn - hubie@ankasa.com
Bill Ker - billker@ankasa.com
212 575 1994

www.ankasa.com

ANKASA

11

harter [♥]

DESIGN TEAMS MOST OFTEN DEVELOP A BRANDING PROGRAM TO SUPPORT AN EXISTING PRODUCT, SERVICE, OR COMPANY. IN THIS CASE STUDY, THE INFLUENCE OF THE DESIGN TEAM EXTENDED TO PRODUCT DESIGN. **HARTER** ENGAGED THE MODERNS NOT ONLY TO REBRAND ITS COMPANY, BUT ALSO TO CURATE A NEW LINE OF PRODUCT FINISHES. ALIGNING THE PRODUCT TEXTURES AND COLOR PALETTES WITH THE BRANDING STRATEGY ADDED DEPTH, DIMENSION, AND CONSISTENCY TO THE BRANDING PROGRAM.

harter [♥]
at the heart of the solution

<< 1
The personality brochure features embossed hearts. The centrally placed logo provides a subtle spot of color.

CLIENT Harter has designed, manufactured, and sold office furnishings for more than seventy years. The company has a strong reputation for producing ergonomic seating and for its distinct design aesthetic. Harter intentionally focuses on lifestyle and solution-based products that meet the changing needs of today's flexible workplace environments.

PROJECT When Harter approached The Moderns, the furniture company had fallen off the radar screen in the design world and was struggling for exposure and relevance in an extremely competitive industry. Harter commissioned The Moderns to develop a holistic brand platform that would reinvigorate and ignite the Harter brand. Deliverables included a logo, a positioning statement, messaging, marketing materials, a website, showroom design, a product color and texture palette, and strategic business consulting services.

KNOW BY HEART The Moderns repositioned Harter as an agile and multilateral solutions provider. They created the positioning statement, "The Heart of the Solution," and used a heart as the main logo symbol. Hearts appear on a variety of collateral material, and the Harter website features customizable Valentine's Day cards.

NEW WORLD Taking their cue from the blurring lines between work and home, designers coined the phrase "work-life universe" and used the concept to define not only the brand positioning, but also Harter's business strategy. Harter's focus shifted away from providing furnishings for traditional office settings and toward designing and engineering flexible solutions for today's mobile workers.

ACTION-ORIENTED The new emphasis on the "work-life universe" transformed the way Harter organizes its product lines. The company now

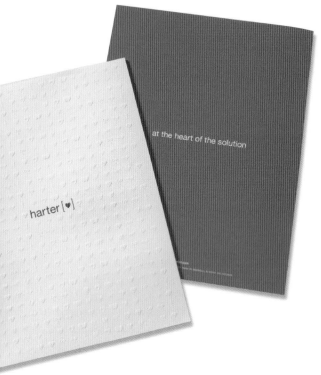

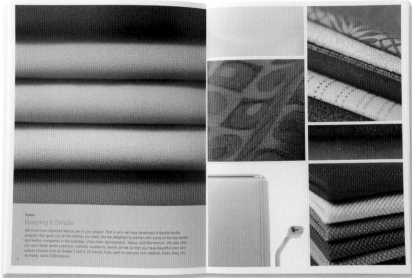

2

presents its product lines based on the ways
people live and work. Function-oriented
categories such as action, side, train, and relax
replaced traditional labels like chair, desk,
and file drawers.

MOOD SELECTION The Moderns brought a fresh
perspective to Harter's understanding of materials
and textiles. Prior to engaging The Moderns,
Harter viewed material and texture as secondary
to ergonomic design and quality manufacturing
of their products. Now, Harter views material and
texture as critical components that can positively
affect the work environment. The Moderns also
curated the color and materials palette for Harter's
product lines to reflect more contemporary
colors and finishes. The Harter furniture designers
worked within the palette, so the product lines
reflect the holistic brand strategy. ■

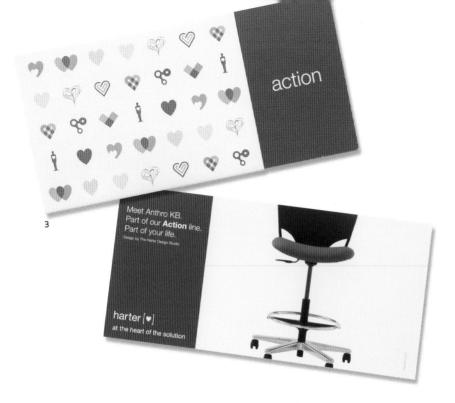

3

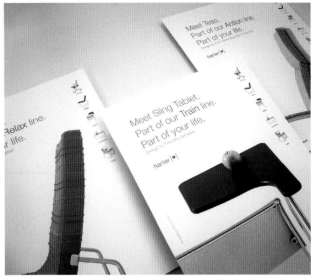

4

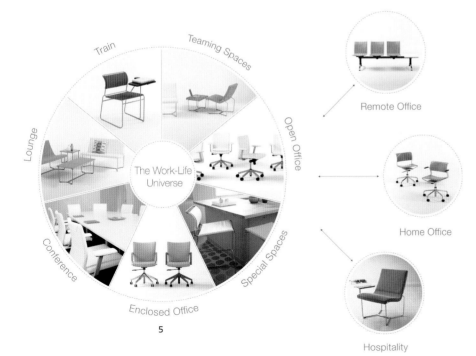

The Work-Life Universe

Train

Teaming Spaces

Open Office

Special Spaces

Enclosed Office

Conference

Lounge

Remote Office

Home Office

Hospitality

5

2

The annual personality brochure introduces product lines and familiarizes customers with the Harter brand.

3

Product cards feature photography and illustration that are also used in the personality brochure.

4

Advertising highlights the work-life universe theme.

5

The design team created the organizing theme of work-life universe to promote Harter's product lines.

6, 8
The Moderns also curated the color and materials palettes for Harter products.

7
The Moderns designed the NeoCon exhibit for Harter, adding consistency to the brand experience.

9
The brand guide provides internal and external resources with strategic and creative direction.

10
This display window created for a major industry event, NeoCon, introduced both the brand and the product lines.

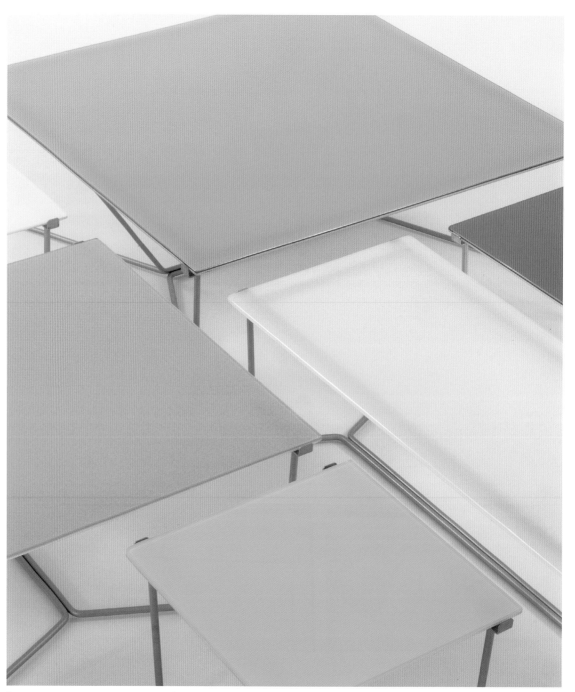

6

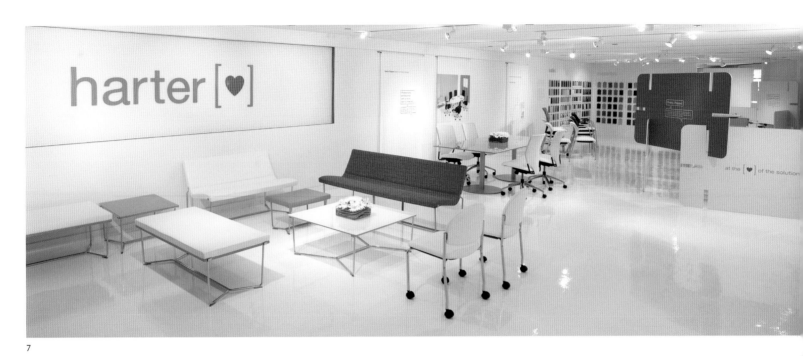

7

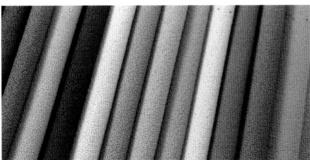

8

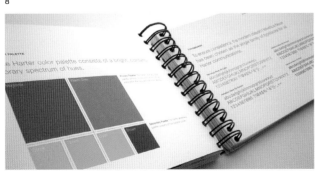

9

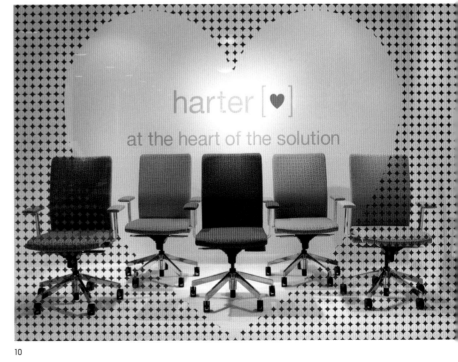

10

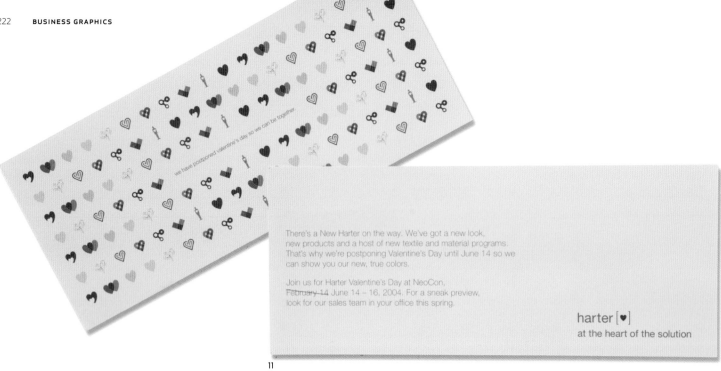

There's a New Harter on the way. We've got a new look,
new products and a host of new textile and material programs.
That's why we're postponing Valentine's Day until June 14 so we
can show you our new, true colors.

Join us for Harter Valentine's Day at NeoCon,
February 14 June 14 – 16, 2004. For a sneak preview,
look for our sales team in your office this spring.

harter [♥]
at the heart of the solution

11

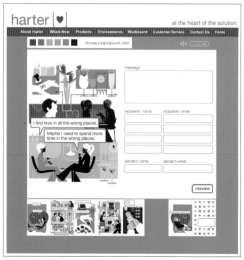

12

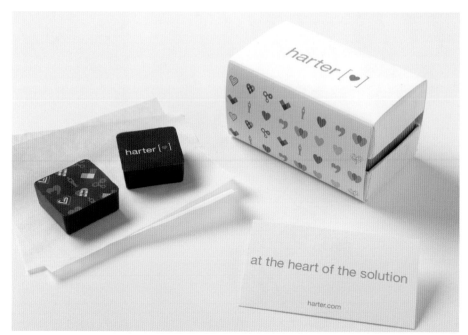

13

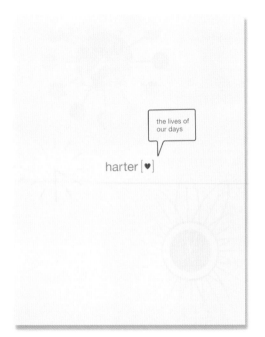

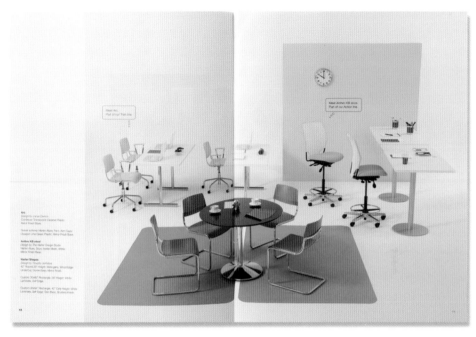

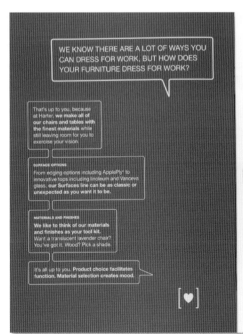

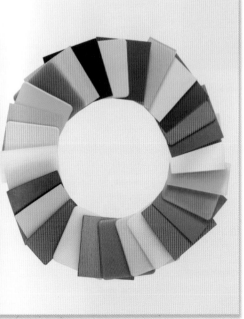

11
The brand launched at NeoCon on June 14, and was positioned as a postponed Valentine's Day event.

12
Custom e-cards for Valentine's Day are a natural fit with Harter's heart-driven identity.

13
Branded give-aways include custom-made chocolates.

14
The personality brochure reveals product vignettes that contextualize the product lines. Speech bubbles punctuate Harter's friendly and conversational editorial voice.

CLIENT: Harter
DESIGN FIRM: The Moderns
ART DIRECTORS: Janine James, Kevin Szell
DESIGNER: Kevin Szell

14

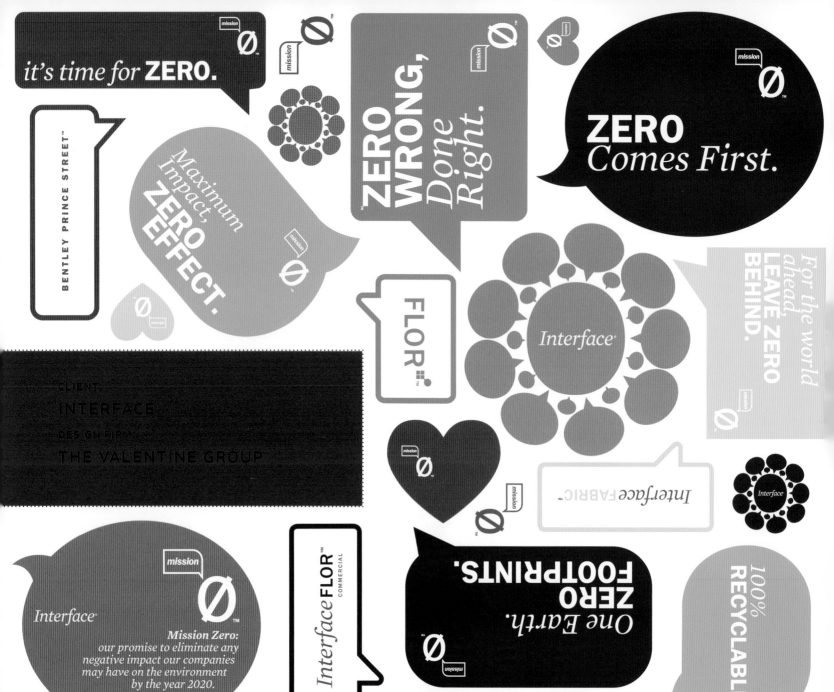

DESIGNERS CONDUCT MULTIFACETED RESEARCH BEFORE DETERMINING A CENTRAL FOCUS FOR A BRANDING PROGRAM. THEY CONSIDER CLIENT VALUES AND ATTRIBUTES, TARGET AUDIENCES, COMPETITOR POSITIONING, CULTURAL TRENDS, PRODUCT QUALITIES, AND DIFFERENTIATING CHARACTERISTICS. IN THIS CASE STUDY, DESIGNERS AT THE VALENTINE GROUP CHOSE TO BUILD A REBRANDING PROGRAM AROUND A SINGLE COMPANY VALUE THAT MOST DIFFERENTIATES **INTERFACE:** A CORPORATE COMMITMENT TO SUSTAINABILITY.

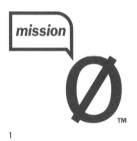

1

1
The Mission Zero logo incorporates the voice bubble from the client's existing brand program.

<< 2
Floor decals at an industry trade show introduced the client's new look and reinforced the Mission Zero messaging.

CLIENT Interface designs, produces, and sells modular carpet, broadloom carpet, panel fabrics, and upholstery. The company is publicly traded, with sales in more than 110 countries worldwide. Interface's position is unique; the company is not only committed to minimizing its impact on the environment, but it also strives to restore the environment. Interface diligently pursues its corporate goal of eliminating any negative impact it may have on the environment by the year 2020—a sizeable task and an admirable promise from the world's largest producer of modular flooring.

PROJECT The global rebranding program needed to work on many levels. Primary goals included streamlining the Interface brand portfolio and integrating the company's already well-developed message of sustainability, known as "ZERO." The design team had the added requirement of creating a flexible branding program that would

appeal globally. Deliverables included identity design, corporate collateral, print and outdoor advertising, showroom graphics, exterior signage, packaging, a website, PowerPoint presentations, press kits, trade show collateral, and a global standards manual.

EXISTENTIAL PHILOSOPHY The Valentine Group thoroughly reviewed the existing brand program to determine if it contained elements that could be leveraged in the rebranding effort. Its analysis revealed two components of significant value: the "voice bubble" element from InterfaceFLOR (Interface's consumer brand), and the message of sustainability, ZERO. The design team incorporated both components to create the Mission Zero concept and identity.

ENVIRONMENTAL GRAPHICS Environmental concerns have been central to Interface for many years. The design team brought the company's

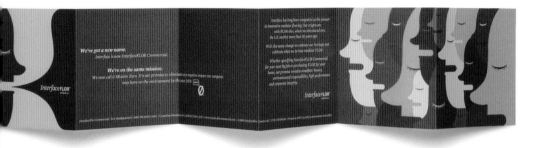

3

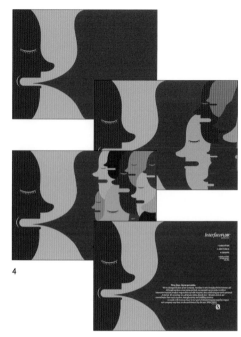

4

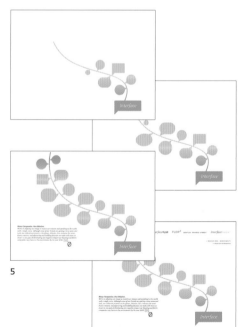

commitment front and center, both visually and verbally. This message clearly differentiates Interface from its competitors and unifies the company around its ambitious goal of minimizing its corporate environmental footprint. Each division of Interface adopted the sustainability promise and incorporated the Mission Zero graphic identity into its visual system.

GLOBAL POSITIONING Interface manufactures and sells its products in more than 110 countries. The design team needed to be aware of design trends across cultures, create visual and verbal language that would translate easily, and convey appropriate and contemporary meaning in different countries.

FAMILY TRAITS In addition to developing the Mission Zero identity, The Valentine Group rebranded the five divisions of Interface.

This process involved developing a master brand identity system that aligned each division more closely with the global Interface brand. This also included renaming two divisions, InterfaceFabric and InterfaceFLOR Commercial.

POP-UP The design team incorporated the existing voice bubble concept into the rebranding program. The voice bubble communicates Interface's voice and suggests its readiness to interact with customers. Designers applied the element to several communication pieces, including the Mission Zero identity, flash animation, bags, and floor decals. The voice bubbles combine to form a series of vine shapes that communicate that Interface is growing organically. They also appear as a component of a "multi-face" graphic used by InterfaceFLOR Commercial to communicate its new face to the industry. ■

5

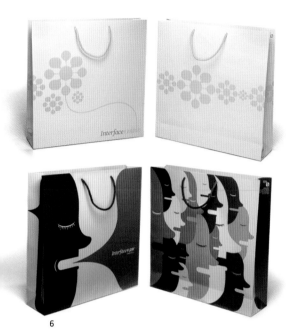

6

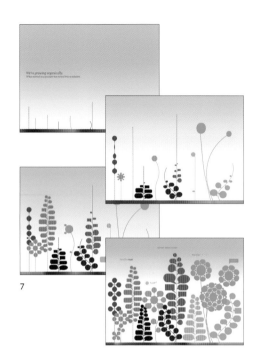

7

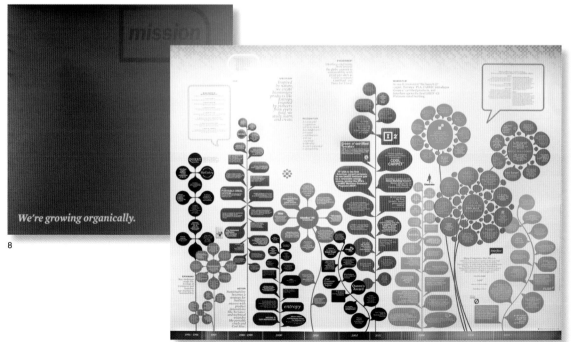

8

3
The direct mail piece uses the "multi-face" graphic to announce the new name and identity of one of Interface's divisions, InterfaceFLOR Commercial.

4
The website for the InterfaceFLOR Commercial division uses the "multi-face" graphic to communicate the company's approachability and introduce its new face to the industry.

5
The global website homepage opens with a flash animation that promotes the rebranding program.

6
The versatile use of graphic elements and color palettes allow both consistency and variety across different product lines.

7
To reinforce the rebrand internally, branded screensavers and a wallpaper application were installed on Interface's employee computers.

8
The corporate timeline poster features vines constructed of voice bubbles that reinforce messages of sustainability and growth.

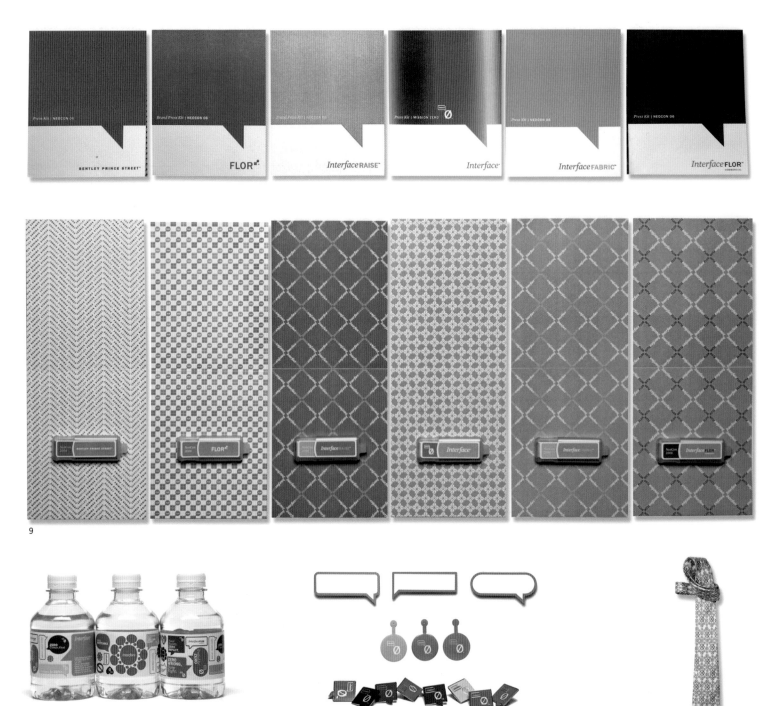

9

10

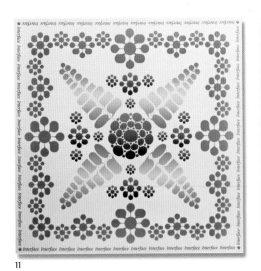

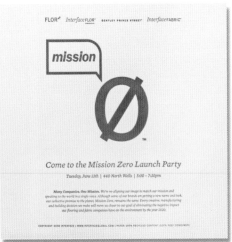

11

9

The design team customized press kits for each product line and the Mission Zero campaign. The digital kits contain USB drives that are pre-loaded with relevant information.

10

Branded items include water bottles, nametags, "museum" tabs, pins, shopping badges, napkins, silk ties, and scarves.

11, 12

Branded items at the Mission Zero launch party introduced the new visual system.

13

Company trucks also received a new design treatment, adding visibility to the brand.

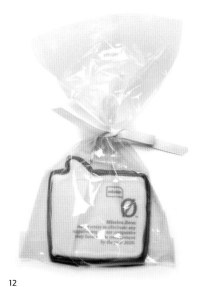

12

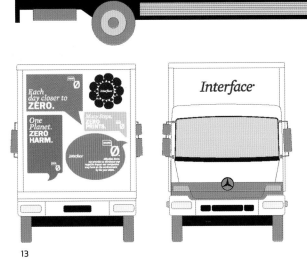

13

14

InterfaceFLOR Commercial's advertising incorporates the "multi-face" graphic and communicates the company's differentiating focus on sustainability.

CLIENT: Interface
DESIGN FIRM: The Valentine Group
ART DIRECTOR: Robert Valentine
DESIGNERS: Robert Valentine,
Brooke Romney

14

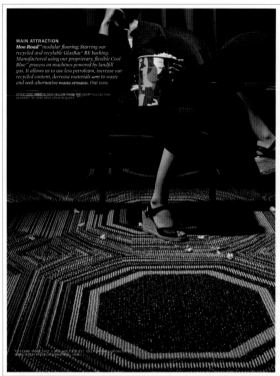
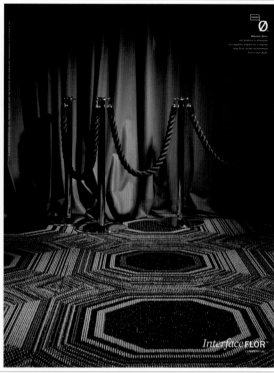

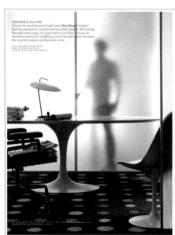
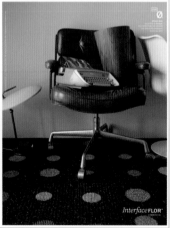
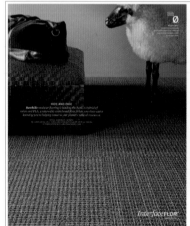
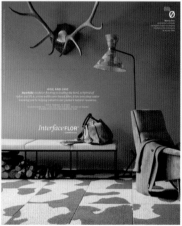

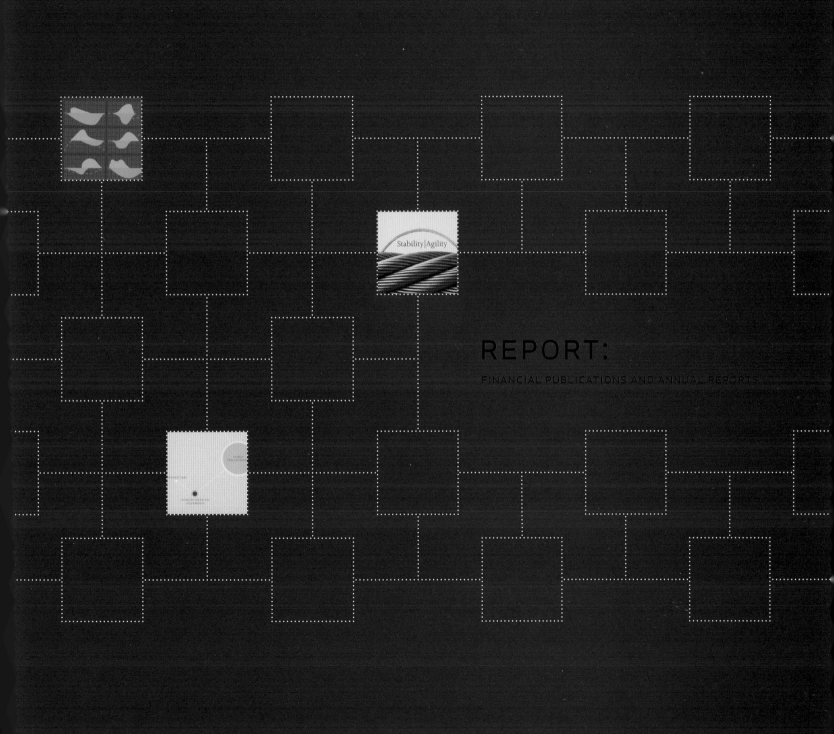

REPORT:

FINANCIAL PUBLICATIONS AND ANNUAL REPORTS

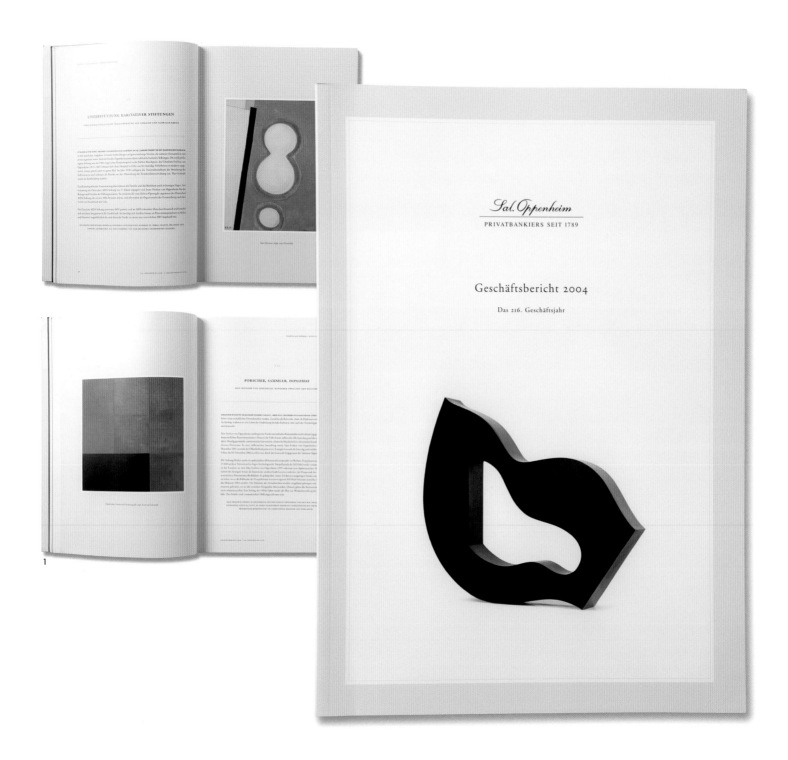

1

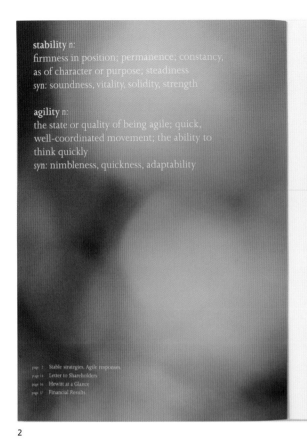

stability n:
firmness in position; permanence; constancy, as of character or purpose; steadiness
syn: soundness, vitality, solidity, strength

agility n:
the state or quality of being agile; quick, well-coordinated movement; the ability to think quickly
syn: nimbleness, quickness, adaptability

Hewitt is a world leader in human capital management. We help companies and the people who work for them succeed—together—and by doing so, we help make the world a better place to work.

Much has changed. Much hasn't.

2

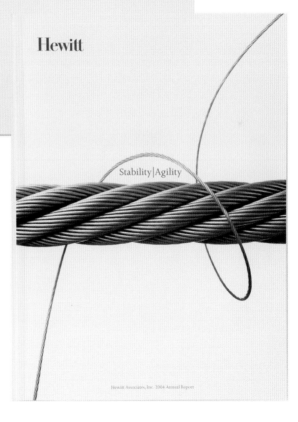

1
CLIENT: Sal. Oppenheim jr. & Cie. KGaA
DESIGN FIRM: Simon & Goetz Design GmbH & Co. KG

2
CLIENT: Hewitt Associates
DESIGN FIRM: Crosby Associates

234

3
CLIENT: VF Corporation
DESIGN FIRM: And Partners

4
CLIENT: CWS Capital
Partners, LLC
DESIGN FIRM: Ramp Creative

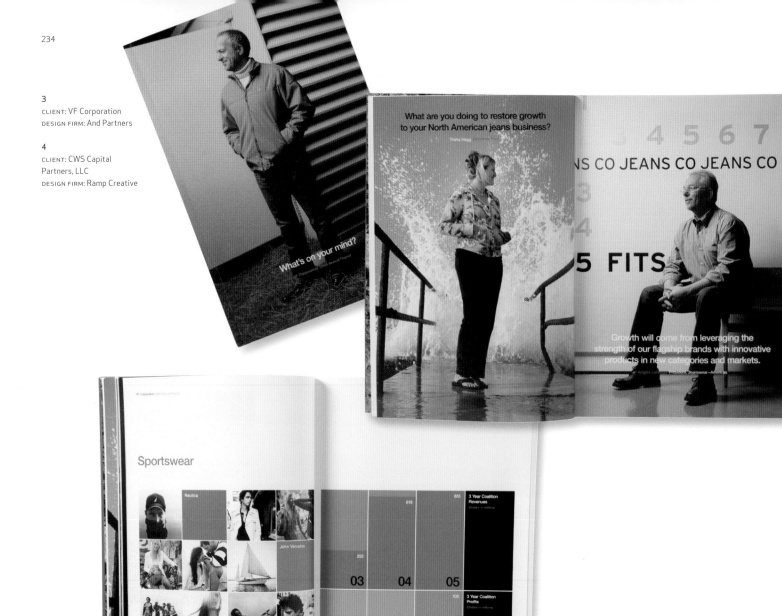

3

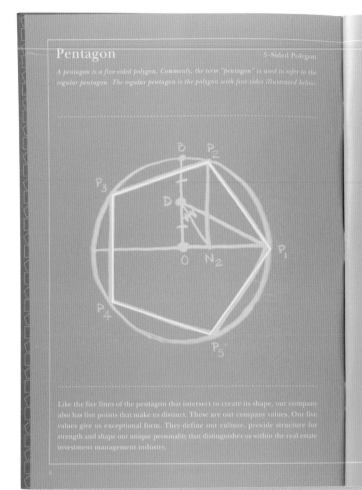

Pentagon

5-Sided Polygon

A pentagon is a five-sided polygon. Commonly, the term "pentagon" is used to refer to the regular pentagon. The regular pentagon is the polygon with five sides illustrated below.

Like the five lines of the pentagon that intersect to create its shape, our company also has five points that make us distinct. These are our company values. Our five values give us exceptional form. They define our culture, provide structure for strength and shape our unique personality that distinguishes us within the real estate investment management industry.

Our Core Values

Our core values are based on five key principles. These values are the foundation of our company culture. By building on a core of trust and open communication, we generate insightful investment opportunities, superior customer service, and long-term relationships with our investors, residents and employees.

1. A demand for excellence with a sense of urgency.
2. A respect for people.
3. A requirement for profitability.
4. Honoring our word.
5. Ethical dealings are paramount.

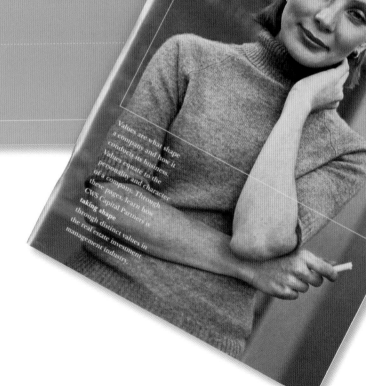

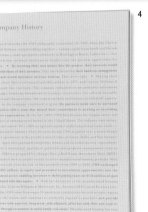

Company History

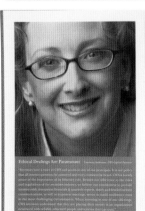

Ethical Dealings Are Paramount

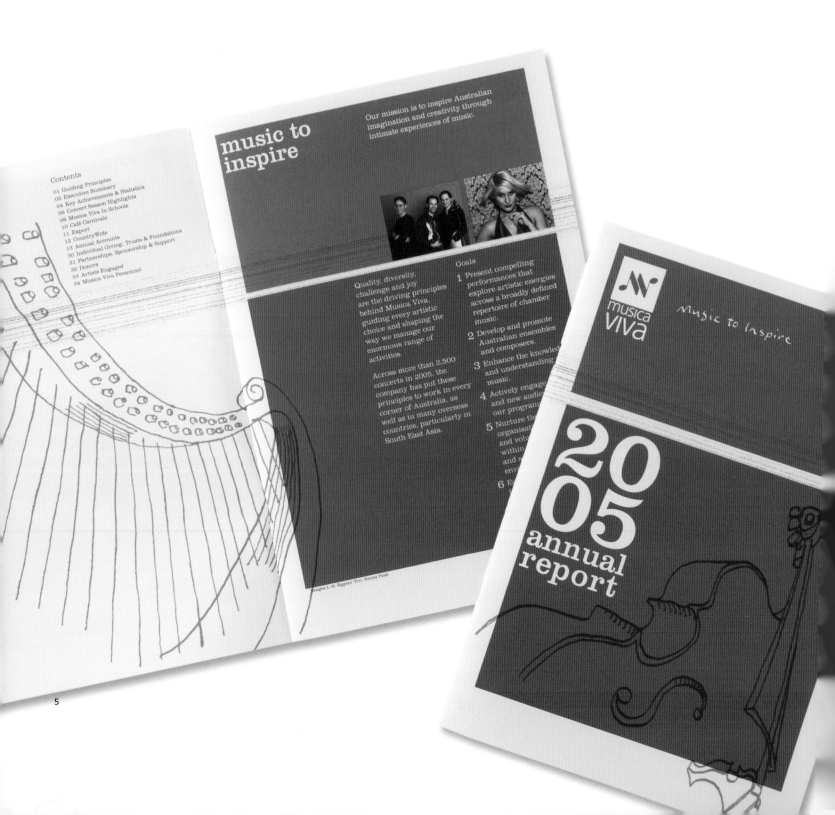

Contents

music to inspire

Our mission is to inspire Australian imagination and creativity through intimate experiences of music.

Quality, diversity, challenge and joy are the driving principles behind Musica Viva, guiding every artistic choice and shaping the way we manage our enormous range of activities.

Across more than 2,500 concerts in 2005, the company has put these principles to work in every corner of Australia, as well as in many overseas countries, particularly in South East Asia.

Goals

1 Present compelling performances that explore artistic energies across a broadly defined repertoire of chamber music.

2 Develop and promote Australian ensembles and composers.

3 Enhance the knowled and understanding music.

4 Actively engage and new audie our program

5 Nurture th organisat and volu within and s env

6 E

Images L-R. Eggner Trio, Emma Pask

musica viva

Music to Inspire

20 05 annual report

5

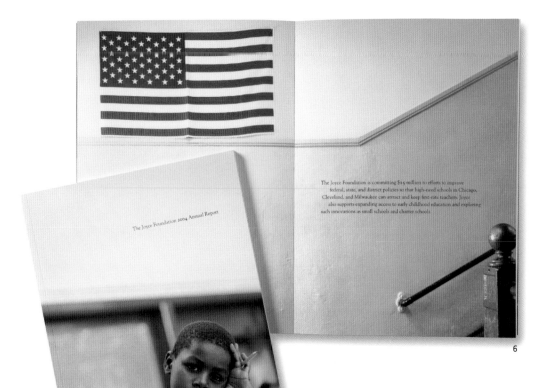

6

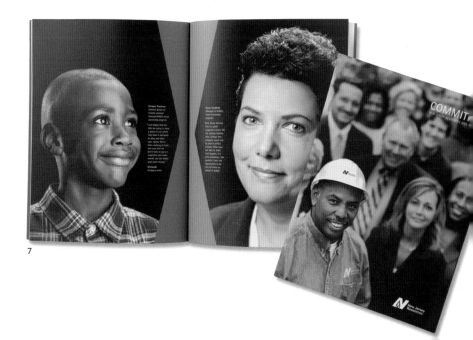

7

5
CLIENT: Musica Viva Australia
DESIGN FIRM: Boccalatte

6
CLIENT: The Joyce Foundation
DESIGN FIRM: Kym Abrams Design

7
CLIENT: New Jersey Resources
DESIGN FIRM: Decker Design

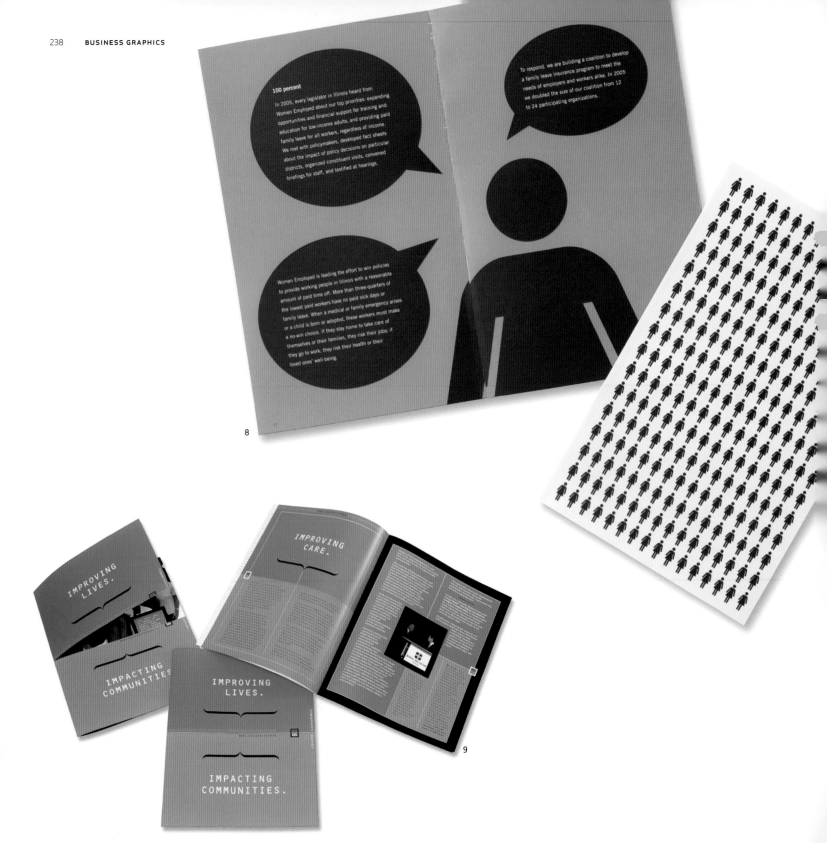

100 percent

In 2005, every legislator in Illinois heard from Women Employed about our top priorities: expanding opportunities and financial support for training and education for low-income adults, and providing paid family leave for all workers, regardless of income. We met with policymakers, developed fact sheets about the impact of policy decisions on particular districts, organized constituent visits, convened briefings for staff, and testified at hearings.

To respond, we are building a coalition to develop a family leave insurance program to meet the needs of employers and workers alike. In 2005 we doubled the size of our coalition from 12 to 24 participating organizations.

Women Employed is leading the effort to win policies to provide working people in Illinois with a reasonable amount of paid time off. More than three-quarters of the lowest paid workers have no paid sick days or family leave. When a medical or family emergency arises or a child is born or adopted, these workers must make a no-win choice. If they stay home to take care of themselves or their families, they risk their jobs; if they go to work, they risk their health or their loved ones' well-being.

8

IMPROVING LIVES.

IMPACTING COMMUNITIES.

IMPROVING CARE.

IMPROVING LIVES.

IMPACTING COMMUNITIES.

9

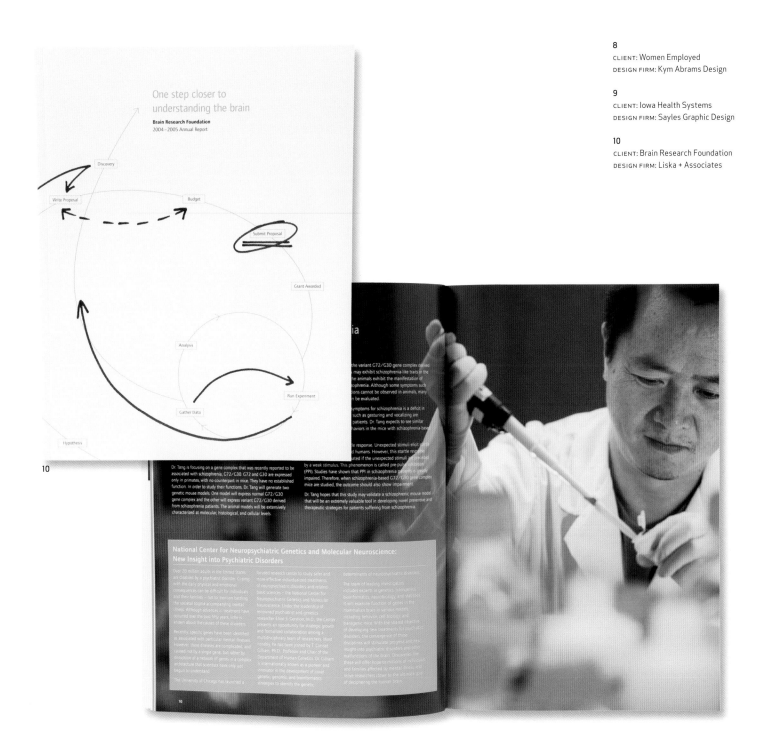

8
CLIENT: Women Employed
DESIGN FIRM: Kym Abrams Design

9
CLIENT: Iowa Health Systems
DESIGN FIRM: Sayles Graphic Design

10
CLIENT: Brain Research Foundation
DESIGN FIRM: Liska + Associates

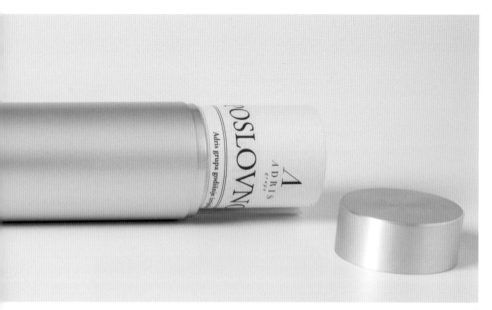

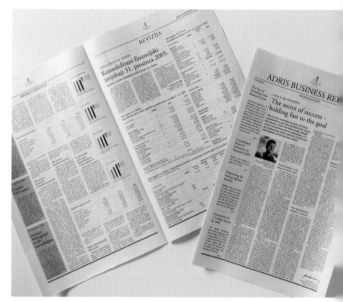

11

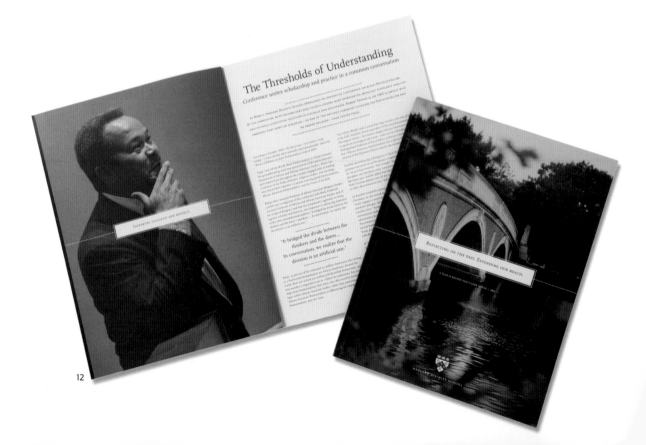

11
CLIENT: Adris Group
DESIGN FIRM: Bruketa & Zinic

12
CLIENT: Harvard Divinity School
DESIGN FIRM: OrangeSeed Design

13
CLIENT: Council of Fashion Designers
of America
DESIGN FIRM: Liska + Associates

12

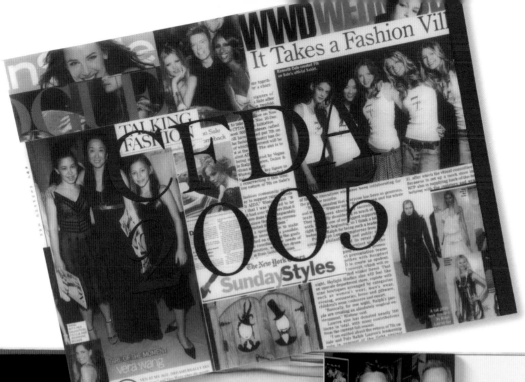

FULL FRONTAL FASHION RETURNS

The CFDA was an instrumental player in bringing *Full Frontal Fashion*, and its wall-to-wall coverage of Fashion Week, back to the tri-state area viewing public. Partnering with NYC TV 25, the new home of the show, and Ultra HD, the CFDA succeeded in securing a place for the show on basic cable, making it more easily available to the area's nine million viewers right in time for the Spring 2007 shows.

FULL FRONTAL FASHION

10

RICHARD AVEDON'S WOMAN IN THE MIRROR

12/6/2005 The CFDA and Theory joined together to host a party celebrating Richard Avedon's "Woman in the Mirror," a collection of the iconic photographer's pictures of women from 1945-2004. The event's casual holiday vibe was enhanced by the invitation to all guests to help themselves to the book's tear sheets which festively decorated the walls of Pastis, and by Theory's generous gift of the coffee-table book to each partygoer. The party was hosted by Andrew Rosen of Theory, Ricky Sasaki, **Stan Herman**, Kal Ruttenstein, Stephanie Seymour, Bruce Weber, and Iman. The evening also marked the debut of the CFDA's new Executive Director, Steven Kolb, whose appointment to the position had been announced that morning.

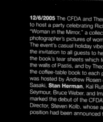

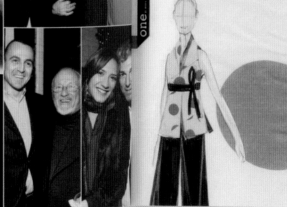

QVC PRESENTS
CFDA New Fashion Designer Showcase

2/24 and **10/28/2005** Always on the look-out for innovative ways to raise the profile of American designers, the CFDA partnered with shopping network QVC to bring six designers to the attention of the network's devoted shoppers. The two QVC Presents CFDA Fashion Designer Showcase shows presented the work of emerging designers **Alice Roi**, **John Bartlett**, **Liz Collins**, and **Maria Cornejo** on the February 24 show, and **Pierre Carrilero** of Pierrot and Steven Cox and Daniel Silver of Duckie Brown on October 28. Each created limited edition capsule collections reflecting their aesthetic, but selling for fashion-friendly prices ranging from $50 to $100. Roi's and Bartlett's appearances were so successful that they each returned with a stand-alone, one-hour program. The endeavor, which donates a portion of the proceeds to the CFDA's educational initiatives, will continue in 2006.

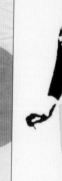

one

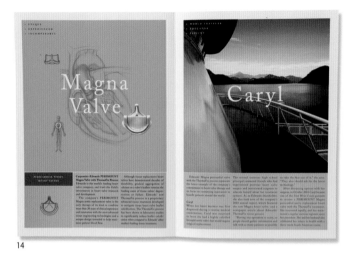

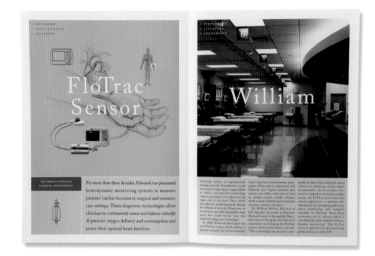

14

14, 15
CLIENT: Edwards LifeSciences
DESIGN FIRM: Ramp Creative

16
CLIENT: The Columbus Foundation
DESIGN FIRM: Base Art Co.

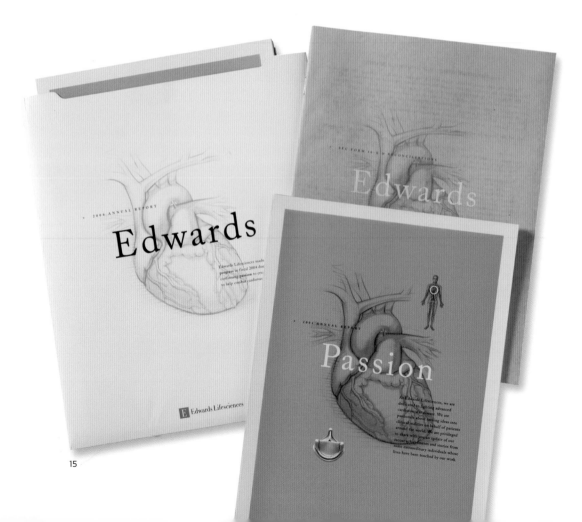

15

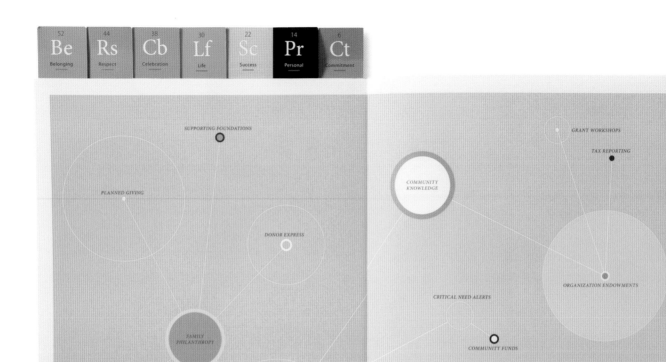

SUPPORTING FOUNDATIONS

GRANT WORKSHOPS

TAX REPORTING

COMMUNITY KNOWLEDGE

PLANNED GIVING

DONOR EXPRESS

ORGANIZATION ENDOWMENTS

CRITICAL NEED ALERTS

FAMILY PHILANTHROPY

COMMUNITY FUNDS

E-NEWSLETTERS

AUDITED FINANCIAL STATEMENTS

DONOR ADVISED FUNDS

We are your natural resource

All that we offer—an experienced staff guiding donors through legal, tax, and financial issues; a pulse on local community needs; relationships with community leaders and programs; and a focus on research and the future—makes The Columbus Foundation a natural fit as the community's resource for all questions, services, and needs surrounding charitable giving. And it's not simply because we exist; it's because we work every day to help you help your community through the most effective philanthropy possible.

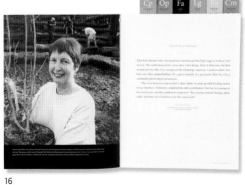

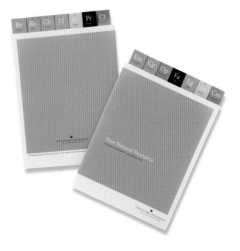

16

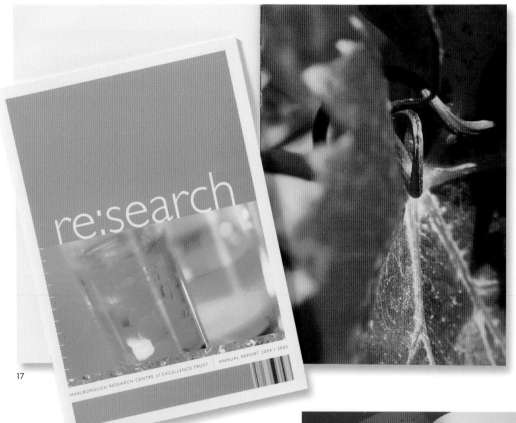

17

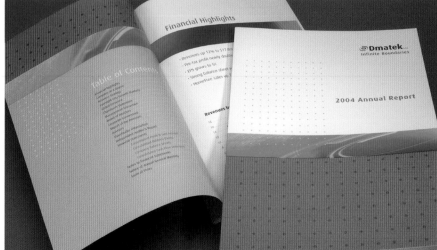

18

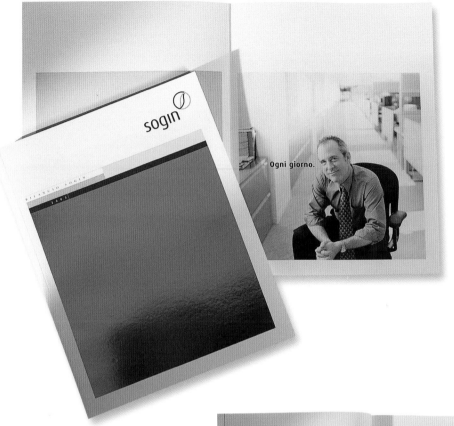

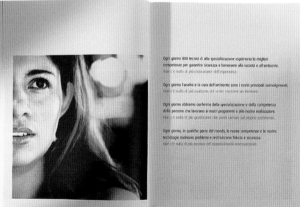

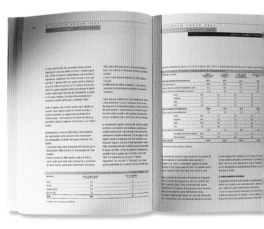

19

17
CLIENT: Marlborough Wine Research Centre
DESIGN FIRM: Lloyd's Graphic Design Ltd.

18
CLIENT: Dmatek
DESIGN FIRM: Jason & Jason

19
CLIENT: SOGIN
DESIGN FIRM: Carré Noir Roma

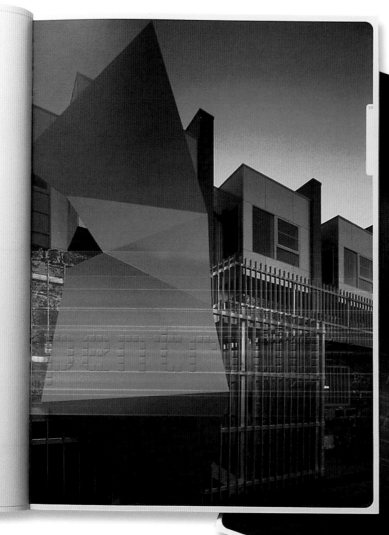

The Benefits

Intermoco's solution will enable the cost effective on-selling of all services to residents and tenants. Electricity will be purchased from suppliers at bulk rates and on-sold to residents and tenants at significantly discounted rates. Gas as well as hot water and rain water will be on-sold with users receiving the one integrated bill. Further, residents and tenants will be able to monitor their daily usage data through a secure website and to use this information to manage their usage more cost effectively.

The bodies corporate and precinct management on the site will also benefit through significantly reduced costs for the supply of energy to common and public areas.

Intermoco's billing software application provides occupiers and tenants with a detailed account of their energy usage on a monthly basis and graphical comparison of consumption for the same period last year.

Ecologically Sustainable Development

One of the Pentridge Piazza's key objectives is to implement the best standards of ecologically sustainable development (ESD) and accordingly, a number of ESD strategies have been incorporated into the overall design. These strategies include installation of rainwater tanks, recycling of rainwater, five star energy ratings for buildings, glazing and insulation techniques and solar panels. Consistent with this philosophy has been the selection of Intermoco's Utiligy solution.

Utilisation of this solution enables residents and tenants to more effectively manage their energy usage and reduce their consumption and cost.

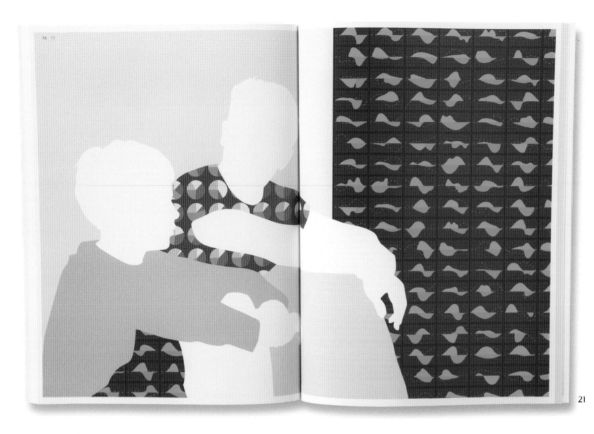

21

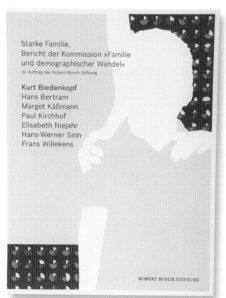

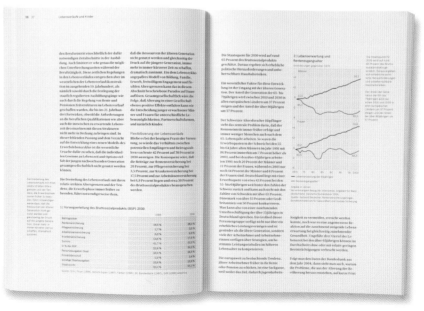

20
CLIENT: Intermoco Limited, Monitoring & Control Systems
DESIGN FIRM: Octavo Design/Spark Studio

21
CLIENT: Robert Bosch Stiftung
DESIGN FIRM: Hesse Design

22, 24
CLIENT: Podravka
DESIGN FIRM: Bruketa & Zinic

23
CLIENT: Endeavor Global
DESIGN FIRM: Goodesign

22

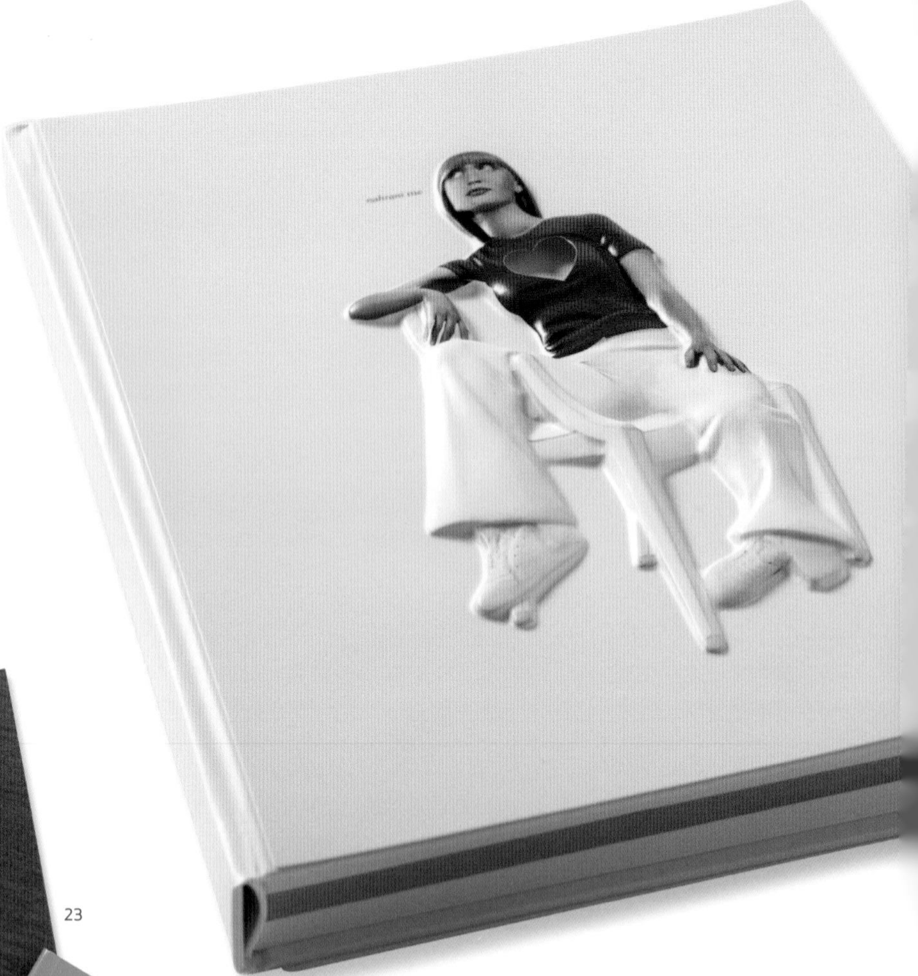

23

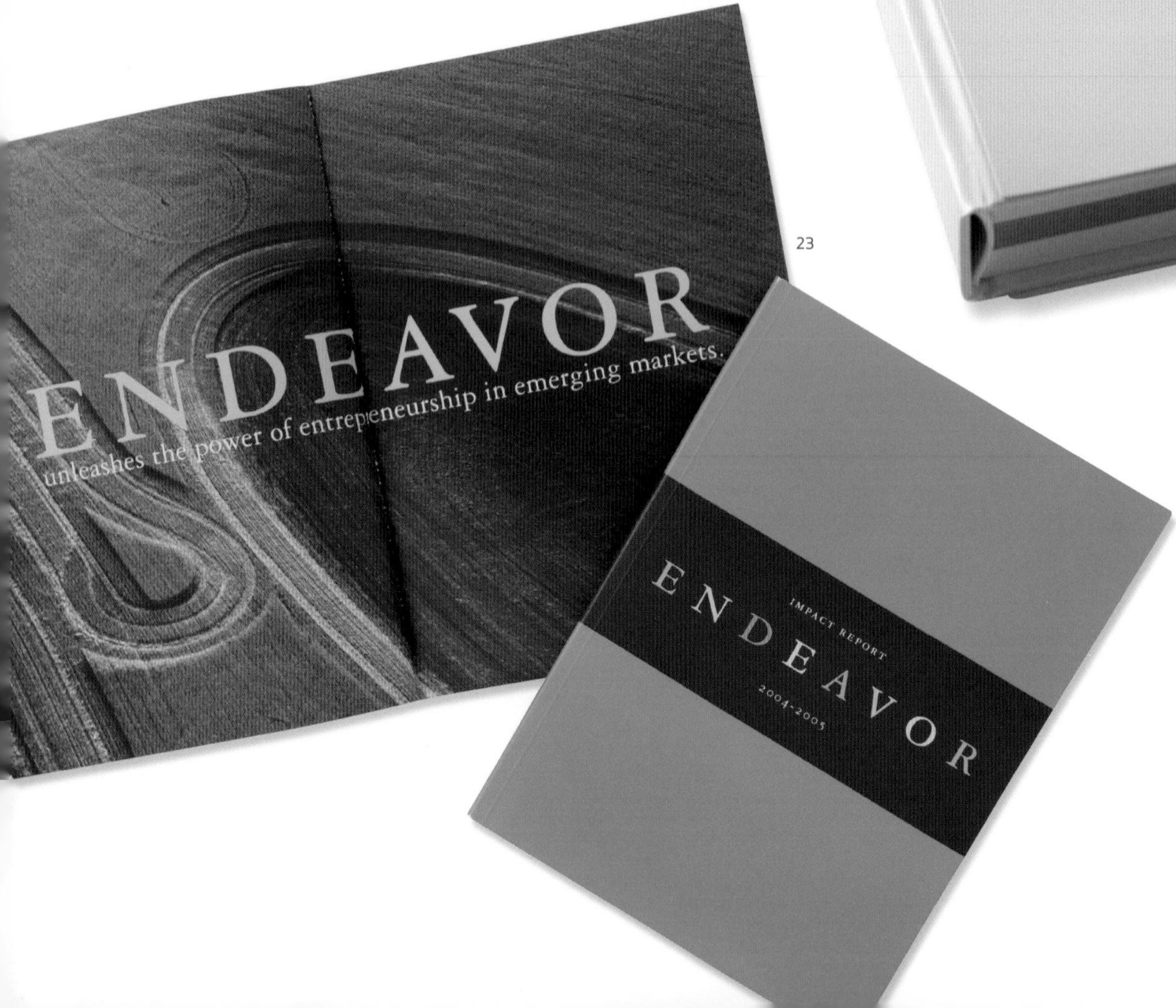

ENDEAVOR
unleashes the power of entrepreneurship in emerging markets.

IMPACT REPORT
ENDEAVOR
2004–2005

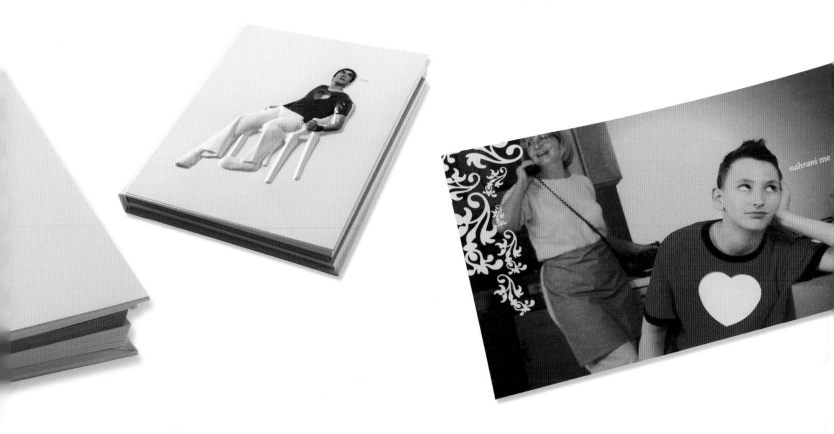

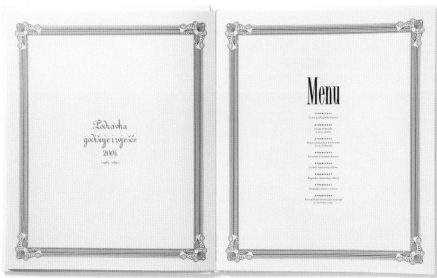

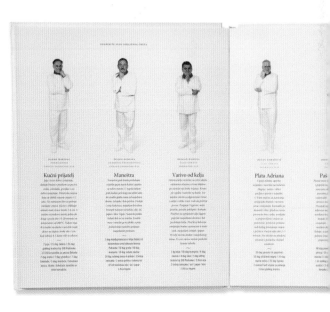

24

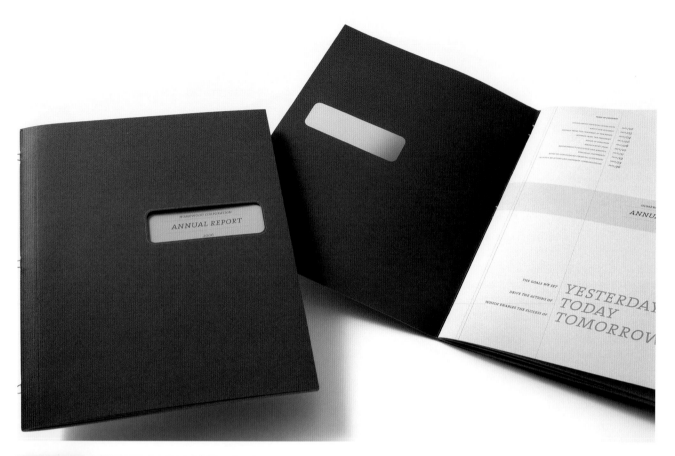

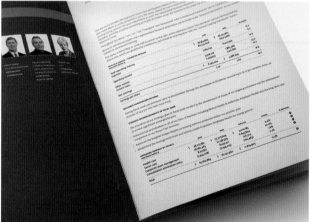

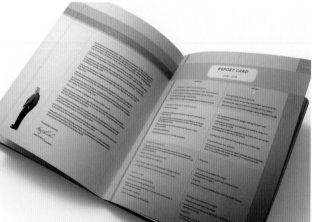

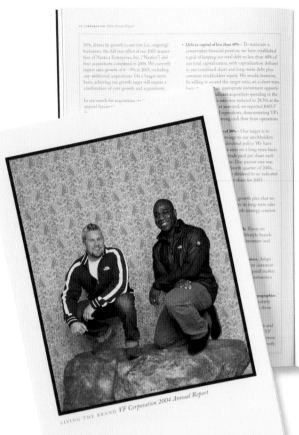

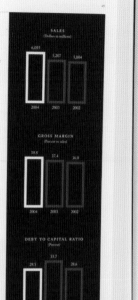

25
CLIENT: Homewood Corporation
DESIGN FIRM: Riordon Design

26
CLIENT: VF Corporation
DESIGN FIRM: And Partners

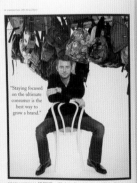

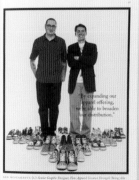

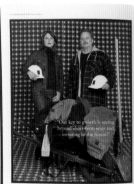

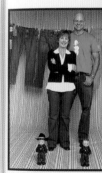

26

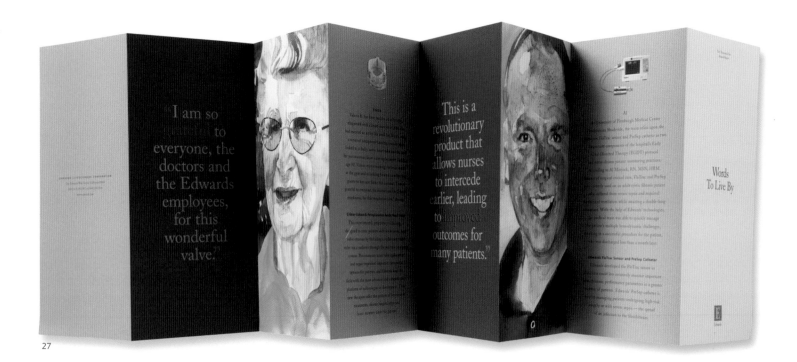

27

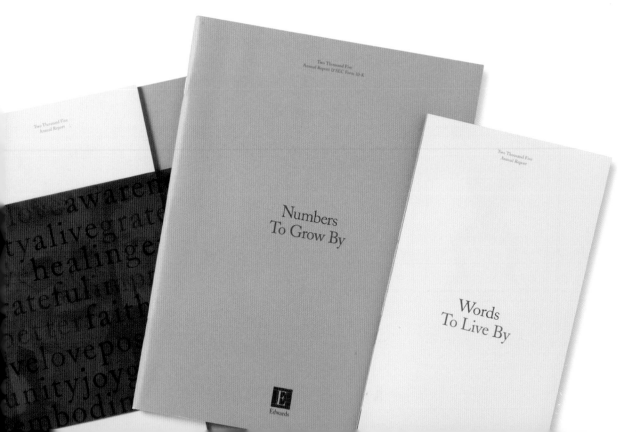

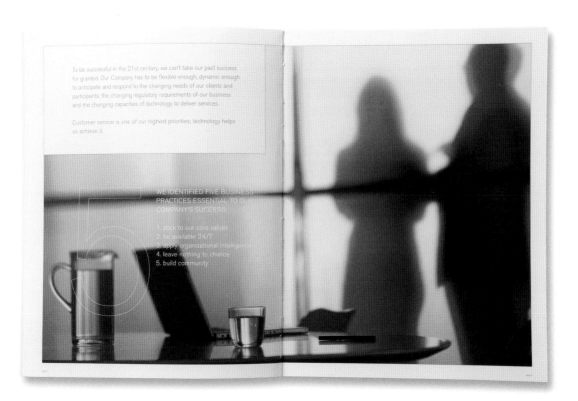

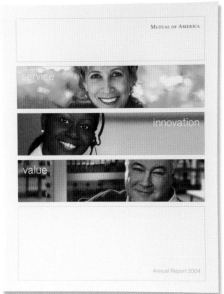

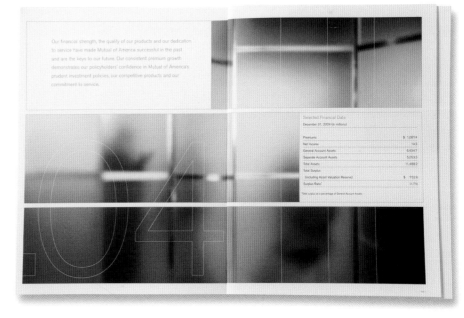

27
CLIENT: Edwards LifeSciences
DESIGN FIRM: Ramp Creative

28
CLIENT: Mutual of America
DESIGN FIRM: Decker Design

28

29, 30
CLIENT: Northwestern Memorial
HealthCare
DESIGN FIRM: Liska + Associates

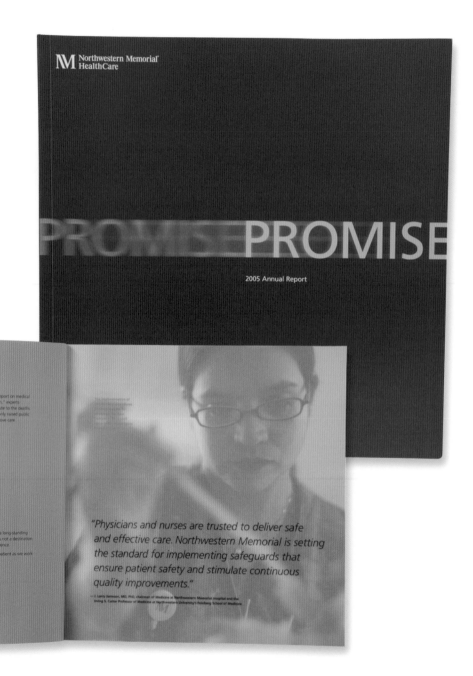

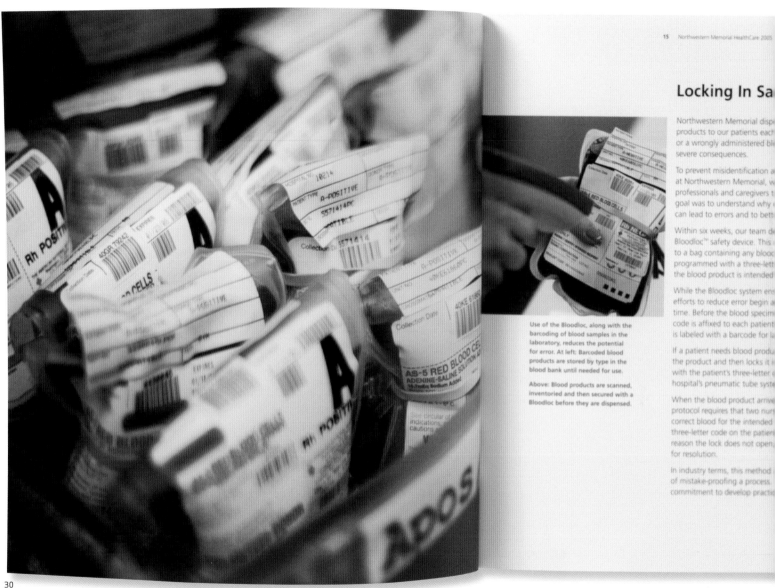

Locking In Sa

Northwestern Memorial disp
products to our patients each
or a wrongly administered bl
severe consequences.

To prevent misidentification a
at Northwestern Memorial, w
professionals and caregivers t
goal was to understand why
can lead to errors and to bett

Within six weeks, our team de
Bloodloc™ safety device. This
to a bag containing any blood
programmed with a three-lett
the blood product is intended

While the Bloodloc system en
efforts to reduce error begin
time. Before the blood specim
code is affixed to each patient
is labeled with a barcode for la

If a patient needs blood produ
the product and then locks it i
with the patient's three-letter
hospital's pneumatic tube syste

When the blood product arrive
protocol requires that two nurs
correct blood for the intended
three-letter code on the patien
reason the lock does not open,
for resolution.

In industry terms, this method
of mistake-proofing a process.
commitment to develop practic

Use of the Bloodloc, along with the barcoding of blood samples in the laboratory, reduces the potential for error. At left: Barcoded blood products are stored by type in the blood bank until needed for use.

Above: Blood products are scanned, inventoried and then secured with a Bloodloc before they are dispensed.

31
CLIENT: Melbourne Pacific
Airports Corporation
DESIGN FIRM: Perks Design Partners

32
CLIENT: New Century Financial
DESIGN FIRM: Ramp Creative

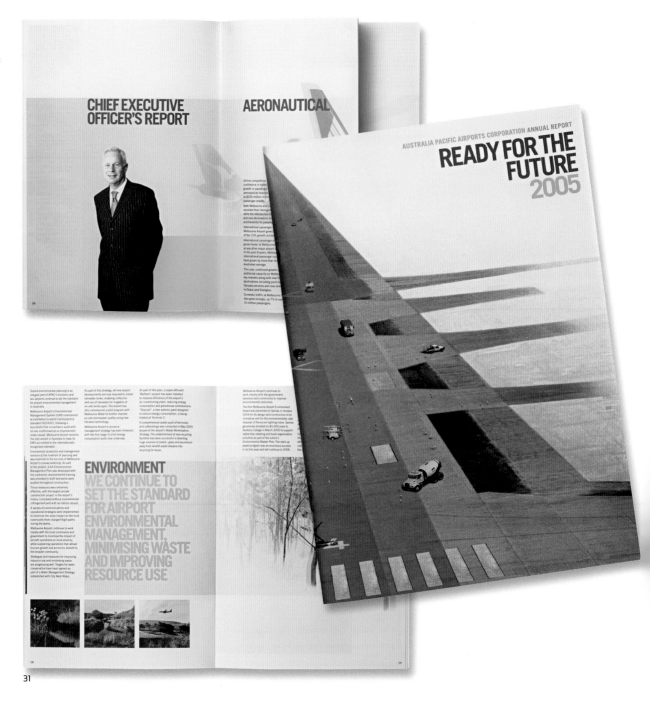

31

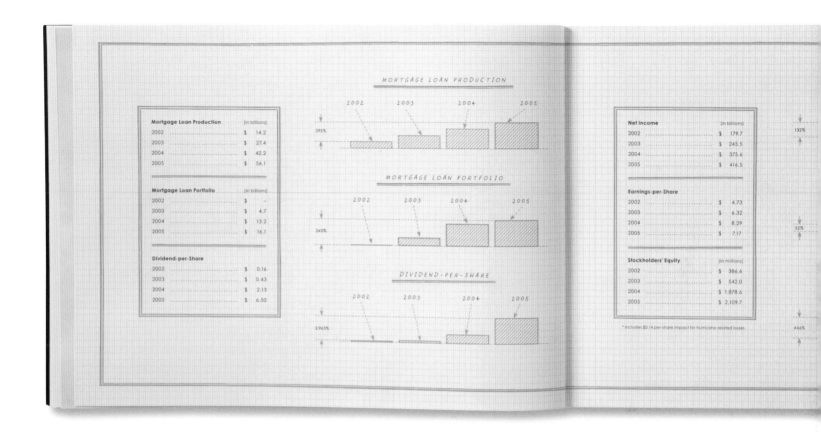

Mortgage Loan Production	(in billions)
2002	$ 14.2
2003	$ 27.4
2004	$ 42.2
2005	$ 56.1

Mortgage Loan Portfolio	(in billions)
2002	$ –
2003	$ 4.7
2004	$ 13.2
2005	$ 16.1

Dividend-per-Share	
2002	$ 0.16
2003	$ 0.43
2004	$ 2.13
2005	$ 6.50

MORTGAGE LOAN PRODUCTION

MORTGAGE LOAN PORTFOLIO

DIVIDEND-PER-SHARE

Net Income	(in billions)
2002	$ 179.7
2003	$ 245.5
2004	$ 375.6
2005	$ 416.5

Earnings-per-Share	
2002	$ 4.73
2003	$ 6.32
2004	$ 8.29
2005	$ 7.17

Stockholders' Equity	(in millions)
2002	$ 386.6
2003	$ 542.0
2004	$ 1,878.6
2005	$ 2,109.7

* Includes $0.14 per-share impact for hurricane-related losses

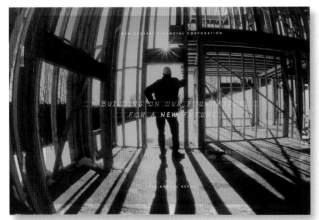

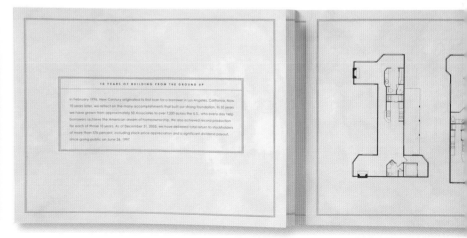

32

BEGINNING

CUTTING FROM THE
ROUGH TO CREATE
GREATER VALUE

STRENGTH

COMMITMENT

Diamond Bank

THIS CASE STUDY ILLUSTRATES TWO ELEMENTS OF THE DESIGN PROCESS: HOW A DESIGN TEAM CAN CREATE A VARIETY OF MATERIALS FROM A SINGLE SOURCE OF INSPIRATION, AND HOW A SINGLE THEME CAN CREATE A REMARKABLY CONSISTENT, YET BROAD, VISUAL LANGUAGE. IN THIS CASE, THE SOURCE OF INSPIRATION CAME FROM THE NAME OF THE CLIENT, **DIAMOND BANK**. THE DESIGN TEAM FOCUSED ON DEVELOPING A HOLISTIC BRANDING PROGRAM THAT RELATES CHARACTERISTICS OF DIAMONDS TO THE CLIENT'S ATTRIBUTES, PRODUCTS, AND SERVICES.

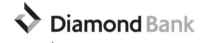

1

1
The logo incorporates the lowercase letter "d" and the shape of an ideal cut diamond. The faceting adds dimension and African patterning.

CLIENT Diamond Bank is one of Nigeria's largest retail banks. The company positions itself as sound, professional, flexible, and purpose-driven. After a recent merger and legislative changes within the Nigerian financial market, the company chose to upgrade its visual system to reflect its stature and breadth of service, while still maintaining a sense of approachability.

PROJECT Diamond Bank engaged Enterprise IG to design a comprehensive brand program that would set the bank apart from—and above—its competitors. The design team developed the visual system around the most prominent image in the existing identity, a diamond. Diamonds inspire each element of the brand, from the shape of the logo and a custom typeface to the spectrum of color and the use of diamond-oriented patterns. Enterprise IG expanded the diamond concept to provide the branding

program with depth while maintaining consistency by focusing each piece on various elements of a diamond. Deliverables included a logo, a custom typeface (appropriately named *Facet Face*), stationery, corporate collateral, a brand manual, signage, and retail and corporate interior design.

OPERATING SYSTEMS Enterprise IG used diamond-related color palettes to generate collateral for each operating division. For the Diamond Bank Group, the team used a graphite color palette. Graphite is derived from carbon, which is expressed in its purest form as a diamond. Design for the Private Banking division reflects the valuation component of diamonds; the less color a diamond contains, the greater its value. The collateral for this division appears colorless and makes use of varnishes and clear foils. The design team selected a range of color

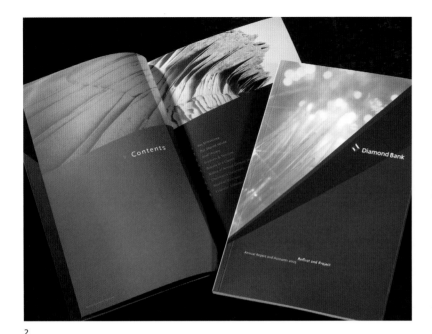

2

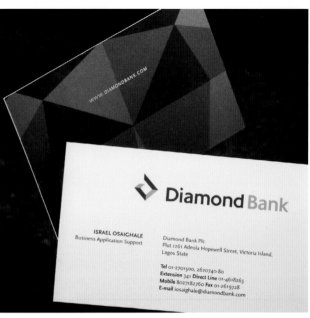

3

for the most public-facing division, Diamond
Bank Retail, because a diamond radiates a
spectrum of color when held up to the light.

DIAMOND CUT Diamond shapes inspired many
of the pieces, including the primary identity.
The logo combines the lowercase letter "d" and
the shape of an ideal cut diamond. The faceting
contributes added depth and dimension to the
identity. The press kit also relies on diamond
shaping for its design. It is folded in an origami
style that re-creates the process of cutting a
diamond. When fully opened, the kit radiates
brilliant color and vibrant stories, like an expertly
cut diamond reflects a spectrum of light.

CHANGING THE LANDSCAPE Diamond Bank's
new identity demonstrates notable consistency
within a holistic branding project. Relative to
international competitors, this could be seen as
standard practice; however, it is groundbreaking
and exceptional within the Nigerian market. ∎

4

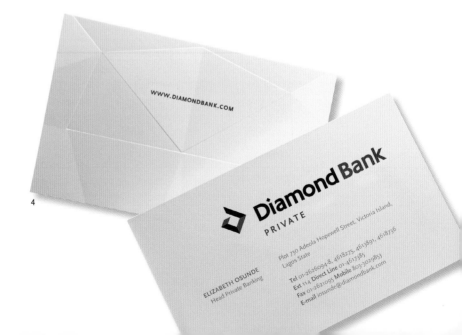

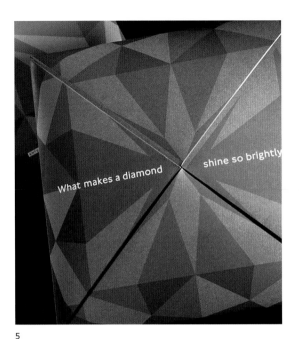

5

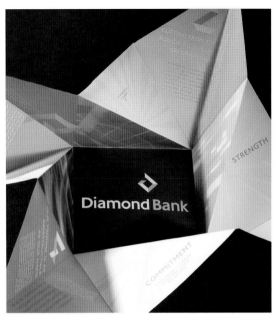

2

The annual report uses a graphite color palette, inspired by a diamond's elemental source, carbon.

3

The double-sided business card combines metallic inks and spot varnishes to create facets of a diamond that sparkle differently when held at different angles.

4

The less color a diamond has, the greater its value. Diamond Bank Private Banking collateral reflects this by using varnishes and clear foils.

5

The press kit unfolds in stages, re-creating the process of cutting a diamond. When fully opened, it radiates brilliant color and communicates vibrant stories.

6

The Private Banking folder is die-cut in the shape of an ideal cut diamond.

7

The decorative typeface, Facet Face, was designed exclusively for Diamond Bank.

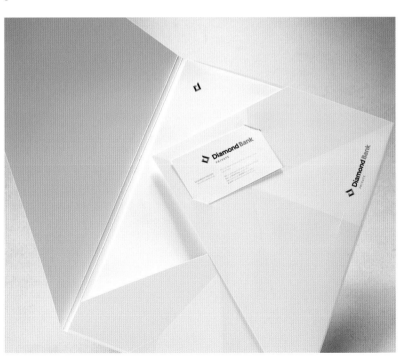

6

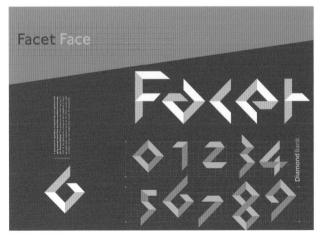

7

8

Each chapter of the brand manual, Facets, begins with a story about an aspect of a diamond that relates to the chapter at hand.

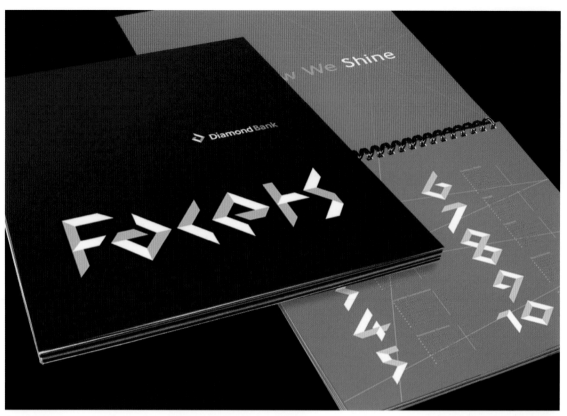

8

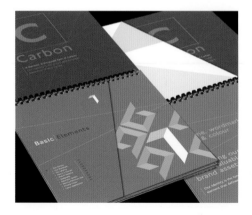

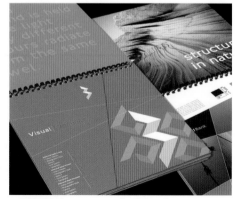

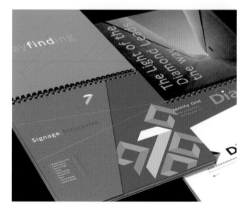

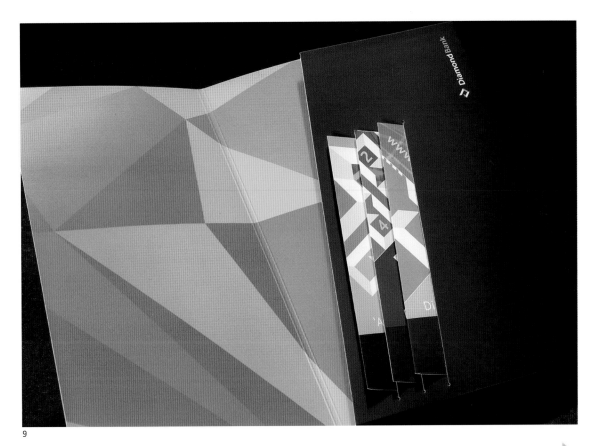

9

9
The most public-facing division uses collateral with brilliant colors because when a diamond is held to the light, it reflects a spectrum of light.

10
The logo is iconic and translates well through all brand materials, from stationery to signage.

11
In its holiday cards, the Diamond Bank symbol is transformed into seasonal iconography. Each accordion panel features a one-word message, ending with the word prosperity.

CLIENT: Diamond Bank
DESIGN FIRM: Enterprise IG
ART DIRECTOR: Dave Holland
DESIGNERS: Bronwen Rautenbach, Leoni Watson

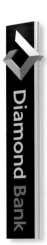

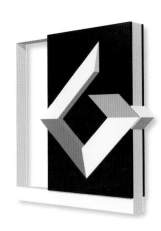

10

11

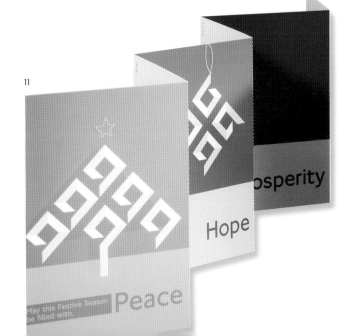

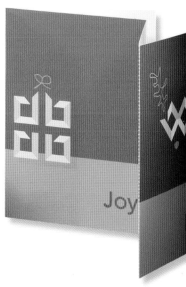

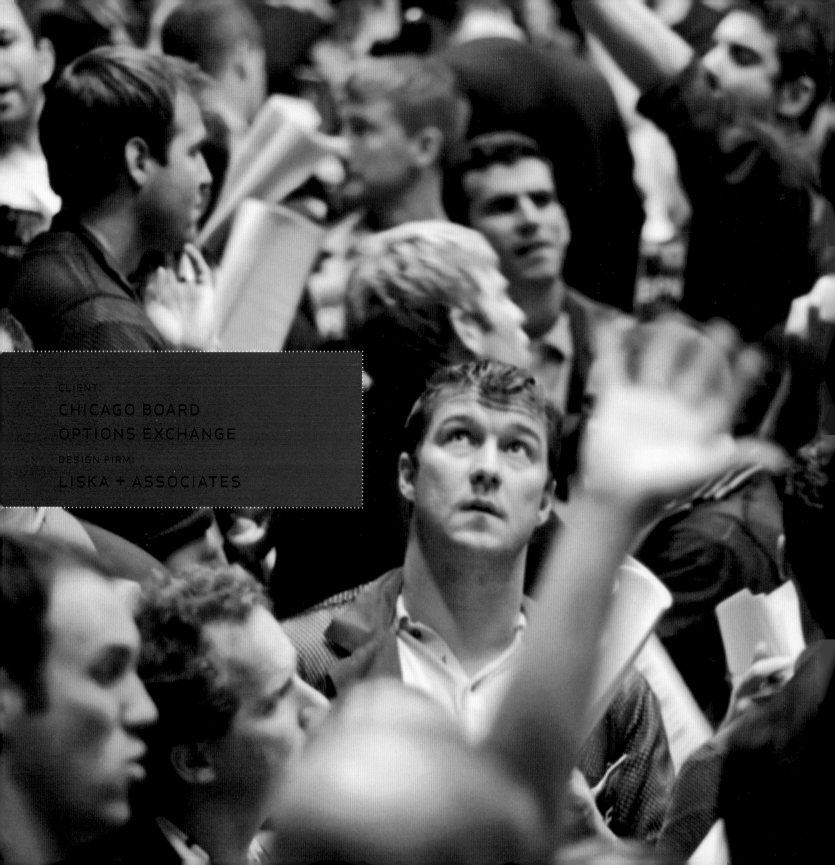

CLIENT:

CHICAGO BOARD
OPTIONS EXCHANGE

DESIGN FIRM:

LISKA + ASSOCIATES

VISUAL AND VERBAL SYSTEMS WORK TOGETHER TO COMMUNICATE A CLEAR, ACCURATE, AND CONSISTENT MESSAGE. THE CONTENT, OR MESSAGE, DRIVES THE DESIGN SOLUTION; THE VISUAL DESIGN SUPPORTS AND REINFORCES THE CORE MESSAGE. WHEN A CLIENT'S CONTENT REMAINS VIRTUALLY THE SAME OVER THE COURSE OF SEVERAL YEARS, DESIGNERS FACE THE CHALLENGE OF COMMUNICATING THE MESSAGE ACCURATELY WHILE ALSO EVOLVING THE VISUAL DESIGN. THIS CASE STUDY SHOWCASES DESIGN SOLUTIONS CREATED FOR THE **CHICAGO BOARD OPTIONS EXCHANGE** (CBOE), A BUSINESS WHOSE MESSAGE REMAINS RELATIVELY CONSTANT.

CBOE is the largest and most successful options marketplace in the world.

CLIENT Founded in 1973, the Chicago Board Options Exchange was the first U.S. options exchange. Every year since its inception, CBOE has been the world leader in options volume. The company is positioned as an options exchange with multiple products, as well as the first exchange to develop a successful hybrid trading system that truly marries floor-based (open outcry) trading with screen-based, electronic trading.

PROJECT For several years, CBOE has engaged Liska to design a variety of corporate communication materials. The central design challenges remain the same from project to project. CBOE's messaging is relatively constant; the business model may evolve, but the overall income-generating activity of options trading remains the same. Yet while the core message remains consistent, the design needs to suggest a sense of difference and progress from year to year.

INCOME GENERATOR CBOE develops markets and platforms that generate new options, literally and figuratively, for trading. The drive to create new products and enhanced methods of trading is elemental to the CBOE brand and critical to CBOE's long-term success. Liska uses a combination of illustrations, photography, and diagrams to communicate CBOE's active process of generating new markets and enhanced trading methods.

ABSTRACT ART The business of CBOE is extremely complex and abstract. Liska focuses intently on developing visual solutions that help display the complicated processes and products of CBOE. The design team presents key performance data in clear and straightforward ways.

HYBRID OPTION The core business of CBOE is facilitating options trading; it provides the mechanisms and venues that traders use to

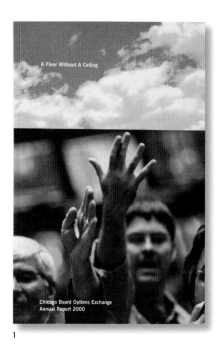

1

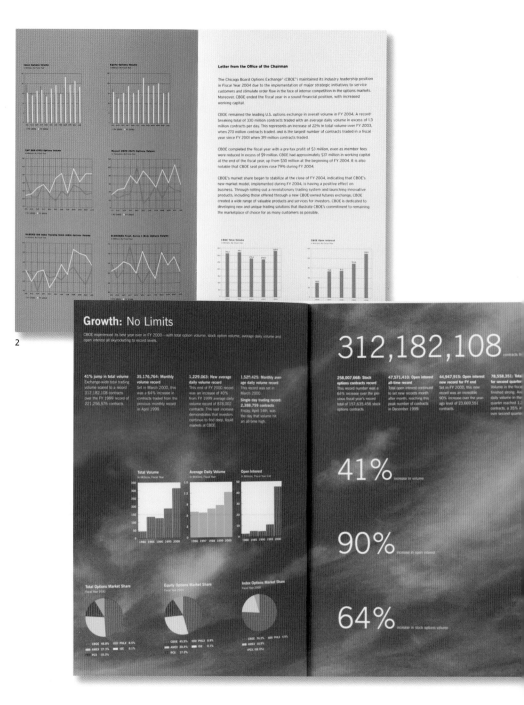

2

make transactions. As CBOE integrated the hybrid system, which combines both open outcry and electronic trading, Liska incorporated photography that communicates the simultaneous presence of human interaction and technology.

LONG-TERM ENGAGEMENT Designers face the challenge of communicating CBOE's consistent core message in accurate and clear ways that are also editorially stimulating. The challenge is compounded by the finite audience for most of CBOE's communications; the audience remains very similar from year to year. Liska resolves this issue by supporting the messaging with visual cues that communicate a variety of aspects of the CBOE experience. From photographs of the trading jackets to dramatic images of the trading floor, the design team engages the reader and demonstrates the richness and depth of CBOE. ■

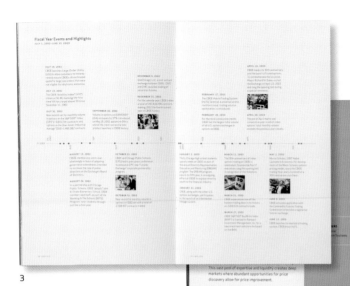

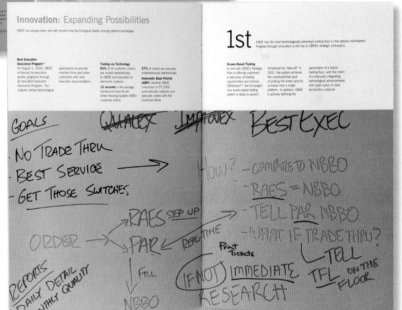

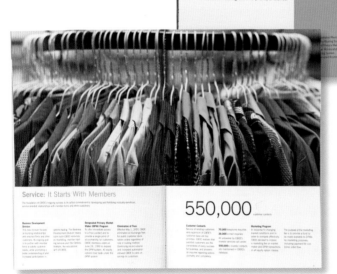

1
This annual report cover balances the intensity and immediacy of floor-based trading with the open and visionary attributes of CBOE.

2
The need for clarity drives the visual presentation of financial data.

3
Liska's design solutions present CBOE's complex processes, financial performance, and key events in visually engaging and memorable ways.

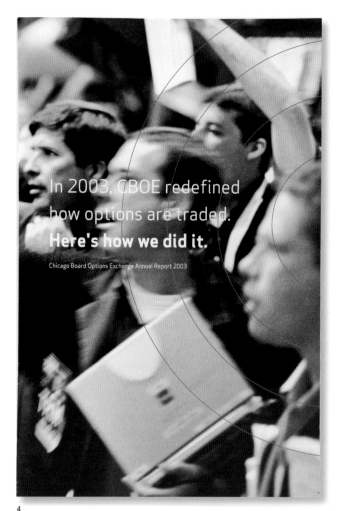

In 2003, CBOE redefined
how options are traded.
Here's how we did it.

Chicago Board Options Exchange Annual Report 2003

4

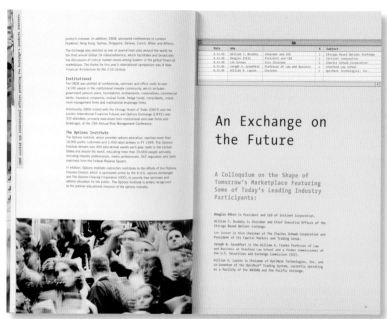

An Exchange on the Future

A Colloquium on the Shape of
Tomorrow's Marketplace Featuring
Some of Today's Leading Industry
Participants:

Douglas Atkin is President and CEO of Instinet Corporation.

William J. Brodsky is Chairman and Chief Executive Officer of the
Chicago Board Options Exchange.

Len Gorman is Vice Chairman of The Charles Schwab Corporation and
President of its Capital Markets and Trading Group.

Joseph A. Grundfest is the William A. Franke Professor of Law
and Business at Stanford Law School and a former Commissioner of
the U.S. Securities and Exchange Commission (SEC).

William A. Lupien is Chairman of OptiMark Technologies, Inc. and
co-inventor of the OptiMark™ Trading System, currently operating
as a facility of the NASDAQ and the Pacific Exchange.

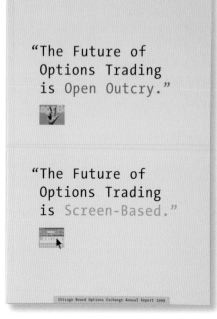

"The Future of
Options Trading
is Open Outcry."

"The Future of
Options Trading
is Screen-Based."

Chicago Board Options Exchange Annual Report 1999

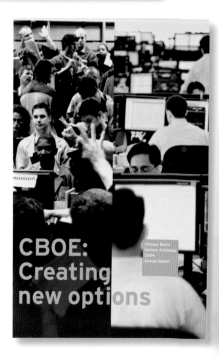

CBOE:
Creating
new options

Chicago Board
Options Exchange
2004
Annual Report

CHICAGO BOARD OPTIONS EXCHANGE 2005 ANNUAL REPORT

5

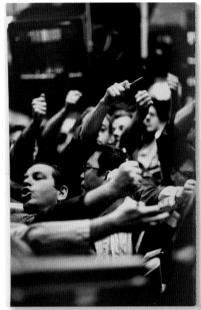

6

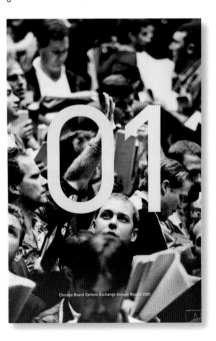

4

As CBOE introduced electronic trading and other high-tech processes, Liska began to integrate images that show both the human experience of the trading floor and the ubiquitous support of technology.

5

The design for this annual report follows the core message and communicates that 2005 brought significant change to CBOE's business model.

6

Dramatic photography communicates the dynamic energy of open outcry trading.

CLIENT: Chicago Board Options Exchange
DESIGN FIRM: Liska + Associates
ART DIRECTOR: Steve Liska
DESIGNERS: Kim Fry, Amy Hogan, Tory Knappenberger

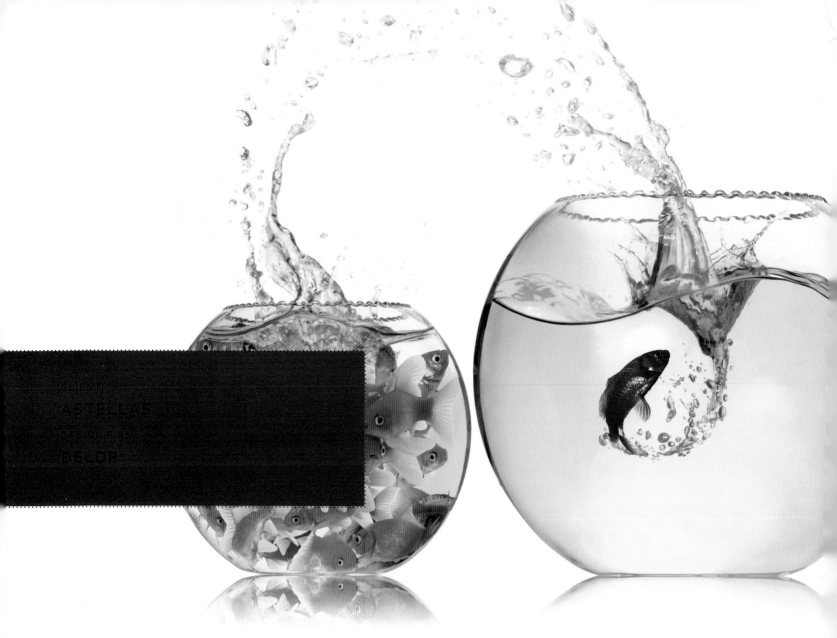

CLIENT

ASTELLAS

DESIGN FIRM

DELOR

different from the

INDUSTRIES TEND TO DEVELOP PARTICULAR TRENDS IN VISUAL AND VERBAL COMMUNICATION. FINANCIAL SERVICES COMPANIES, FOR EXAMPLE, TEND TO REFLECT A SERIOUS, CONSERVATIVE TONE WHEREAS THE FASHION INDUSTRY RELIES HEAVILY ON LIFESTYLE IMAGERY. THE PHARMACEUTICAL INDUSTRY TENDS TO BE DOMINATED EITHER BY IMAGES OF HAPPY, SMILING PATIENTS OR PLAYFUL CARTOON ILLUSTRATIONS. **ASTELLAS** WANTED TO SET ITSELF APART AND BE TRUE TO ITS CORE ATTRIBUTE OF BEING A DIFFERENT KIND OF PHARMACEUTICAL COMPANY. THE DESIGN TEAM AT DELOR ROSE TO THE CHALLENGE.

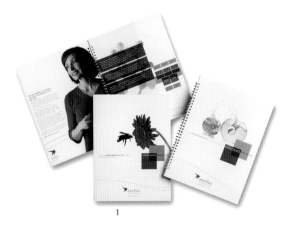

1

1

The corporate brochure uses smart, iconic images to communicate the Astellas brand.

CLIENT Astellas is a pharmaceutical products company formed by the merger of two related companies: Fujisawa and Yamanouchi. Although Astellas does not share the size of major pharmaceutical corporations, it still competes globally with companies such as Pfizer, Astra Zeneca, and Lilly. It does so by focusing on niche categories in contrast to "big pharma's" emphasis on volume-driven products.

PROJECT Astellas approached DeLor with the task of building a branding program for the United States market. Astellas requested that the branding program honor the existing name and logo and appropriately integrate the global tag line, "Leading Light for Life." Project deliverables included sales and marketing materials, corporate communications, global brand guidelines, and multimedia collateral for internal sales.

SMALLER AND SLOWER, BY DESIGN DeLor focused its design on demonstrating clearly that Astellas is not what healthcare professionals have come to expect from big pharma. Big pharma tends to be impersonal and volume-driven and operates from a speed-to-market perspective; Astellas approach is relationship-driven, niche-product oriented, and slow-to-market, ensuring that every possible variable has been tested in its clinical trials. These attributes led DeLor to position Astellas as a refreshing contrast to big pharma.

APPLES, EGGS, AND GOLDFISH The design team used primarily iconic imagery to communicate the Astellas brand—a striking difference from the cartoon illustrations and smiling patients that dominate the industry. They supported the theme of difference by presenting Astellas as the sole item that stands out. One image presents

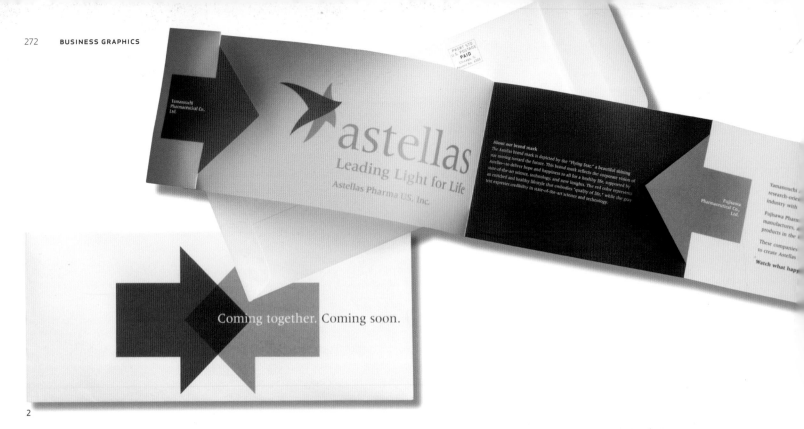

2

three eggs, with one colored differently. Another shows a single goldfish leaping from the full bowl into a larger bowl where it is the only fish.

DIFFERENT APPLICATIONS The design team developed the branding program based on the theme, "Different from the Start" and extended the idea of difference throughout the communication pieces. For example, sales collateral for various product categories incorporated customizable headlines that begin with, "Making a Difference in…" (i.e., dermatology, cardiology, immunology). Launch teasers for the internal sales team used the headline "You're not one of the crowd."

CORE IDENTITY In addition to the central theme of difference, Astellas needed to communicate its other core attributes: disciplined, efficient, respected, and creative. The design team incorporated the brand attributes with smart, iconic images to add depth to the Astellas brand image. Words like "fresh" and "trusted" accompany the images and are designed to draw the reader's attention. ∎

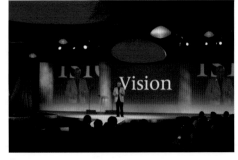

3

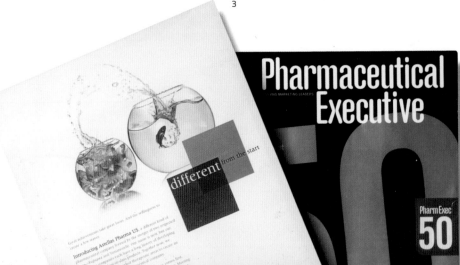

4

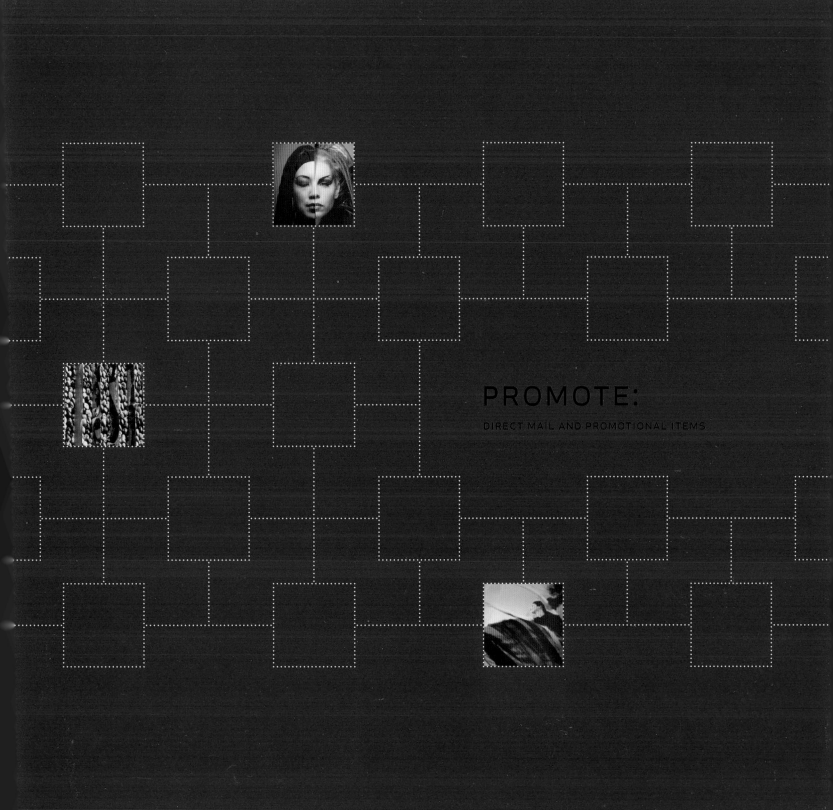

PROMOTE:

DIRECT MAIL AND PROMOTIONAL ITEMS

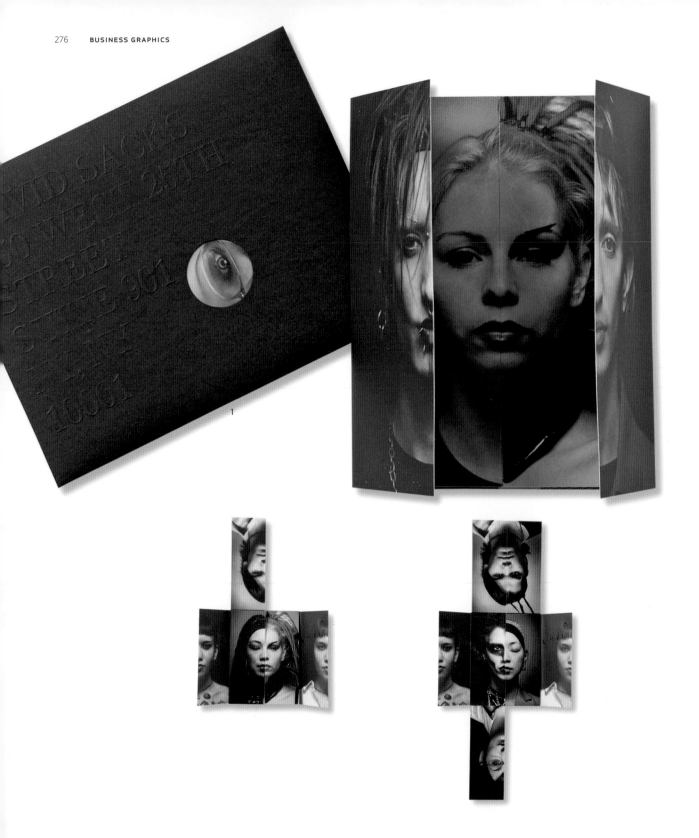

1

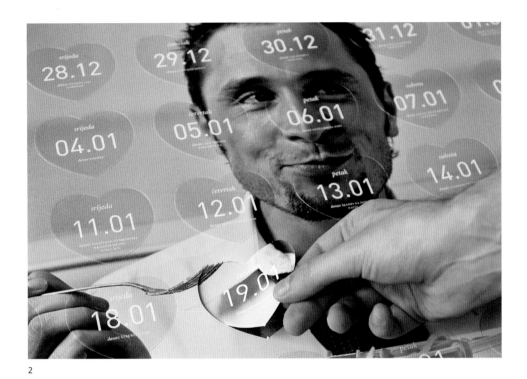

2

1
CLIENT: David Sacks
DESIGN FIRM: The Buddy Project/
Squarehand

2
CLIENT: Podravka
DESIGN FIRM: Bruketa & Zinic

3
CLIENT: Lenovo 2006 Winter Olympics
DESIGN FIRM: Stoller Design Group

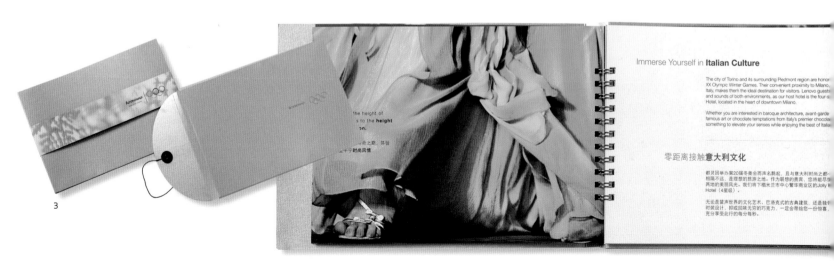

3

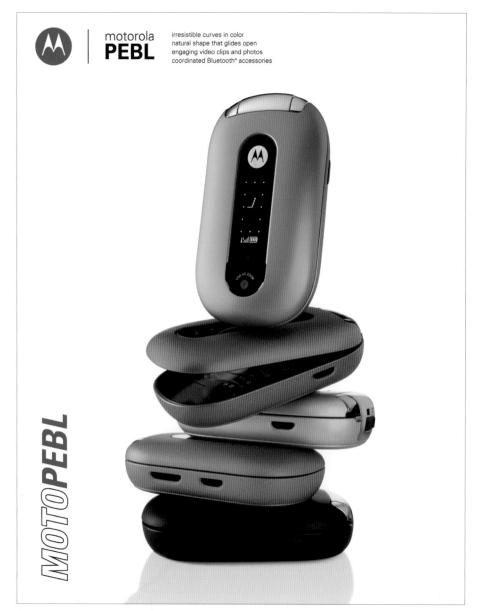

motorola
PEBL

irresistible curves in color
natural shape that glides open
engaging video clips and photos
coordinated Bluetooth® accessories

MOTOPEBL

4

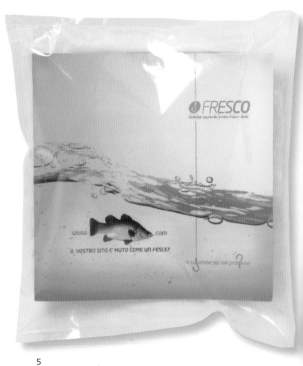

5

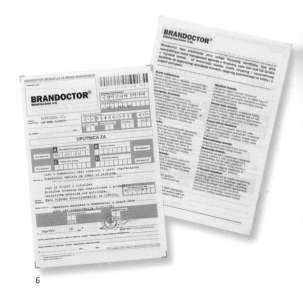

6

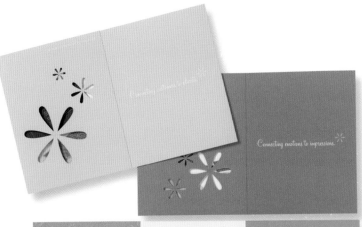

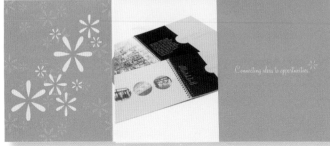

7

4

5

6

7

8

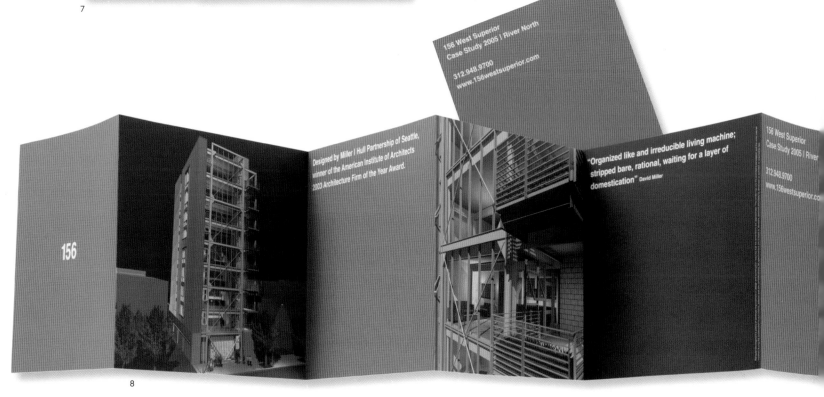

8

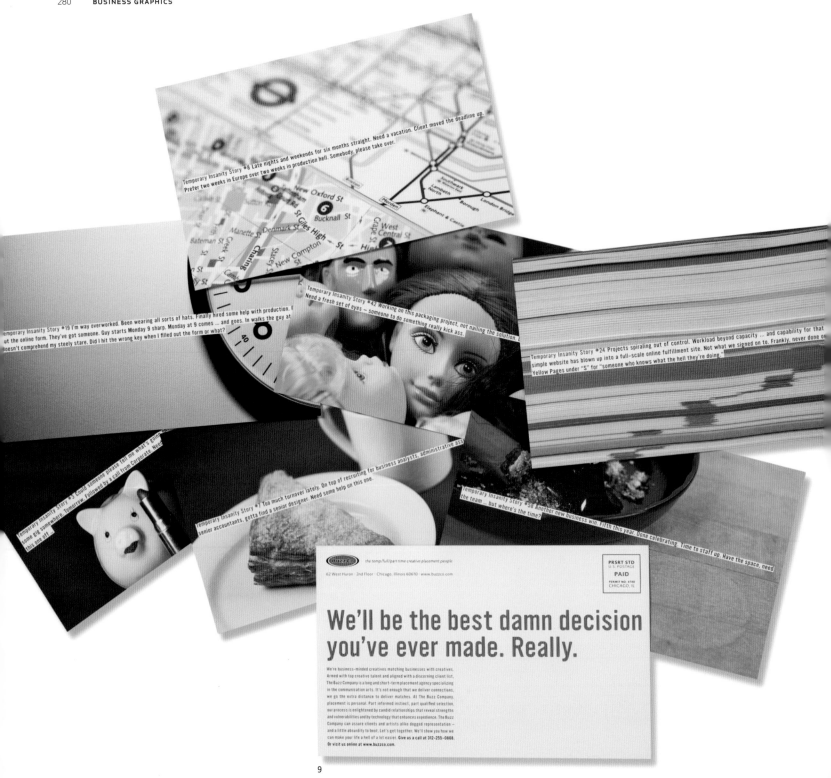

9

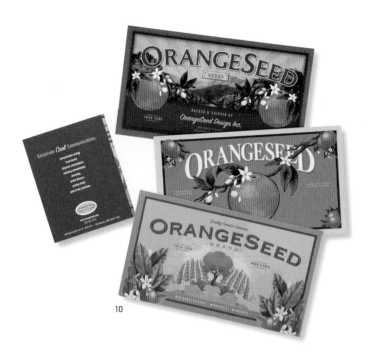

10

9
CLIENT: The Buzz Company
DESIGN FIRM: Faust Associates

10
CLIENT: OrangeSeed Design
DESIGN FIRM: OrangeSeed Design

11
CLIENT: IntraSpec Solutions
DESIGN FIRM: Sussner Design Company

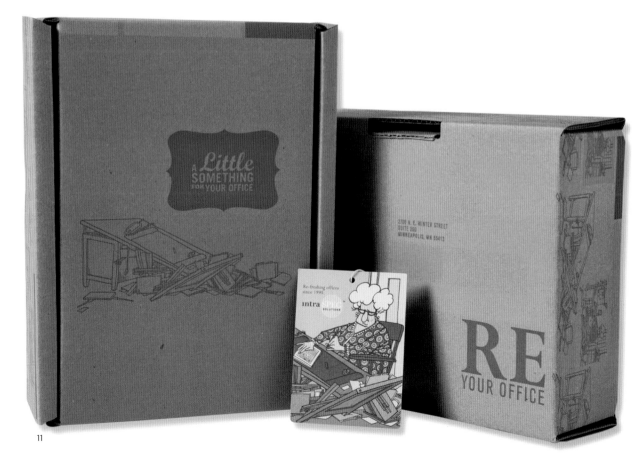

11

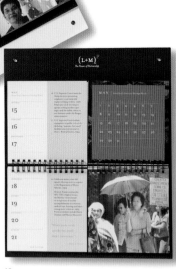

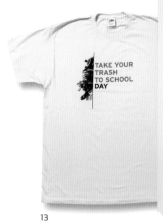

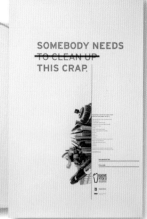

12
CLIENT: Kaiser Permanente
DESIGN FIRM: Stoller Design Group

13, 15
CLIENT: Creative Pitch
DESIGN FIRM: Brainforest, Inc.

14
CLIENT: Yes Design Group
DESIGN FIRM: Yes Design Group

16
CLIENT: Riordon Design
DESIGN FIRM: Riordon Design

12

13

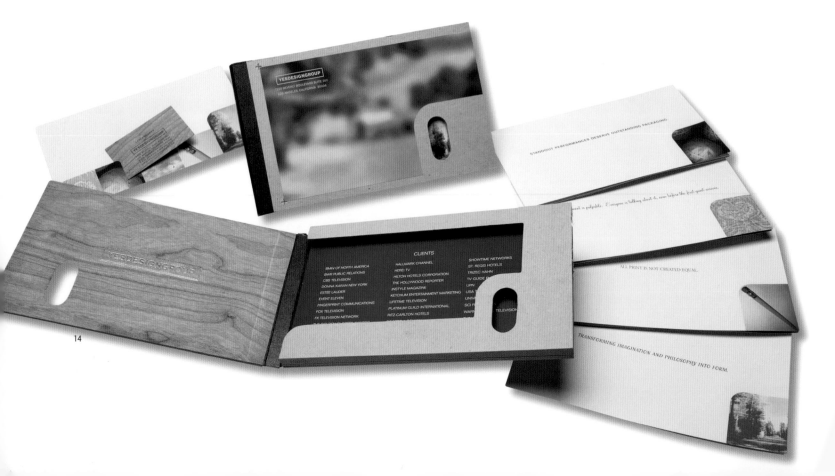

14

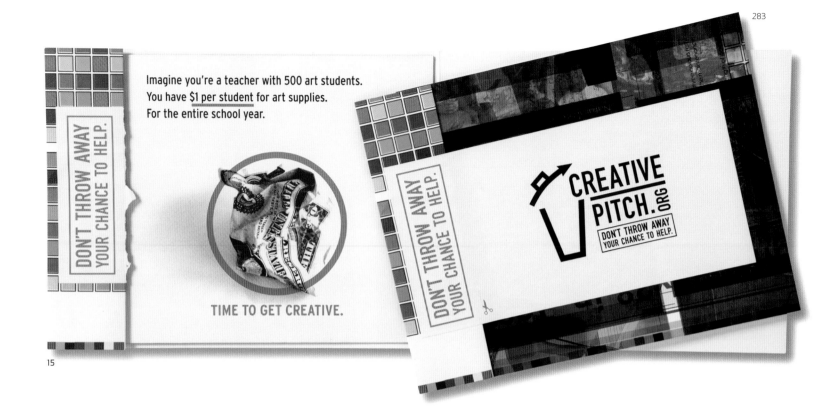

Imagine you're a teacher with 500 art students.
You have $1 per student for art supplies.
For the entire school year.

DON'T THROW AWAY
YOUR CHANCE TO HELP.

TIME TO GET CREATIVE.

DON'T THROW AWAY
YOUR CHANCE TO HELP.

CREATIVE
PITCH.ORG

DON'T THROW AWAY
YOUR CHANCE TO HELP.

15

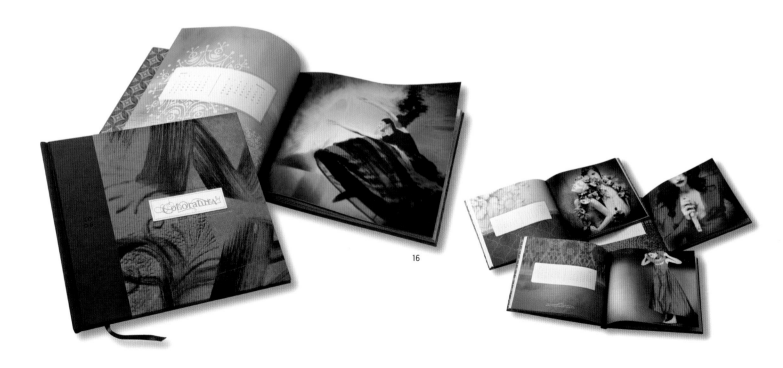

16

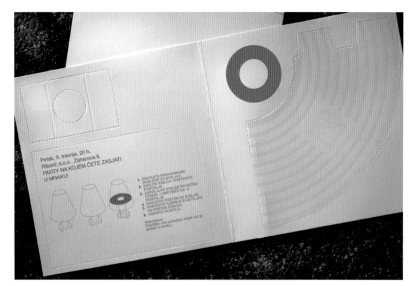

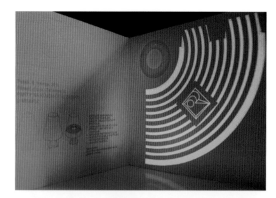

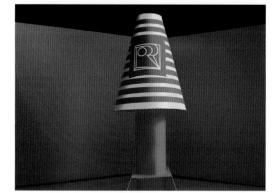

17

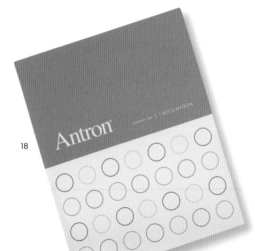

18

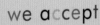

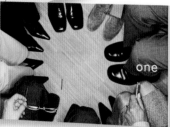

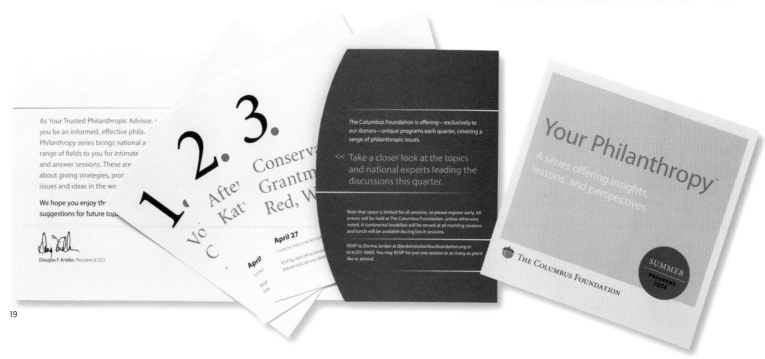

19

20

17
CLIENT: Ribarić d.o.o.
DESIGN FIRM: Bruketa & Zinic

18
CLIENT: Antron
DESIGN FIRM: Wages Design

19
CLIENT: The Columbus Foundation
DESIGN FIRM: Base Art Co.

20
CLIENT: USA Network
DESIGN FIRM: Yes Design Group

21
CLIENT: Clemenger BBDO
DESIGN FIRM: Clemenger BBDO

22
CLIENT: Reflections Printing
DESIGN FIRM: Sussner Design Company

23
CLIENT: Target Commercial Interiors
DESIGN FIRM: Sussner Design Company

24
CLIENT: Hubbard Street Dance Chicago
DESIGN FIRM: Liska + Associates

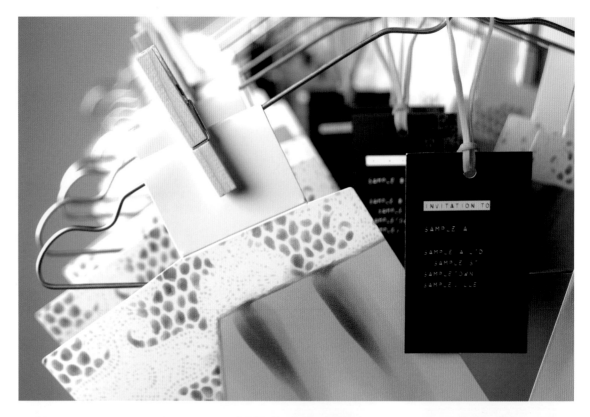

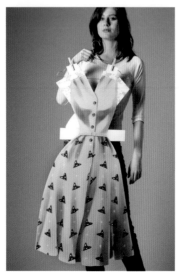

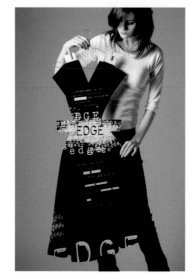

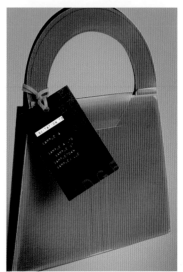

21

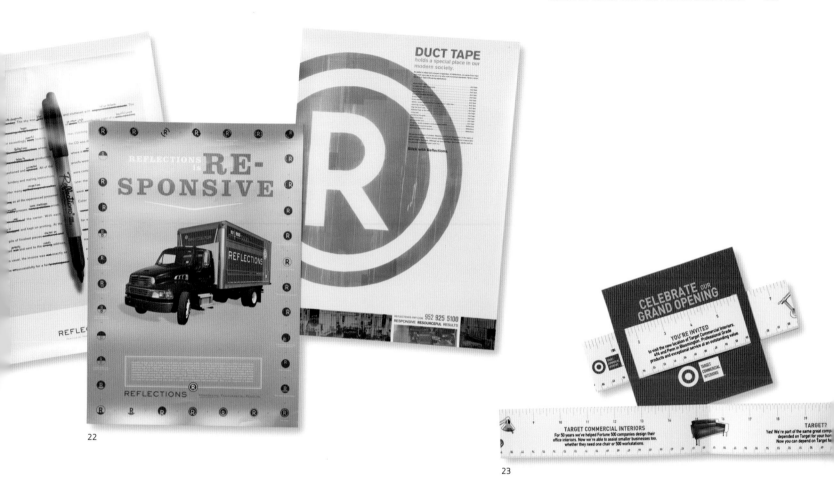

22

23

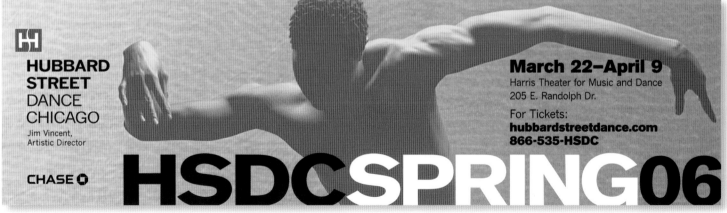

24

25
CLIENT: Fine Art & Antiques
DESIGN FIRM: Curious

26
CLIENT: Croatian National Tourist Board
DESIGN FIRM: Studio International

27
CLIENT: Showtime
DESIGN FIRM: Yes Design Group

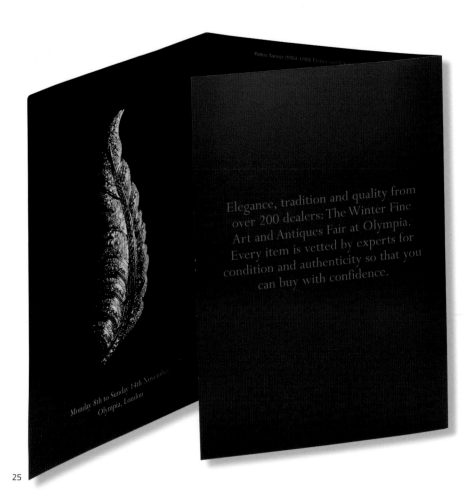

Robin Tanner (1904–1988) Etching and Drypoint

Elegance, tradition and quality from over 200 dealers: The Winter Fine Art and Antiques Fair at Olympia. Every item is vetted by experts for condition and authenticity so that you can buy with confidence.

Monday 8th to Sunday 14th November
Olympia, London

25

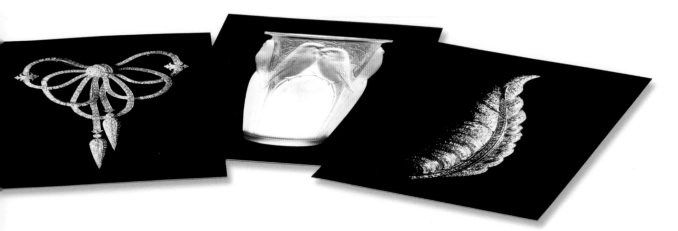

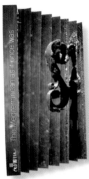
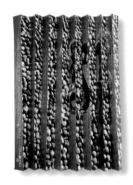
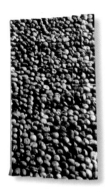
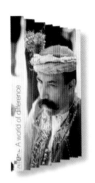
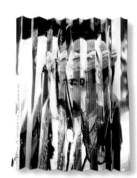
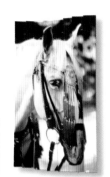

26

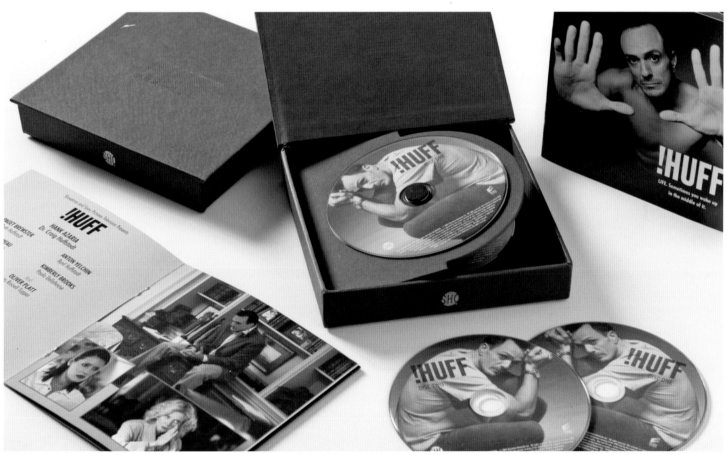

27

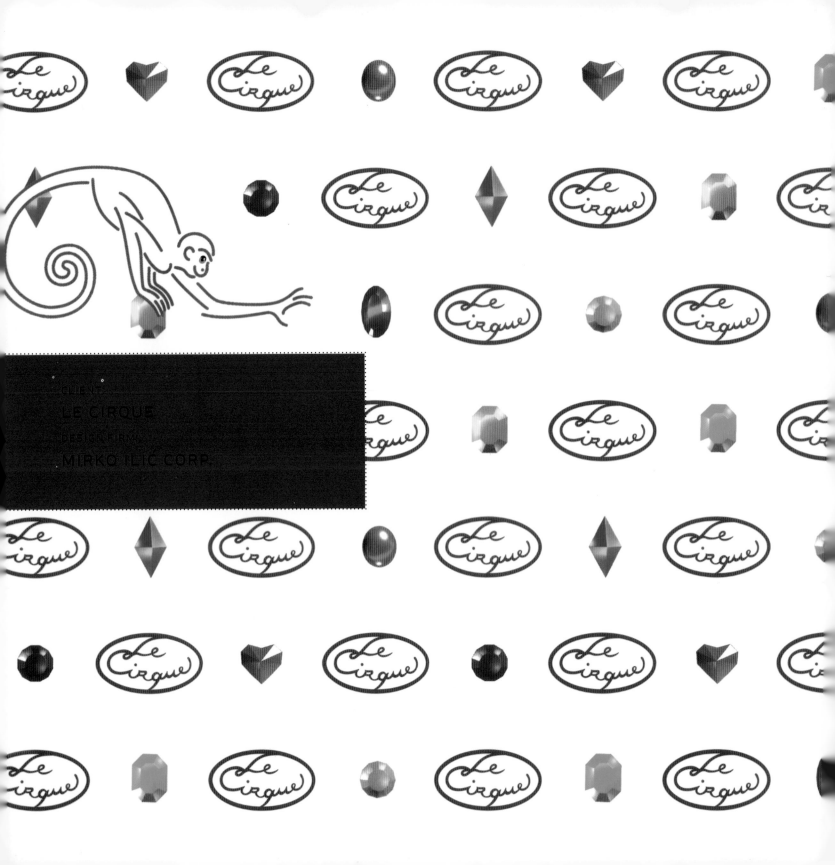

CLIENT

LE CIRQUE

DESIGN FIRM:

MIRKO ILIĆ CORP.

FOR A BRAND TO ACHIEVE LONGEVITY, IT NEEDS TO COMMUNICATE ACCURATELY WHAT A CUSTOMER WILL EXPERIENCE WHEN INTERACTING WITH A PARTICULAR COMPANY, PRODUCT, OR SERVICE. **LE CIRQUE** IS A RESTAURANT THAT PROMISES BOTH A REFINED DINING EXPERIENCE AND A "CIRCUS" OF ACTIVITY—ENERGY, FUN, AND A LEVEL OF QUALITY THAT MAKE AN EVENING A MEMORABLE EVENT. THE VISUAL SYSTEM IN THIS CASE STUDY CLEARLY COMMUNICATES THE BRAND PROMISE THAT LE CIRQUE DELIVERS.

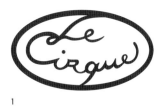

1

1
Le Cirque is as venerable as it is fashionable, a place for exquisite food and fashionable clientele. The visual system communicates that the location is both lively and refined.

CLIENT Le Cirque is one of the most venerable "A-list" restaurants in New York. Newer, yet equally exclusive Le Cirque locations include Las Vegas and Mexico City. The restaurant is positioned as the place where food, fashion, art, and culture converge.

PROJECT For more than thirty years, Le Cirque has been consistently known as one of New York's top restaurants. It's tasteful, established, and always fashionable. Both the food and clientele are noteworthy and elegant. When Le Cirque moved to a new location, the company commissioned Mirko Ilić Corp. to update the existing logo and create a visual system to support the newly designed, yet deeply established restaurant. Deliverables included a logo, a stationery system, menus, place cards, dishes, chocolate boxes, bags, matchbooks, and carry-out packaging.

ICONIC CHANGE This project brought a particular challenge: Le Cirque has a rich history, a strong tradition, and established success. Rebranding a company of legendary status requires retaining elements of the existing brand in the new visual system. The design team achieved congruence with the established brand by focusing the design on the unchanging brand promise.

THREE RING AND FIVE STAR Le Cirque, by name, suggests acrobats, animals, and accessible entertainment. By contrast, the food, clientele, and price points of Le Cirque communicate luxury and haute couture. Ilić found a way to blend both concepts into the visual system. The design team used shapes and colors that are primary and fun, but also communicate elegance and finery. The design is at once playful, refined, light, and lavish.

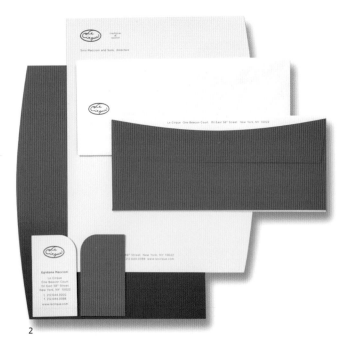

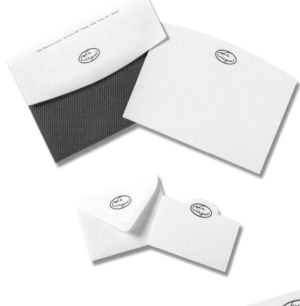

2

MONKEYS ON YOUR PLATE White plates, white linen, and crystal set the standard for most elegant dining establishments. Fueled by a strong client relationship that encourages moving beyond the expected, the design team developed a much less common and far more conceptual approach to the brand. They chose to incorporate a lighter tone into the serious nature of the restaurant, creating illustrated "scenes" that feature monkeys attempting to steal jewels. This playful theme was applied to tableware, menus, bags, and other collateral pieces. By setting aside the standard, designers added a unique and notable personality to the high-end experience at Le Cirque.

COLLABORATION Restaurants rely on a combination of food, service, and ambiance to attract and retain clientele. While the staff manages food and service, designers—both graphic and interior—create the look and feel of the restaurant. Le Cirque needed a visual system that would appropriately reflect the energy and activity that make its restaurant one of the best-known places to see and be seen in New York City. The graphic design team worked closely with the interior designer, Adam Tihany, to develop a unified brand experience. ■

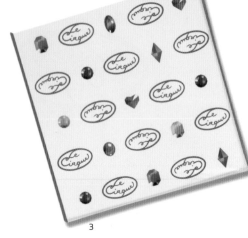

3

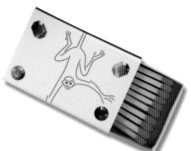

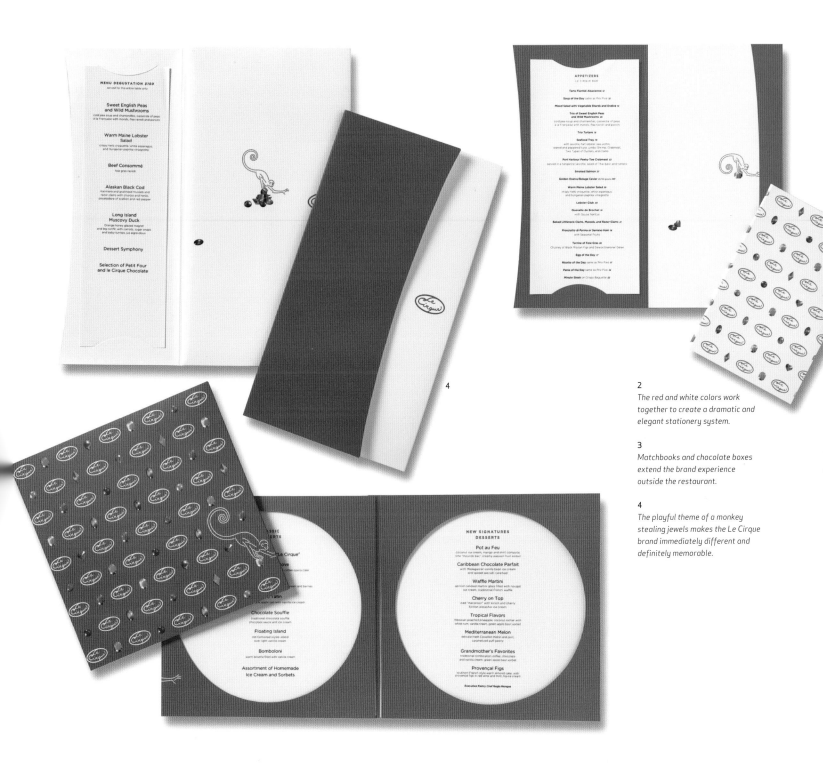

2
The red and white colors work together to create a dramatic and elegant stationery system.

3
Matchbooks and chocolate boxes extend the brand experience outside the restaurant.

4
The playful theme of a monkey stealing jewels makes the Le Cirque brand immediately different and definitely memorable.

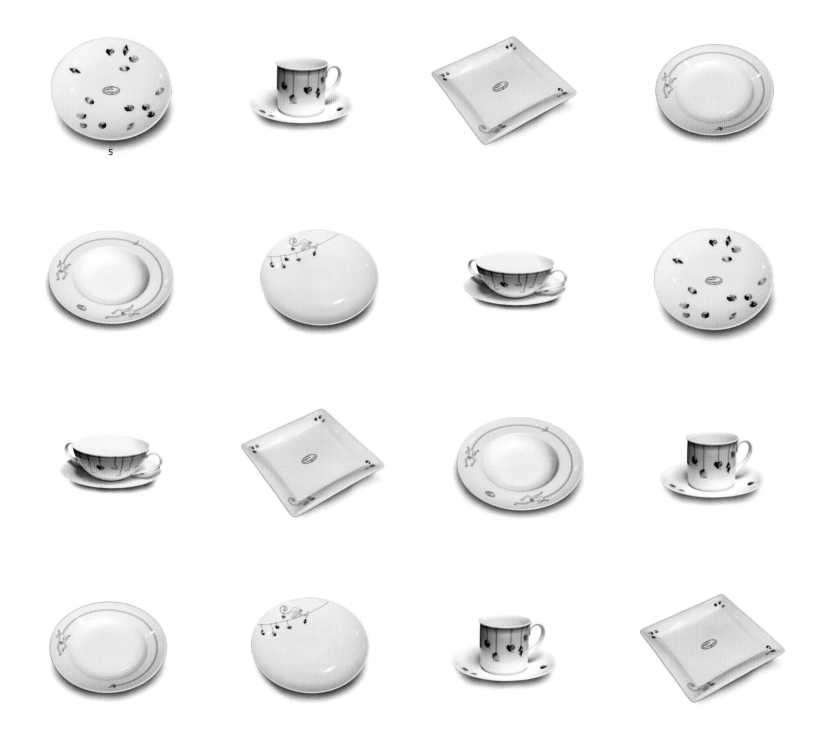

5

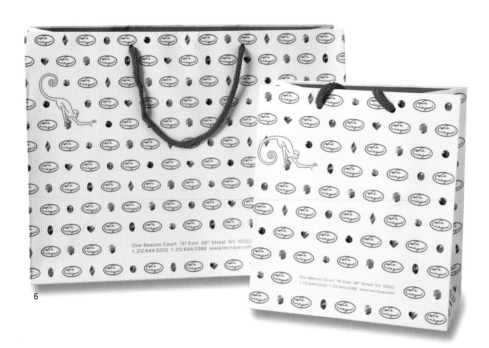

6

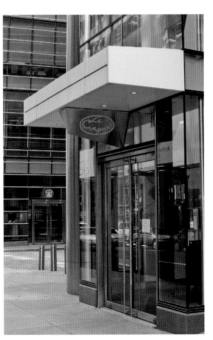

5
*The visual system extends intimately
into the actual dining experience,
where monkeys attempt to steal the
jewels that dot the plates and cups.*

6, 8
*Bags and carry-out boxes create a
patterned appearance by repeating
the logo and jewels, and feature
the illustrated monkey.*

7
*The curved lines for the logo find new
expression in the illustrated monkeys.*

CLIENT: Le Cirque
DESIGN FIRM: Mirko Ilić Corp.
ART DIRECTOR: Mirko Ilić
DESIGNER: Mirko Ilić

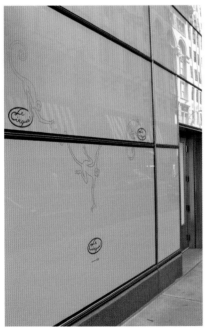

7

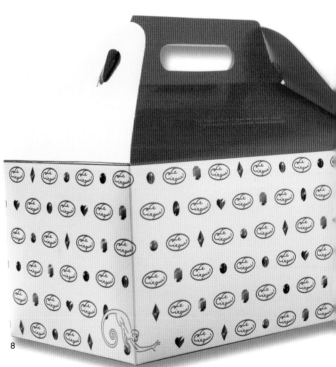

8

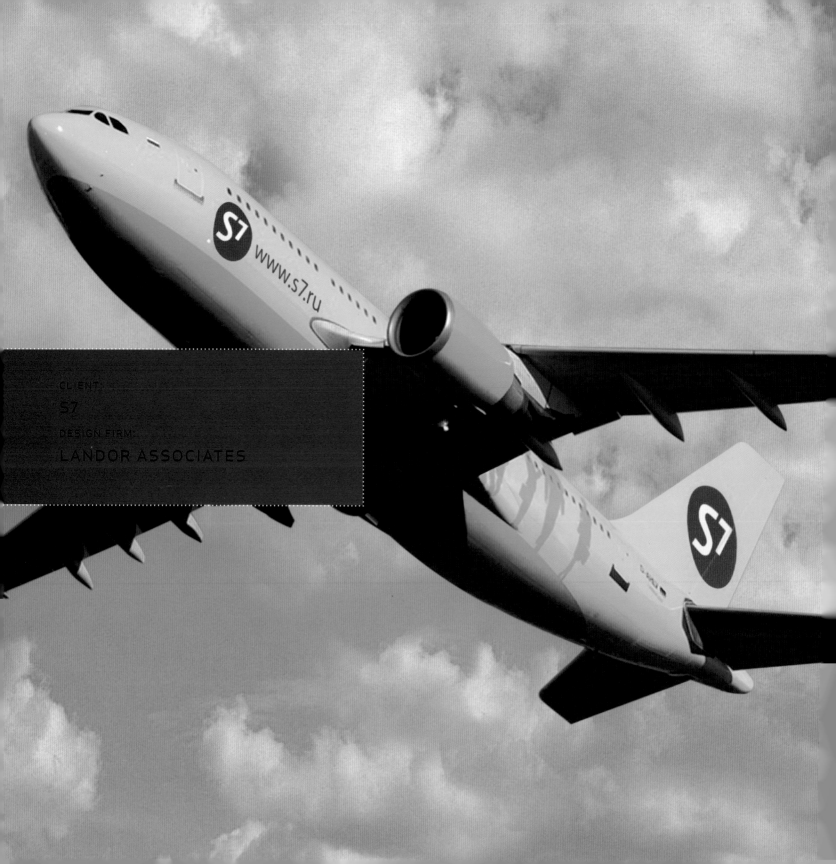

CLIENT:
S7

DESIGN FIRM:
LANDOR ASSOCIATES

PRIOR TO THE LAUNCH OF S7, FORMERLY SIBERIA AIRLINES, THE RUSSIAN
DOMESTIC AIRLINE MARKET WAS DOMINATED BY VERY "GRAY" EXPERIENCES,
LITERALLY AND FIGURATIVELY. AIR TRAVEL FUNCTIONED MORE AS A COMMODITY
AND, NOT SURPRISINGLY, CUSTOMER EXPECTATIONS WERE EXTREMELY LOW.
THE LAUNCH OF THE **S7** BRAND CHANGED ALL THAT—FOR GOOD. THIS CASE STUDY
SHOWS HOW A HOLISTIC BRANDING PROGRAM CAN COMMUNICATE BOTH THE
TANGIBLE FEATURES AND THE INTANGIBLE SPIRIT OF A COMPANY, PRODUCT,
OR SERVICE.

<< 1

*The livery departs radically from
Russian airline conventions (using two
bright greens and red) and ensures that
the aircraft stand out on the tarmac.*

CLIENT Siberia Airlines competes in a
marketplace where most airlines, or at least the
aircraft, look alike. The early 1990s breakup of
the state airline, Aeroflot, created thousands of
local and regional airlines, often made up of just
one or two aircraft. Many of the small airlines
couldn't afford to repaint their aircraft, so the
blue and white design of the ex-Aeroflot aircraft
remains the norm and national standard.

Siberia Airlines emerged from this environment
as the largest domestic airline in Russia and the
fifth fastest growing airline in the world. The
state of the airline industry in Russia created
enormous opportunity for Siberia Airlines to
stand out from competitors by developing and
executing a comprehensive brand program.

PROJECT Landor Associates began by gathering
research and hosting collaborative workshops
with Siberia Airlines management. Collectively,

the team discovered the relevant differentiating
factor for Siberia Airlines. The design team
centered their approach on the brand position,
"A breath of fresh air," based on the existing
perception of air travel in Russia and the
potential to significantly improve consumer
experiences. Project deliverables included a
strategic brand review, naming, visual identity,
collateral brand manual and environmental
design for livery, lounges, aircraft interiors,
check-in desks, ticketing offices, and uniforms.

ALPHANUMERIC Part of the rebranding efforts
included creating a new name. The previous
name communicated strength, health, and
simplicity, but also identified the airline as
regional and provincial. The new name needed
to indicate the size of the airline; appeal to
younger, more cosmopolitan Russians; and be
elastic enough to move beyond the airline
category. It also had to use letters common to

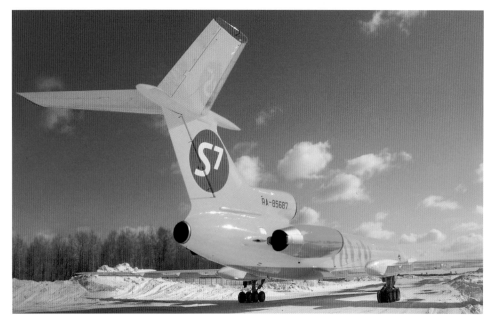

2

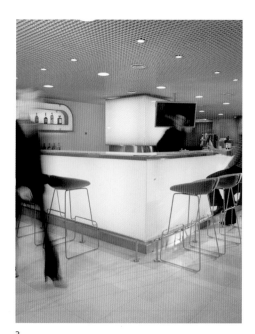

3

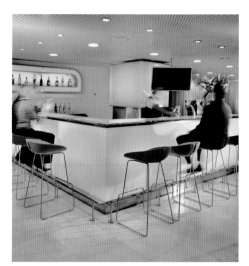

4

both Cyrillic and Roman alphabets, heightening the challenge.

The name S7 meets each requirement and offers the added bonus of existing awareness. S7 is the airline's IATA code, the prefix to the airline's flight numbers and the existing Web address. Using S7 as the airline name builds on the awareness and infuses the airline with a new and modern image. It also gives the brand the "stretch factor" needed as the airline's business expands.

JET SET The look of the aircraft dramatically represents the design theme, "A breath of fresh air." The design team selected two shades of vibrant green for the livery to communicate without question that S7 is new, modern, and distinctive. The colors stand out for miles on the tarmac, particularly in the snow—especially important in the eastern regions of Russia. The use of green provides a striking contrast to the red logo that appears on the fuselage and fin. The core value of customer care is represented by the use of silhouettes in a deeper shade of green above the wing. The differentiating design continues throughout the interior of the aircraft, where the seats feature colorful fabrics covered in dots, a reference to the S7 mark. ∎

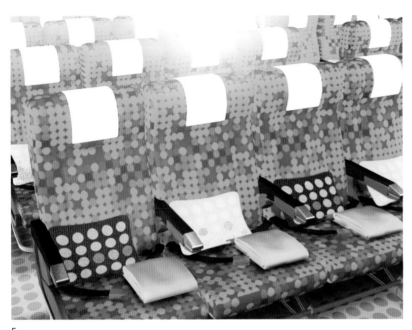

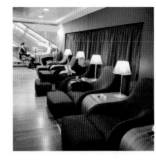

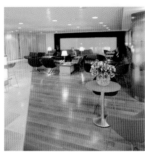

5

6

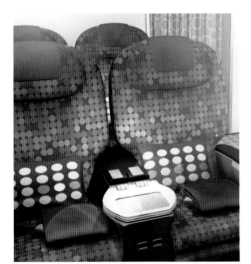

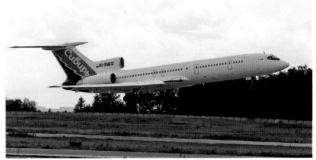

7

8

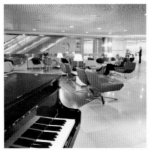

9

2
The S7 livery is strikingly different from other Russian airlines, especially in the snow.

3, 4
The brand experience carries through into the Business Class lounge in Moscow's Domodedovo Airport. Lighting changes the environment and mood over the course of the day.

5
The brand positioning, "A breath of fresh air," carries through into the economy-class cabins, revealing a multicolored, multidimensional passenger experience.

6
The office/home space of the Business Class lounge has an upscale, modern design, and incorporates colors from the S7 brand palette.

7
Seats in Business Class feature colorful fabrics covered in dots—a reference to the S7 mark.

8
The previous Siberia Airlines identity presented a "gray" experience and did not stand out among regional competitors. S7 branding dramatically changed that.

9
Live piano music creates the ambience of being in an intimate club in S7's Business Class lounge.

CLIENT: S7
DESIGN FIRM: Landor Associates
ART DIRECTOR: Peter Knapp
DESIGNER: John Stanley

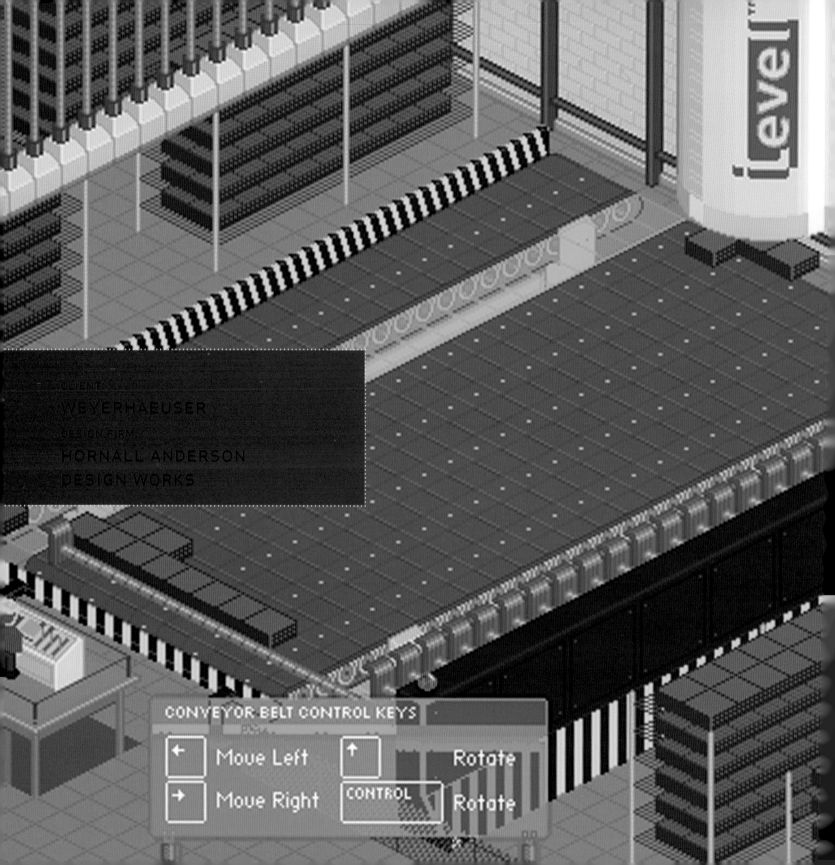

CLIENT
WEYERHAEUSER
DESIGN FIRM
HORNALL ANDERSON
DESIGN WORKS

CONVEYOR BELT CONTROL KEYS

← Move Left

↑ Rotate

→ Move Right

CONTROL Rotate

EFFECTIVE BRAND PROGRAMS REQUIRE CONSISTENT MESSAGING AT EVERY CUSTOMER TOUCH POINT. EMPLOYEES AT EVERY LEVEL OF THE ORGANIZATION MUST HAVE A THOROUGH UNDERSTANDING OF THE BRAND ATTRIBUTES AND EDITORIAL VOICE. INSPIRED AND EDUCATED EMPLOYEES ARE THE MOST VALUABLE BRAND ADVOCATES, EFFECTIVELY PROMOTING AND CONTRIBUTING TO THE SUCCESS OF A BRAND PROGRAM. THIS CASE STUDY FOCUSES ON THE AMBITIOUS AND INNOVATIVE INTERNAL LAUNCH OF **WEYERHAEUSER'S** ILEVEL BRAND PROGRAM.

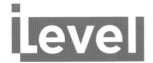

CLIENT Weyerhaeuser Company is an international forest products company and one of the 100 largest companies in the United States. The company decided to consolidate five operating units into a single, unified business—iLevel. iLevel provides residential builders and dealers with a single source for integrated, structural frame products and related software resources.

PROJECT Weyerhaeuser engaged Hornall Anderson Design Works to name the company and develop its visual brand program. Since iLevel is a new entity, the brand program focused on building a corporate culture to support the emerging iLevel brand. Project deliverables included the new name, identity, website, corporate collateral, external launch materials, convention signage, an internal launch strategy including the iLevel 2006 interactive game, promotional game collateral, posters, and a brand movie.

TEAM PLAYERS The ultimate goal of the internal launch was to link the brand personality with the daily working decisions of iLevel employees—all 16,000 of them. The design team chose a video game (and corresponding offline version of the game) as the primary tool for achieving the goal. The innovative approach worked amazingly well. Over eighty percent of iLevel employees participated, and feedback throughout the organization was universally positive.

CONSTRUCTION TOOLS The interactive game met three strategic objectives. First, it provided an active and engaging way to educate employees about the structures, goals, and attributes of iLevel. Second, the game provided a chance for employees to interact with one another, regardless of title, division, or physical location. Third, the game provided a real-life demonstration of the brand attributes: innovation, integration, interaction, and information.

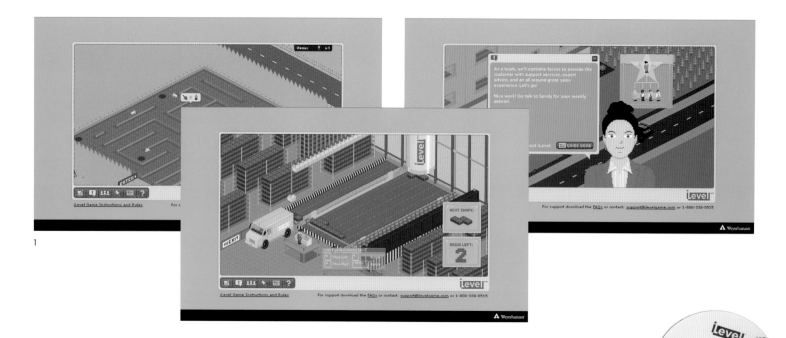

1

RULES OF ENGAGEMENT Employees formed teams across all disciplines and management levels to learn about and demonstrate understanding of key brand messages. The game lasted four weeks, and each week focused on a different brand attribute. The themes were hardwired into the game's DNA. For example, when employees registered to play, they were grouped into teams (integration). Teams worked together (interaction) to perform tasks. Teams reached different levels of play based on correct answers about the new company (information). The game itself served as an example of the fourth attribute (innovation).

THREE IN ONE The internal launch slogan, "All In One," encompassed three dimensions of the iLevel story. It expressed the functional benefits of iLevel products, the synergy and mutual interdependence of an integrated organization, and the company values of camaraderie and shared effort.

BUILDING FOUNDATION The design team integrated the core business of iLevel, construction, into its choice of launch items. Branded items included building blocks, thermoses, and hard hats. The iLevel game is also built around the daily work of the construction business. ■

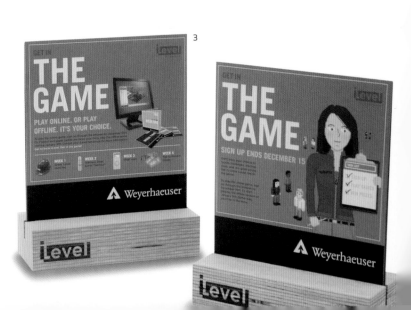

2

3

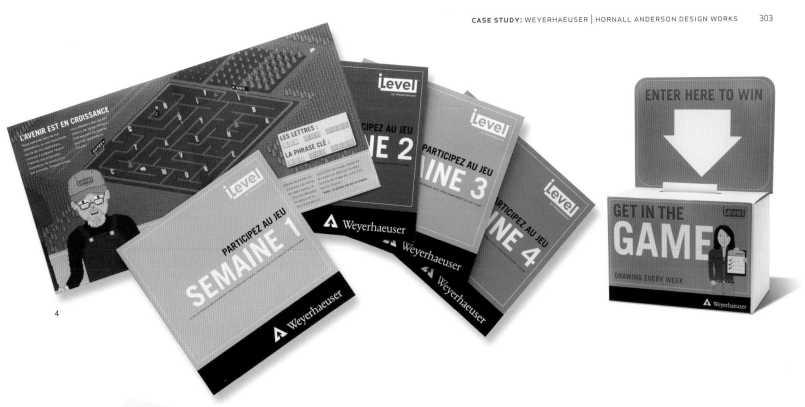

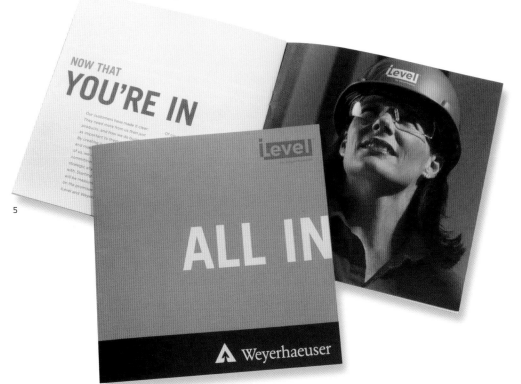

1
The iLevel game provided an interactive way for employees to learn about the iLevel brand.

2
The design team created two CD-ROM movies to help introduce the new brand.

3
Table toppers with a "building block" base provided information about the iLevel game and other launch events.

4
Designers created offline versions (in English and French) of the game so that those without computer access could participate. Perforated raffle tickets were included in the back of the brochures, which could be filled out and deposited into the game box.

5
"All In One" functioned as the internal launch slogan.

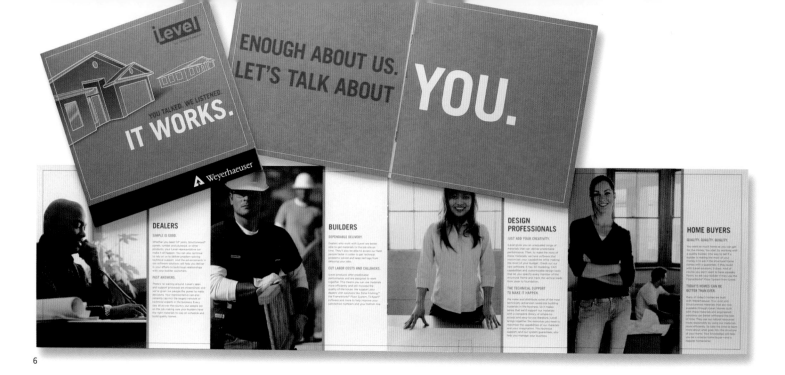

6

6

"It Works" is an external brochure sent to iLevel customers after the launch.

7

The "Starting Now" brochure, shown here in English and French, provided in-depth information about the new brand for iLevel employees.

8

The iLevel website uses a combination of photography and illustration and features a unique interface.

9

The square shape and vibrant green color palette are repeated across several launch items to provide consistency for the brand program.

7

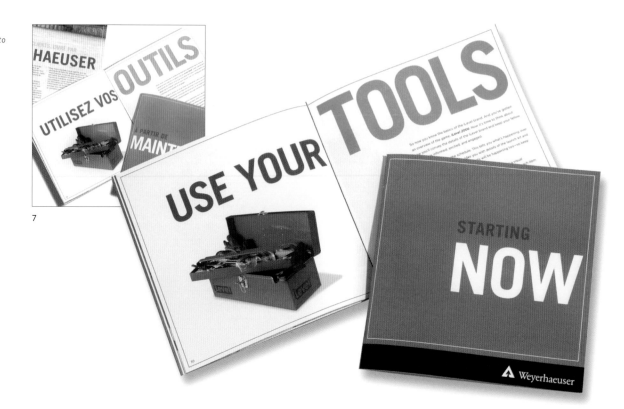

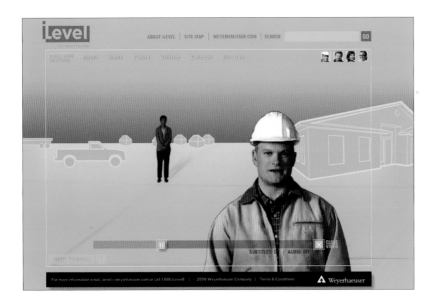

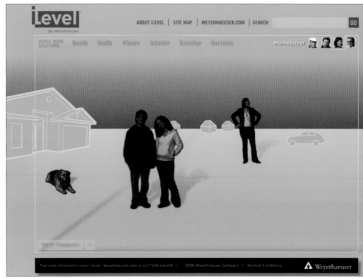

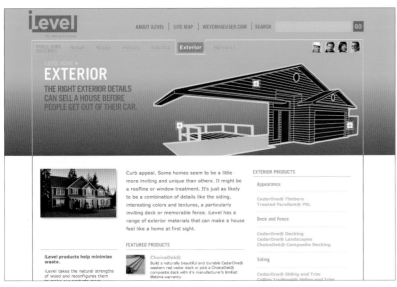

EXTERIOR

THE RIGHT EXTERIOR DETAILS
CAN SELL A HOUSE BEFORE
PEOPLE GET OUT OF THEIR CAR.

Curb appeal. Some homes seem to be a little
more inviting and unique than others. It might be
a roofline or window treatment. It's just as likely
to be a combination of details like the siding,
interesting colors and textures, a particularly
inviting deck or memorable fence. iLevel has a
range of exterior materials that can make a house
feel like a home at first sight.

EXTERIOR PRODUCTS

Appearance

CedarOne® Timbers
Treated Parallam® PSL

Deck and Fence

CedarOne® Decking
CedarOne® Landscapes
ChoiceDek® Composite Decking

Siding

CedarOne® Siding and Trim
Collins TruWood® Siding and Trim

**iLevel products help minimize
waste.**

iLevel takes the natural strengths
of wood and reconfigures them

FEATURED PRODUCTS

ChoiceDek®
Build a naturally beautiful and durable CedarOne®
western red cedar deck or pick a ChoiceDek®
composite deck with it's manufacturer's limited
lifetime warranty.

8

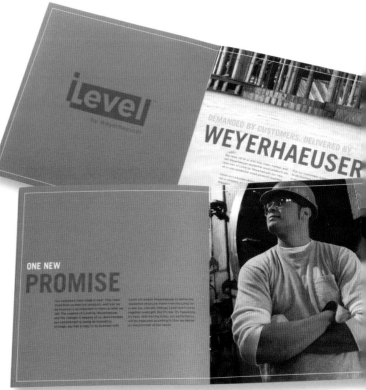

ONE NEW
PROMISE

9

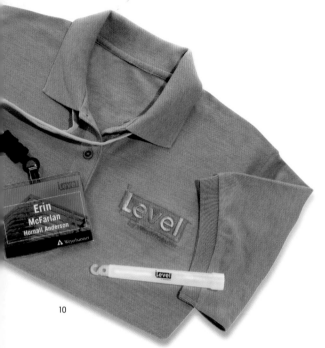

10

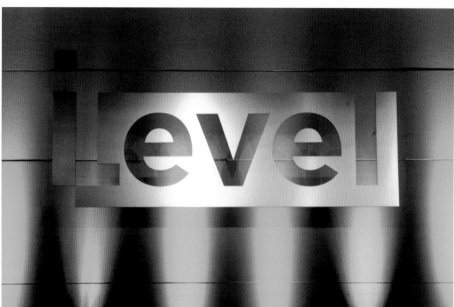

11

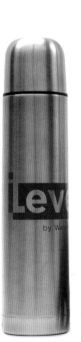

12

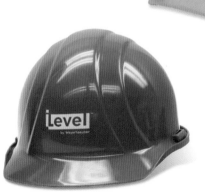

13

10
Brand champions, named Transition Agents, received branded polo shirts, promotional glow sticks, and name badge holders.

11
Designers provided signage and multimedia collateral for the Transition Agent launch conference.

12
The design team chose hard hats and thermoses as prizes for the iLevel game to reflect the company's core construction business.

13
All 16,000 employees received a branded T-shirt, cap, pencil, and level key chain.

CLIENT: Weyerhaeuser
DESIGN FIRM: Hornall Anderson Design Works
ART DIRECTORS: Jack Anderson, James Tee
DESIGNERS: James Tee, Andrew Wicklund, Elmer Dela Cruz, Holly Craven, Jay Hilburn, Hayden Schoen, Belinda Bowling, Yuri Shvets, Michael Conners

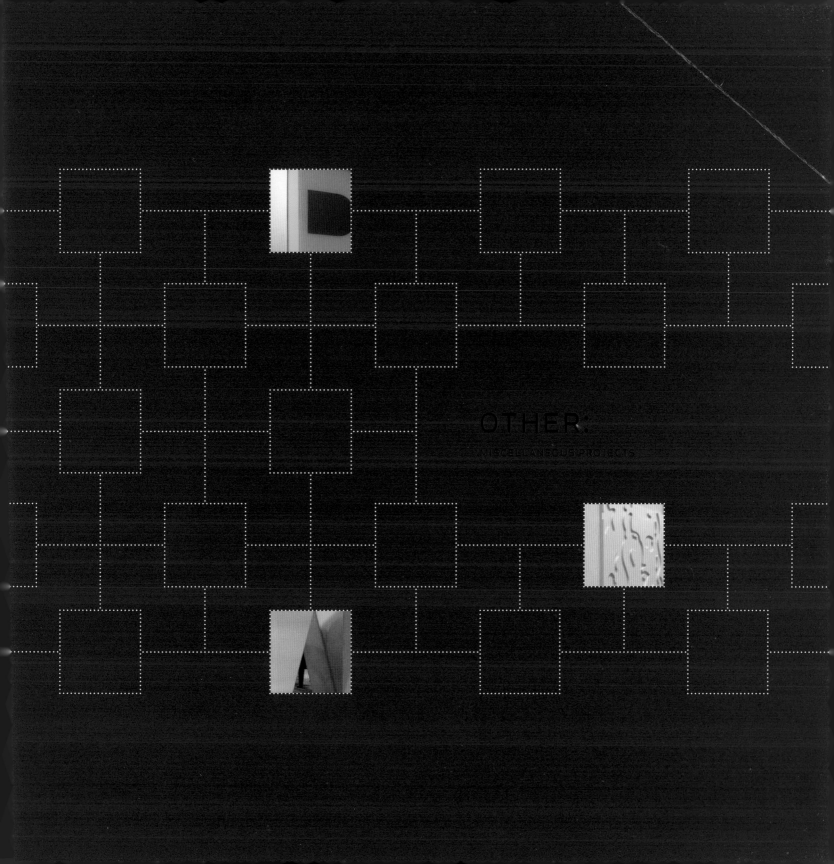

OTHER:
MISCELLANEOUS PROJECTS

1
CLIENT: Target Commercial Interiors
DESIGN FIRM: Sussner Design Company

2
CLIENT: Tower 23 Hotel
DESIGN FIRM: Hollis Brand
Communications

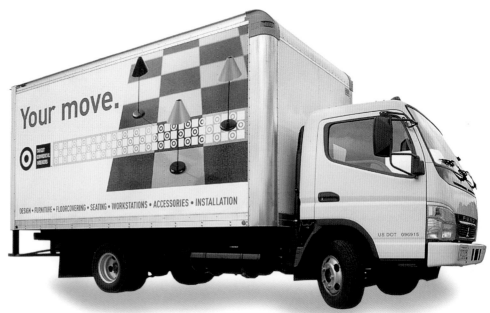

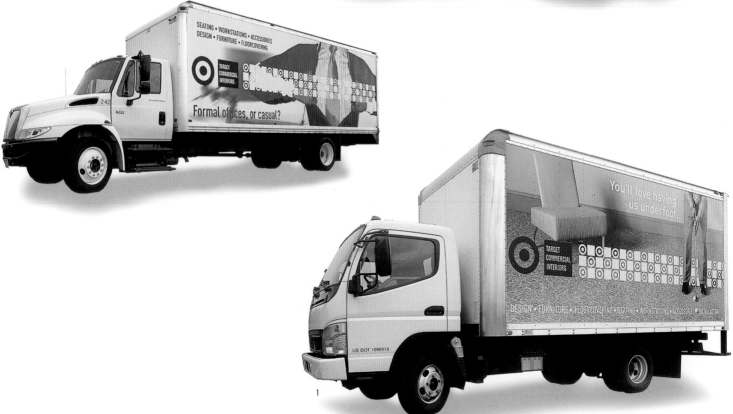

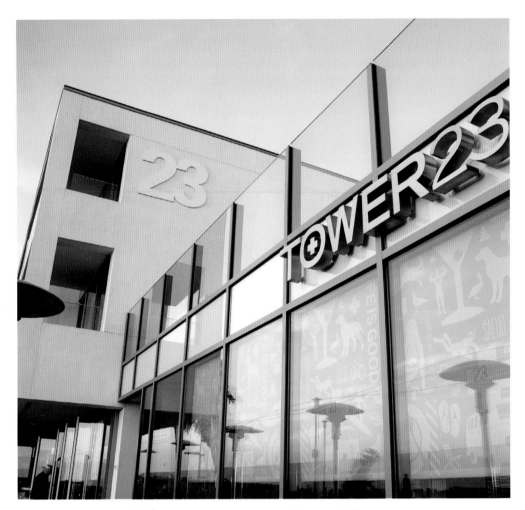

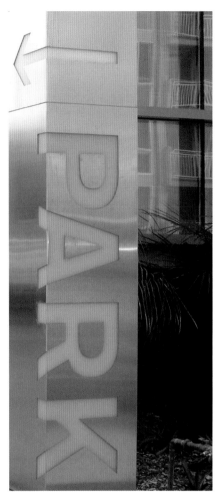

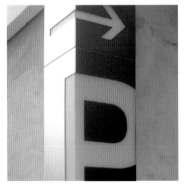

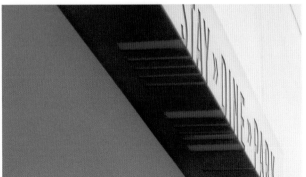

2

3
CLIENT: Time Warner, Inc.
DESIGN FIRM: Poulin + Morris Inc.

4
CLIENT: EOS Airlines
DESIGN FIRM: Hornall Anderson
Design Works

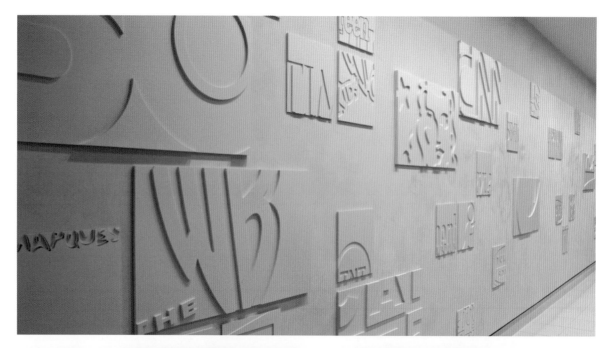

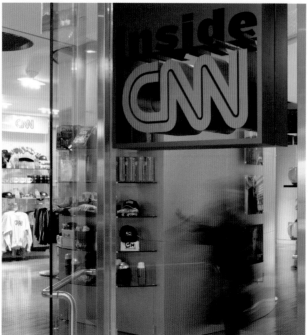

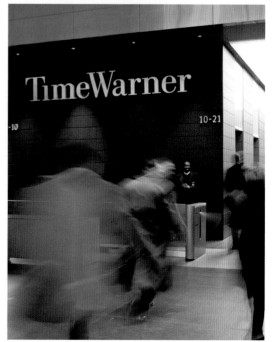

3

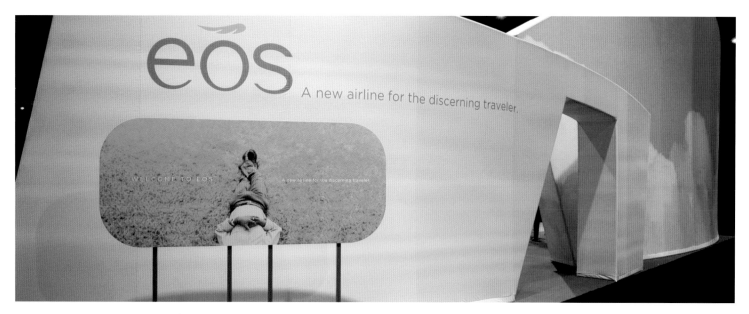

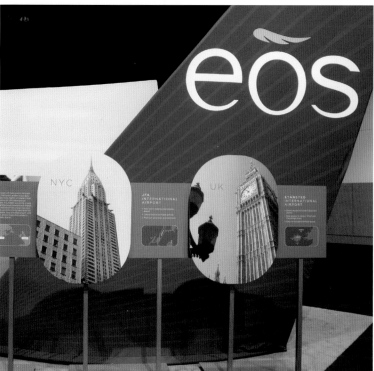

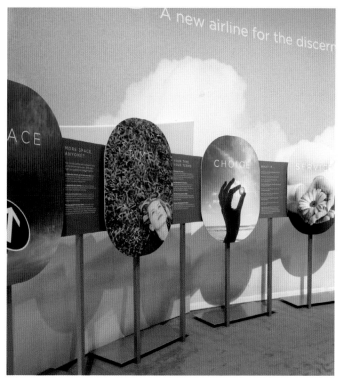

4

5
CLIENT: Mirvac, HPA Architects
DESIGN FIRM: Perks Design Partners

6
CLIENT: America Online
DESIGN FIRM: sky design

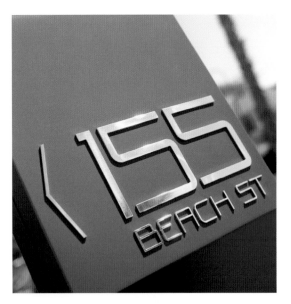

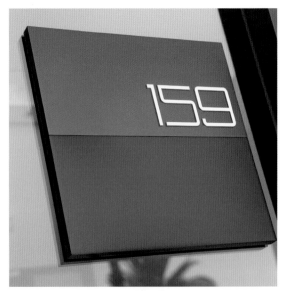

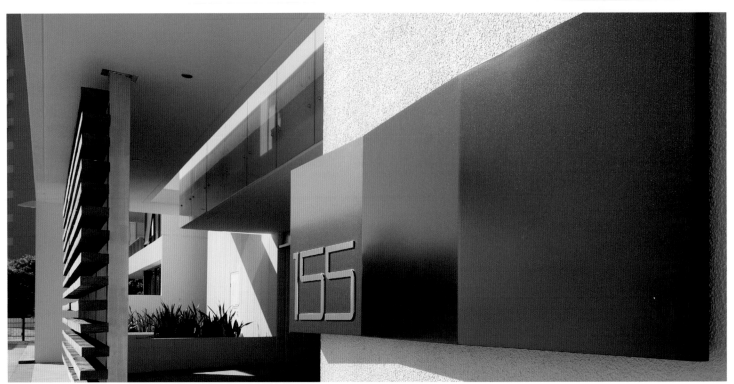

5

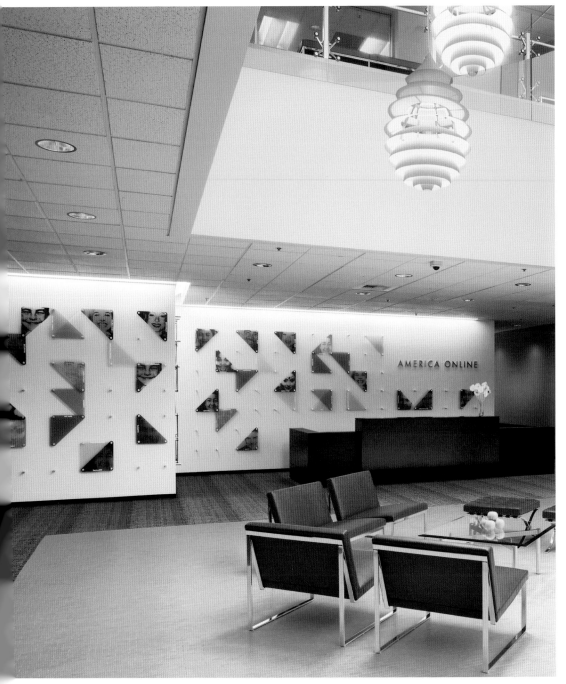

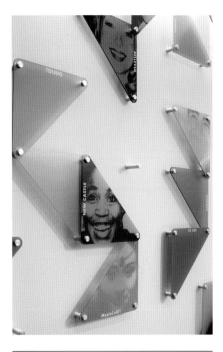

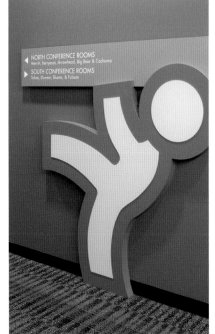

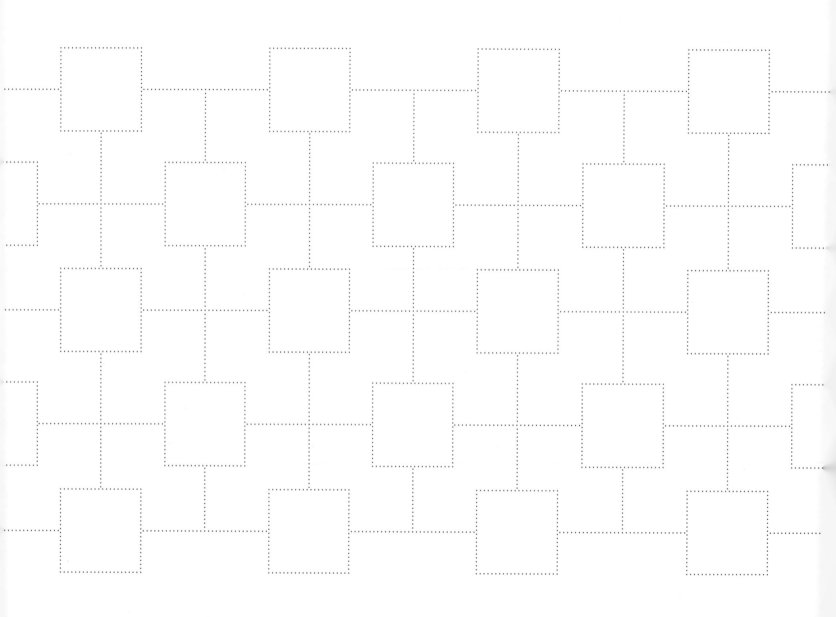

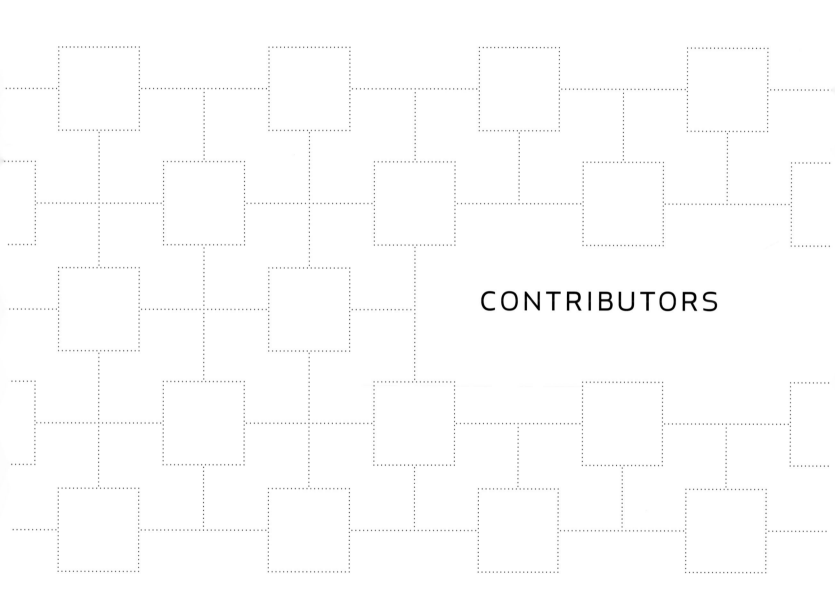

CONTRIBUTORS

3
8220 La Mirada NE
Suite 500
Albuquerque, NM 87109
USA
505.293.2333
www.whois3.com
PAGES 16, 26–27

3rd Edge Communications
162 Newark Avenue
Jersey City, NJ 07302
USA
201.395.9960
www.3rdedge.com
PAGE 91

98pt6
443 Greenwich Street
Suite 5A
New York, NY 10013
USA
212.625.2054
www.98pt6.com
PAGES 25, 55, 64–65

AdamsMorioka
8484 Wilshire Blvd.
Beverly Hills, CA 90211
USA
323.966.5990
www.adamsmorioka.com
PAGES 20–21, 38, 45, 92–97, 156

Addis Creson
2515 Ninth Street
Berkeley, CA 94710
USA
510.704.7500
www.addiscreson.com
PAGES 14, 44, 49, 89, 120, 202

And Partners
158 West 27th Street
7th Floor
New York, NY 10001
USA
212.414.4700
www.andpartsnersny.com
PAGES 161, 234, 251

Ant Industrial Design Pte. Ltd
31 Toh Guan Road East
Lw Technocentre 07-07
Singapore 608608
Singapore
65.6425.3181
www.ant.sg
PAGE 77

Archrival
720 "O" Street
Lincoln, NE 68508
USA
402.435.2525
www.archrival.com
PAGES 42–43, 188

AS|D Labs, Inc.
110 Greene Street
Suite 605/Nasty Little Man
New York, NY 10012
USA
212.866.4402
www.asdlabs.com
PAGES 62, 159

Ayse Celem Design
Birinci Cadde No. 89
Arnavutkoy
Istanbul, 34345
Turkey
90.212.358.20.93
www.aysecelemdesign.com
PAGES 144, 160

Base Art Co.
623 High Street
Worthington, OH 43085
USA
614.841.7480
www.baseartco.com
PAGES 243, 285

BIZ-R
35A Fore Street
Totnes
Devon TQ95Hn
Great Britain
UK
44(0).1803.868.989
www.biz-r.co.uk
PAGE 87

Boccalatte
P.O. Box 370
Surry Hills
Sydney, New South Wales, 2010
Australia
61.2.9310.4149
www.boccalatte.com
PAGES 155, 236

Brainforest, Inc.
2211 N. Elston
Suite 301
Chicago, IL 60614
USA
773.395.2500
www.brainforest.com
PAGES 282–283

Brandoctor
Zavrtnica 17
Zagreb 10000
Croatia
385.1.6064.006
www.brandoctor.com
PAGES 39, 84, 112, 278

Bruketa & Zinic
Zavrtnica 17
Zagreb 10000
Croatia
385.1.6064.000
www.bruketa-zinic.com
PAGES 10, 36, 240, 248–249, 277, 284

Carbone Smolan Agency
22 West 19th Street
10th Floor
New York, NY 10022
USA
212.807.0011
www.carbonesmolan.com
PAGES 178–180

Carré Noir Roma
Via Giovanni Miani 37/b
Roma 00154
Italy
39.06.571784.1
www.carrenoir.com
PAGES 66, 164, 245

CDI Studios
2215A Rennaissance Drive
Las Vegas, NV 89119
USA
702.876.3316
www.cdistudios.com
PAGE 28

CFX Creative
259-3495 Cambie Street
Vancouver, BC V5Z 4R3
Canada
604.676.1866
www.cfxcreative.com
PAGE 90

Clemenger BBDO
8 Kent Terrace
Wellington
New Zealand
64.4.802.3362
www.clemengerbbdo.co.nz
PAGES 50, 56, 145, 148–149, 286

Crosby Associates
203 N. Wabash
Chicago, IL 60601
USA
312.346.2900
www.crosbyassociates.com
PAGES 98–103, 233

Curious
19A Floral Street
London, WC2E 9D5
UK
44(0).20.7240.6251
www.curiousdesign.com
PAGES 136, 153, 162, 191, 288

Davidson Design
Level 1, Bldg 5
658 Church Street
Richmond, Victoria 3121
Australia
61.3.9429.1288
www.davidsondesign.com.au
PAGES 46, 63, 151, 194, 197

Decker Design
14 W. 23rd Street
3rd Floor
New York, NY 10010
USA
212.633.8588
www.deckerdesign.com
PAGES 31, 58, 80, 116, 137, 182, 193, 203, 207, 253

DeLor
613 W. Main Street
Louisville, KY 40202
USA
502.584.5500
www.delor.com
PAGES 270–274

Design Source East
235 Birchwood Avenue
Cranford, NJ 07016
USA
908.653.9797
www.dsebrand.com
PAGES 59, 127, 138

Di depux
Eratous 4
Dafni-Athens 17235
Greece
30.210.975.5850
www.depux.com
PAGE 57

Diseño Dos Asociados
Privada 25 A sur 913-6 Col. La Paz
Puebla, Puebla 72160
Mexico
522 (222) 231.34.73
www.disenodos.com
PAGES 44, 55, 74, 165, 188

Elevator
B.Berislavica 7
Split 21000
Croatia
385.98.434.556
www.elevator.hr
PAGES 68, 78

Emmi Salonen
Studio 17
310 Kingsland Road
London E8 4 DB
UK
44(0).77.5200.1311
www.emmi.co.uk
PAGES 23, 63, 84, 113, 123

Enterprise IG
19 Tambach Street
Sunninghill, Uhb
South Africa
27.011.319.8000
www.enterpriseig.co.za
PAGES 60, 258–263

Faust Associates
360 Utedale Road
Riverside, IL 60546
USA
708.447.0608
www.faustltd.com
PAGES 134, 280

Fluid Design Lab
36 Cavazzoni Street
Tezze sul Brenta
Vicenza 36056
Italy
33.3472.8116
www.fluiddesignlab.com
PAGES 48, 142, 165, 278

Front Media Studio
Courtyard Offices
Braxted Park
Great Braxted, Essex CM8 3GA
UK
44(0).1621.890220
www.frontmedia.co.uk
PAGES 139, 183

Goodesign
68 Jay Street
Suite 901
Brooklyn, NY 11201
USA
718.254.8738
www.goodesignny.com
PAGE 248

Go Welsh
987 Mill Mar Road
Lancaster, PA 17601
USA
717.569.4040
www.gowelsh.com
PAGE 123

Hardy Design
Rua Araguari 1541/5º andar
Belo Horizonte/Minas Gerais
Brazil
55.31.3275.3095
www.hardydesign.com.br
PAGES 12, 19, 35, 72, 73, 82,
85, 89, 184

Hartford Design
954 W. Washington
4th Floor
Chicago, IL 60607
USA
312.563.5600
www.hartfordesign.com
PAGES 11, 44, 49

Heath Kane Design
35 Muswell Hill Road
London 10 3J8
UK
44(0).208.374.0576
www.heath-kane.com
PAGES 166–171

Hesse Design
Duesseldorfer Str 16
Erkrath 40699
Germany
49.211.2807.200
www.hesse-design.de
PAGE 247

Hollis Brand Communications
680 West Beech Street
Suite 1
San Diego, CA 92101
USA
619.234.2061
www.hollisbc.com
PAGES 66, 67, 158, 309

Hornall Anderson Design Works
710 2nd Avenue
Suite 1300
Seattle, WA 98104
USA
206.826.2329
www.hadw.com
PAGES 14, 16, 28, 36, 84, 127,
189, 190, 193, 198, 206, 209,
300–306, 311

Jason and Jason
7713 Hayetzira Street
Ra'anana 43663
Israel
972.7444.282
www.jandj.co.il
PAGES 150, 152, 244

JDAnthony
945 Liberty Avenue
16th Floor
Pittsburg, PA 15222
USA
800.983.6792
www.jdanthony.com
PAGES 70, 74, 84

John Wingard Design
925 Bethel Street
Suite 306
Honolulu, HI 96813
USA
808.529.8833
www.johnwingarddesign.com
PAGE 48

KASHI_design
Fröbelgasse 33/10, A-1160
Vienna
Austria
43.699.12.915.349
www.kashi.at
PAGE 162

KesselsKramer
Lauriergrachat 39
1016 RG Amsterdam
The Netherlands
31(0)20.5301060
www.kesselskramer.com
PAGES 104–110

Kinesis
P.O. Box 683
Ashland, OR 97520
USA
544.482.3600
www.kinesisinc.com
PAGE 28

Kinetic
2 Leng Kee Road
Thye Hong Centre 04-03A
Singapore 159086
65.637.957.92
www.kinetic.com.sg
PAGES 11, 13, 54, 63, 185, 192

KROG, Ljubljana
Krakovski nasip 22
1000 Ljubljana
Slovenia
386.41.780.880
PAGES 163, 205

Kym Abrams Design
213 West Institute Place
Suite 608
Chicago, IL 60610
USA
312.654.1005
www.kad.com
PAGES 131, 200, 237, 238, 279

Lain Livingston Marketing Studio
3595 Canton Road
Suite 49, 191
Marietta, GA 30066
USA
404.550.5508
www.lainlivingston.com
PAGE 119

Landini Associates
42 Davies Street
Surry Hills, Sydney, NSW 2010
Australia
612.9360.3899
www.landiniassociates.com
PAGES 172–177

Landor Associates
Klamath House
18 Clerkenwell Green
London EC1R ODP
UK
44.20.7880.8000
www.landor.com
PAGES 296–299

Lienhart Design
939 W. Huron
Suite 310
Chicago, IL 60622
USA
312.738.2200
www.lienhartdesign.com
PAGE 89

Liska + Associates
515 North State Street
23rd Floor
Chicago, IL 60610
312.644.4400
www.liska.com
PAGES 23, 28, 36, 89, 130, 135,
144, 146, 154, 157, 187, 195,
208, 239, 241, 254–255,
264–269, 278, 287

Lloyd's Graphic Design Ltd.
17 Westhaven Place
Bienheim 7301
New Zealand
643.578.6955
PAGES 76, 244

Lowercase, Inc.
213 West Institute Place
Suite 311
Chicago, IL 60610
USA
312.274.0652
www.lowercaseinc.com
PAGES 88, 151, 160

Mad Dog Graphx
1443 W. Northern Lights Blvd.
Suite U
Anchorage, AK 99503
USA
907.276.5062
www.thedogpack.com
PAGES 52, 62

Manasteriotti Design Studio
Sestinsky dol 99A
Zagreb 10000
Croatia
385.98.253.466
www.mds01.com
PAGES 62, 70

Matthew Schwartz Design Studio
611 Broadway
Suite 430
New York, NY 10012
USA
212.925.6460
www.ms-ds.com
PAGES 49, 52, 91, 141, 150

mCube
11 Zaver Mahal
5th Floor
66 Marine Drive
Mumbai 400020
India
91.98811.49455
www.mcubedesign.com
PAGES 15, 210–215

Michele Moore Design
4885 Avoca Street
Los Angeles, CA 90041
USA
323.528.7404
www.mooregraphicdesign.com
PAGE 67

Mindseye Creative
21 B Anand Darshan
13 Peddar Road
Mumbai 400026
India
201.377.2494
www.mecstudio.com
PAGE 84

Mirko Ilić Corp.
207 E. 32nd Street
New York, NY 10016
USA
212.481.9737
www.mirkoilic.com
PAGES 17, 22, 290–295

The Moderns
900 Broadway
Suite 903
New York, NY 10003
USA
212.387.8852
www.themoderns.com
PAGES 216–223

Monderer Design
2067 Massachusetts Avenue
Cambridge, MA 02140
USA
617.661.6125
www.monderer.com
PAGE 147

Morla Design, Inc.
1008A Pennsylvania Avenue
San Francisco, CA 94107
USA
415.543.6548
www.morladesign.com
PAGE 163

Nazy Alvarez
12321 Ocean Park Blvd.
Los Angeles, CA 90064
USA
310.270.7576
www.nazyalvarez.com
PAGE 76

Nita B. Creative
991 Selloy Avenue
St. Paul, MN 55104
USA
651.644.2889
www.nitabcreative.com
PAGE 279

Nothing: Something: NY
242 Wythe Avenue
Studio 3
Brooklyn, NY 11211
USA
646.221.9972
www.nothingsomething.com
PAGES 34, 47, 183, 186, 196, 207

Oliver Russell
217 S. 11th Street
Boise, ID 83702
USA
208.287.6528
www.oliverrussell.com
PAGE 28

One Method Inc.
7145 West Credit Avenue
Mississauga, Ontario L5N6J7
Canada
905.603.0180
www.onemethod.com
PAGES 49, 86

OrangeSeed Design
800 Washington Avenue N.
Suite 461
Minneapolis, MN 55401
USA
612.252.9757
www.orangeseed.com
PAGES 113, 240, 281

p11 Creative
20331 Irvine Avenue
Suite E5
Santa Ana Heights, CA 92707
USA
714.641.2090
www.p11.com
PAGES 30, 43, 52, 70, 80, 203,
205, 207

Perks Design Partners
333 Flinders Lane
2nd Floor
Victoria 3000
Australia
613.9620.5911
www.perksdesignpartners.com
PAGES 198, 204, 206, 256, 312

Poulin & Morris, Inc.
286 Spring Street
6th Floor
New York, NY 10013
USA
212.675.1332
www.poulinmorris.com
PAGES 60, 155, 310

Ramp Creative
453 South Spring Street
Suite 819
Los Angeles, CA 90013
USA
213.623.7267
www.rampcreative.com
PAGES 235, 242, 252, 257

The Republik
313 West Main Street
Durham, NC 27701
USA
919.956.9400
www.therepublik.net
PAGES 83, 203

Riordon Design
131 George Street
Oakville, Ontario L6J3B9
Canada
905.339.0850
www.riordondesign.com
PAGES 250, 283

Ross Levine Design
2237 Parker Street
Berkeley, CA 94704
USA
510.665.4551
www.rosslevinedesign.com
PAGE 28

Root Idea
Flat 2304
Progress Commercial Bldg
9 Irving Street, Causeway Bay
Hong Kong
852.9707.0066
www.rootidea.com
PAGE 53

Sayles Graphic Design
3701 Beaver Avenue
Des Moines, IA 50310
USA
515.279.2922
www.saylesdesign.com
PAGE 238

Seltzer Design
45 Newbury Street
Suite 406
Boston, MA 02116
USA
617.353.0303
www.seltzerdesign.com
PAGES 40, 73, 117

Sharp Communications, Inc.
425 Madison Avenue
New York, NY 10017
USA
212.829.0002
www.sharpthink.com
PAGES 31, 87, 89

Simon & Goetz Design GmbH & Co. KG
Westhafen Pier 1, Rotfeder-Ring 11
Frankfurt am Mai/Hessen/60327
Germany
49(0).69.968855.0
www.brand-equity-group.com
PAGES 121, 132, 232

sky design
50 Hurt Plaza
Suite 500
Atlanta, GA 30303
USA
404.688.4702
www.skydesigngraphics.com
PAGE 313

Sockeye Creative
800 NW 6th Avenue
Suite 211
Portland, OR 97209
USA
503.226.3843
www.sockeyecreative.com
PAGES 55, 84, 159

Spark Studio
11 Yarra Street
South Melbourne, Victoria 3205
Australia
613.9686.4703
www.sparkstudio.com.au
PAGES 11, 18, 36, 37, 38, 51, 57,
61, 71, 115, 128, 131, 133, 136,
138, 201, 205, 246

Springboard Creative
5606 Outlook
Mission, KS 66202
USA
913.789.7408
www.springboardcreative.biz
PAGE 76

Squarehand/The Buddy Project
21-38 31st Street
Suite 5P
Astoria, NY 11105
USA
646.285.5600
www.squarehand.com
PAGE 276

Stoller Design Group
1818 Harmon Street
Berkeley, CA 94703
USA
510.658.9771
www.stollerdesigngroup.com
PAGES 114, 128, 135, 140,
277, 282

Studio International
Bucomjicarva 43
Zagreb 10000
Croatia
385.137.60171
www.studio-international.com
PAGES 55, 289

Sussner Design Company
212 3rd Avenue N.
Suite 505
Minneapolis, MN 55401
USA
612.339.2886
www.sussner.com
PAGES 11, 23, 24, 69, 70, 81,
133, 136, 142, 186, 194, 202,
281, 287, 308

Taber Creative Group
1693 Eureka Road
Suite 200
Roseville, CA 95661
USA
916.771.6868
www.tabercreative.com
PAGE 23

Talisman Interactive
4169 Main Street
Suite 200
Philadelphia, PA 19127
USA
215.482.6000
www.talismaninteractive.com
PAGES 11, 36, 44, 49, 62, 89,
119, 122, 129

TD2
Ibsen 43
8th Floor
Polanco, Mexico D.F. 11560
Mexico
52.55.5281.6999
www.td2.com.mx
PAGE 143

Timber Design Company
4402 N. College Avenue
Indianapolis, IN 46205
USA
317.213.8509
www.timberdesignco.com
PAGES 23, 41, 44, 62

urbanINFLUENCE Design Studio
423 Second Avenue, Ext. South
Suite 32
Seattle, WA 98104
USA
206.219.5599
www.urbaninfluence.com
PAGES 29, 39, 55, 62, 67, 80, 91,
115, 140

The Valentine Group
555 West 25th Street
Floor 3
New York, NY 10001
USA
212.989.8188
www.valentinegroup.com
PAGES 74–75, 118, 124–125,
126, 224–230

Valiant Media, Inc.
3116 Commerce Street
Suite D
Dallas, TX 75226
USA
214.741.4300
www.valiantmedia.com
PAGES 11, 23, 49, 70

Voice
217 Gilbert Street
Adelaide, SA 5000
Australia
618.8410.8822
www.voicedesign.net
PAGES 32–33, 114

Wages Design
887 West Marietta Street
Suite S-111
Atlanta, GA 30318
USA
404.876.0874
www.wagesdesign.com
PAGES 44, 199, 284

Yes Design Group
7220 Beverly Blvd.
Suite 202
Los Angeles, CA 90036
USA
323.330.9300
www.yesdesigngroup.com
PAGES 59, 282, 285, 289

ABOUT THE AUTHOR

Steven Liska founded Liska + Associates, Inc. in 1980. The visual design firm, based in Chicago and New York, creates strategy-driven, comprehensive branding programs. Liska + Associates partners with and designs for a wide range of clients—from image-conscious businesses to complex corporations—that need help clarifying their brand messages.

ACKNOWLEDGMENTS

We wish to thank enlightened clients everywhere who understand the value of design and appreciate the expertise of designers. Thanks also to the array of professionals who regularly collaborate with designers—from photographers and printers to writers and programmers. Your work is vital to any successful design project. Special thanks to Carole Masse, Jamie Jazdzyk, and all the people at Liska + Associates.